W9-BGK-621

Total Picture Control

by Andreas Feininger

CHILTON BOOK COMPANY
Philadelphia New York London

Other books by ANDREAS FEINIGER

Trees	(1968)
Forms of Nature and Life	(1966)
The Complete Photographer	(1965)
New York	(1964)
The World through my Eyes	(1963)
Maids, Madonnas and Witches	(1961)
Man and Stone	(1961)
Total Picture Control	(1961)
The Anatomy of Nature	(1956)
Changing America	(1955)
The Creative Photographer	(1955)
Successful Color Photography	(1954)
Successful Photography	(1954)
The Face of New York	(1954)
Advanced Photography	(1952)
Feininger on Photography	(1949)
New York	(1945)
New Paths in Photography	(1939)

Published in New York by Amphoto.
Library of Congress Catalog Card Number 69-20466.
Printed in the Federal Republic of Germany.

Contents

This is not a textbook for the beginner

Rather, it is an analytical discussion of photographic controls, addressed to the reader who has experience in black-and-white as well as color photography and is therefore familiar with basic photographic techniques. The whole complex of black-and-white and color photography has been thoroughly treated by this author in two companion volumes to this book, *The Complete Photographer* and *The Color Photo Book*, published by Prentice-Hall Inc., Englewood Cliffs, N. J.

The devices and techniques discussed and illustrated on the following pages have nothing to do with tricks. They are part of the "vocabulary" of any "literate" photographer. Some devices, such as telephoto and wide-angle lenses, color correction filters, or motion-suggesting blur, are used daily by most experienced photographers. Other devices, such as cylindrical and spherical perspective, will seldom be needed. However, the danger exists that the more spectacular devices and controls, particularly, will be misused for the production of meaningless effects. Red filters in black-and-white photography and extreme wide-angle lenses, especially, are often used, without the slightest justification, to produce "black skies" and "interesting distortions." In many photographs, unsharpness and grain are not used creatively to symbolize specific subject qualities, but are present merely as the result of poor technique. I even know of instances in which photographers have shot pictures through the grid of an exposure meter in a desperate attempt to be original and create novel effects.
This kind of thing is pathetic. Such practices add nothing to the growth in significance or the widening of the scope of photography. Of course, growth is inseparable from change, and change has never been brought about by those who believed in playing it safe and sticking to the rules. Without a constant search for new and better ways of expression, photography would remain at a standstill. But unless this search is led by creative thought and reflection is given to photography as a means of communication, the danger exists that the means will overshadow the meaning. To help avoid this, in the picture part of this book I have illustrated as many of the different controls as was practicable, with "finished pictures" made by some of the best photographers. Each of these photographs demonstrates how a specific control, imaginatively used, gave a particular graphic effect to the picture and thereby enhanced its meaning.

PART 1

What this Book Can Do for You

The enormous advances of the last decade in the field of phototechnology have made the taking of photographs progressively simpler and easier. The increase in semiautomatic and fully automatic controls and devices has reduced the need for laboriously acquiring skill and experience. Even relatively inexpensive cameras now have features such as: double-exposure prevention; a shutter-coupled diaphragm that, at the moment of exposure, automatically closes down to a preselected stop, sometimes coupled directly to a built-in exposure meter that instantly adjusts it to the prevailing light; a lens-coupled combination rangefinder–viewfinder in the form of a split-image or microprism device; automatic parallax compensation; cross-coupling of diaphragm aperture and shutter speed in accordance with the LVS (Light Value Scale) or EV (Exposure Value) system (see: *The Color Photo Book*, pp. 131–132); an instant-return mirror that minimizes "exposure blackout"; one-stroke operation, which simultaneously cocks the shutter, advances the film, and records the number of exposures. And the two most critical operations in the making of any photograph, exposure and development, are now performed strictly on the basis of readings taken from three control instruments: exposure meter, thermometer, and timer.

As a result of these and other advances in the field of phototechnology, the technical quality of the average photographer's work is at an all-time high. Unfortunately, however, with a few notable exceptions, today's photographs, as far as artistic quality and emotional impact are concerned, are still on a level with pictures taken 10 to 20 years ago. As in many other fields, technical progress has far outpaced progress in creative application.

With all the wonderful means at his disposal, the average photographer should be able to produce more interesting work. Since any subject can be rendered photographically in many different forms, some of them more effective than others, photographers could exert an enormous amount of control over the appearance of their pictures if they were aware of this freedom of rendition. With this fact in mind, I have tried something which, to the best of my knowledge, has not been done before in this way, although its importance should be obvious to anyone connected with photography, that is to describe and evaluate systematically the different forms of photographic expression together with the techniques by which a photographer can control the graphic effect of his picture.

The result is a book, a reference work, which perhaps can be called a dictionary of the picture language of photography. Like a dictionary which defines the usage of a language, this book lists, explains, and critically compares the different photographic forms of expression with one another and gives their applications. Just as any good writer carefully selects those words which will convey not only meaning to his reader but also feeling, so a good photographer must carefully select those particular means of photographic expression which will most completely convey his intentions as well as the essence of a subject to the observer of his picture.

This book should be of help to all photographers who wish to broaden their range of expression. Among other benefits, it provides immediate, definite answers to such constantly asked questions as these:

Which camera type is best for photographing a specific subject? Which kind of lens? Why? pp. 36, 40

Color filters are available in many different hues. What can each one do for me? When should I use a red filter and when a yellow, orange, green, or blue one? How can I make a specific color in a black-and-white photograph appear lighter or darker? How can I improve tonal separation? pp. 52, 242–247

Working with black-and-white film, how, and how much, can I increase the contrast of a contrastless subject (important in telephotography)? How, and how much, can I decrease the contrast of an overcontrasty subject, particularly important in portraiture, closeup, and color photography? pp. 69, 222–241

pp. 268–319 How can I control space rendition and perspective? How can I emphasize, exaggerate, or minimize the feeling of depth? How can I provide pp. 114–119 my picture with scale?

pp. 278–281 How can I prevent perspective distortion; render verticals parallel in angle shots; greatly extend sharpness in depth without stopping down the diaphragm of the lens to prohibitively small stops; get the most out of the "swings" of my view camera?

pp. 302–309 What are the characteristics and differences of rectilinear, cylindrical, and spherical perspectives? What are the advantages and drawbacks of each? What are the means for producing them?

pp. 320–330 What are the different methods for "freezing" high-speed motion? How can I create impressions of motion, action, danger, speed?

pp. 334–337 What are the potentialities and limitations of double and multiple exposures? How, and under what conditions, can I use such "faults" as graininess, flare and halation, or blur to give my pictures extra punch?

p. 348 How can I improve my compositions?

THE NEED FOR PHOTOGRAPHIC CONTROL

The means of modern photography are so highly refined that it is almost impossible *not* to render a subject in the form of a recognizable picture, regardless of the circumstances under which it was made. But there is an enormous difference between a recognizable and an *impressive* photograph of the same subject. The photograph in which the subject is merely recognizable may be adequate for many purposes but it will rarely leave a lasting impression. The difference between that kind of photograph and one that does impress—the kind of picture one remembers because it is thought-provoking, stimulating, *different*—is usually accounted for by the extent of control which a photographer was able to exert over his medium.

In this sense, exerting control over his picture means making the best of pp. 15, 19, 35 one's opportunities in regard to subject selection, approach, and rendition. Any good photographer knows that any subject can be photographed in many different ways, some more effective than others. The first impression may not be the best, nor may the first considered mode of approach or method of rendition be the most effective. If they are immediately obvious, it stands to reason that they are too similar to (if not identical with) those which have already been used by other photographers, and are therefore not likely to capture the attention of an observer whose sensibility has been dulled from picture bombardment by magazines, newspapers, books, movies, and television screens. To give the reader an idea of the innumerable ways in which he can control his pictures, and thereby show even old and familiar subjects in new and interesting forms, was another reason for compiling this book.

A further reason was my desire to dispel the popular myth that photography is a naturalistic medium of rendition and that a photograph is a purely mechanical reproduction of the subject. Actually, it would be difficult to imagine a less naturalistic form of rendition than a black-and-white photograph. With the exception of a photographic reproduction of a page of print, few photographs can truthfully be called reproductions because most photographic subjects have three dimensions: height, width, and depth, whereas a photograph has only two; depth is lost. Furthermore, the world around us appears in color, but a black-and-white photograph shows only shades of gray; color is lost. Also, the majority of photographic subjects move or change appearance, but a photograph is a "still"; motion and life are lost. In reality, direct light is radiant, whereas in photographic rendition it is the same as white; radiance is lost.

A reproduction is a replica which in every important respect is identical with the original. Obviously, then, since a photograph cannot reproduce such vital characteristics of most subjects as depth, motion, radiance, and, if the picture is in black-and-white, color, it is *not* a "reproduction." And because a photograph cannot reproduce reality, speaking of realism in connection with photography is absurd.

The conclusion seems obvious to me. Since the overwhelming majority of photographs can never be realistic in the true sense of the word, we may as well cease to strive for a form of realism that can be no more than superficial. Instead, we should take advantage of the inherent characteristics and potentialities of the photographic medium to present our surroundings in new, exciting ways through the magic of the lens, and take human vision beyond its congenital limits.

To achieve this goal, to translate concepts into picture form, and to choose from the many available means of graphic expression those best suited to characterize particular subject qualities, a photographer must be familiar with all the resources of his medium and able to command them at will. This book intends to show him the way.

THE CONCEPT OF PHOTOGRAPHIC CONTROL

In view of the nature of the photographic medium, it is surprising that it is at all possible to produce *effective* photographs because, as we have seen, *some of the most important subject qualities cannot be rendered directly in photographic form.* Although, in photographic form, most subjects lack some vitally important qualities—depth, motion, radiance, and, if the picture is in black-and-white, color—many photographers still expect their "uncontrolled" pictures to represent the subject effectively p. 86 because they still believe that "the camera does not lie." The fallacy of this notion, of course, is shown again and again in every photograph that didn't "come off"; that disappoints because it lacks the drama and excitement of the actual event; that suffers from perspective distortion, "converging verticals," lack of depth, excess or lack of contrast, insufficient tonal separation, "unnatural" color, unwanted graininess or blur, unsatisfactory illumination, absence of a feeling of motion, or falsification of a characteristic mood.

In black-and-white photography, colors are translated into shades of gray. Because this happens automatically, most photographers accept it without much thought and feel little necessity for controlling the translation. As a result, their pictures, lacking one of the main characteristics of most subjects—color—all too frequently leave the observer with an impression less vivid than that which the subject itself would have created.

In contrast to this approach, creative photographers carefully control the pp. 52–55 transformation of color into shades of gray. By choosing color filters for pp. 55–61 visualized pictorial effects; selecting film for its color sensitivity and pp. 176–215 gradation; using illumination of a particular quality and controlling it in regard to direction, intensity, and contrast; choosing sensitized paper of suitable gradation; and by "dodging" during printing, photographers transform colorful reality into graphically exciting photographs that, through imaginative exploitation of the expressive qualities of black-and-white, achieve impact. Although their pictures also lack color, this loss is compensated for by the *creation of new values*—values which did not exist in this form in reality and which, consequently, the observer could not have seen in the subject itself.

pp. 63–64
pp. 73, 170

Similar considerations also apply to the representation of space within the two-dimensional plane of the photograph. Since most subjects are three-dimensional, and a photograph has only two dimensions, one dimension, depth, is lost during the translation from reality into picture form. As with color in black-and-white photography, space and extension in depth can be expressed photographically only in symbolic form.

pp. 268–319

In any photograph, actual depth is automatically changed into graphic "perspective." And, because this change is automatic, many photographers accept whatever form it happens to take in their pictures, unaware that perspective can be manifest in many forms which can be controlled by the photographer to produce whatever space illusions he may wish to create.

What we call perspective is the apparent converging of horizontal lines toward the horizon, the apparent converging of vertical lines toward height or depth, the apparent diminution of object size with increasing distance from the observer, and the apparent increase in lightness toward depth (aerial perspective). These phenomena can be controlled by any knowledgeable photographer. In his picture, he can either preserve, accentuate, or minimize their appearance in accordance with artistic demands, the characteristics of the subject, and the purpose of the picture. It is for such control that the creative photographer selects a certain subject distance, camera point, and angle of view; that he chooses a lens with a particular focal length and a filter which will produce the desired degree of aerial perspective. The principles which govern such selections are illustrated in this book together with the effects they create.

p. 268
p. 270
p. 318
pp. 278–319
pp. 26–33
pp. 40, 52
pp. 318–319

Two other useful means of photographic expression that are often either

pp. 220, 326–329
neglected or misused are unsharpness and blur. Although at times justly said to be faults, these forms of rendition, properly used, can symbolize subject qualities that, like color in a black-and-white picture or depth in any photograph, cannot be expressed directly in photographic form. Furthermore, pictures that are unsharp or blurred show the subject as the healthy eye can never see it without special aids and thus can enrich our visual experience.

pp. 154, 156
Unsharpness, which is controlled through selective focusing, appropriate use of the diaphragm, or the employment of a soft-focus device, can be used to emphasize a definite, sharply defined picture zone in depth
pp. 316–317
(objects before and behind this zone appear increasingly unsharp), to graphically separate planes situated at different distances from the camera (the subject rendered sharply in front of an unsharp background or behind an unsharp foreground), to create a feeling of space and
pp. 207, 220
depth, to introduce an unrealistic or dreamlike mood, or to symbolize certain intangible qualities such as tenderness or femininity.

pp. 320 326–329
Blur—directional unsharpness—is controlled by a shutter speed appropriate to the movement of the subject or by moving the camera during the exposure. It is the most expressive means for accomplishing a paradox: to create a feeling of motion within the limits of a still. How a feeling of motion, action, and speed can be created by photographic means is part of the subject of this book.

Again and again we find that a "photographic lie" is necessary to make a picture appear "true." For example, in "uncontrolled" architectural photographs that were taken with the lens tilted upward (no matter
p. 280
how slightly), the sides of buildings or the walls of rooms converge toward the top of the picture, producing the impression of leaning. Although this manifestation of perspective is perfectly natural, many people find it objectionable because they haven't trained their eyes to see it consciously in reality. To avoid this effect, a photographer can control perspective rendition in several ways, either on the film or in the
pp. 280, 281
print, as we will see later, and thereby render vertical lines parallel in his picture.

Another time a deliberate "photographic lie" may be required to create a vivid impression would be when an automobile race is being photographed. Many photographers, using fast lenses and high shutter speeds, freeze the action and produce pictures in which the cars appear to be standing still. In this way, of course, they negate the purpose of the picture which is to convey something of the excitement, speed, and drama of a race. Using a different approach, a photographer who is exerting control will either use the technique known as "panning," or select a shutter speed slow enough to produce a carefully considered amount of blur—not enough to make the cars unrecognizable, but sufficient to create a feeling of speed.

p. 330

pp. 326–329

To give a third example, let us suppose that a black-and-white fashion shot of a green dress trimmed with red must be made. In an uncontrolled photograph, the colors green and red would be rendered as more or less identical shades of gray, tonal separation would be lost (and with it the particular character of the dress which largely depends upon the contrast between green and red), and the photograph would appear untrue. However, if control were exerted with the aid of filters, tonal separation could be achieved and thus the outstanding quality of the dress could be symbolized graphically. If an orange filter were used, the green would appear dark and the red aggressively light; conversely, if a green filter were used, the reverse effect would be produced, the green appearing light and the red, dark.

pp. 242–245

In addition to the controls offered by subject selection in accordance with photogenic considerations, subject approach with its many possibilities, and the graphic–artistic complex of expression known as composition, photographers also have the choice of cameras of different types and sizes, different lenses, shutter speeds, diaphragm settings, filters, films, developers, paper gradations, means and methods of illumination—to name only the most important factors that determine the graphic effect of a picture. Now, since each of these controls can be varied to a greater or lesser degree, and any can be combined with others, depending upon the objective of the photographer, an imaginative and resourceful worker has an almost unlimited number of different combinations at his disposal, equivalent to an almost unlimited number of different forms in which any subject can be depicted in a photograph. This partly explains why some photographers are more successful than others. Those who are unsuccessful neglect the creative potentialities of control. Again and again they use pictorial clichés, whereas successful photographers are familiar with and, whenever possible, fully exploit the different means of control.

pp. 15, 19

pp. 35–64

THE PURIST'S ATTITUDE TOWARD CONTROL

To be able to take full advantage of the various photographic symbols that, in the photograph, represent subject qualities that cannot be rendered directly in picture form, a photographer must know how to control his medium. Purists as a rule frown upon the use of symbols and controls, although they themselves, however unknowingly, use most of them: the gray shades that symbolize color; perspective, diminution, overlapping, the symbols of depth and space. The only apparent difference is that they accept the chance appearance of these symbols and make no effort to control (and thus to decide) their final form because they regard "control" as equivalent to faking. However, since photographers are forced by the very nature of their medium to work with symbols, it seems to me that instead of accepting whatever chance may present, it is far more sensible deliberately to select the symbols best suited for expressing specific subject qualities and to control the manifestation of these symbols in accordance with the individual requirements of each subject or event.

What, actually, does the purist mean when he speaks of "straight" photography (as opposed to controlled photography)? Unquestionably, Mathew Brady's Civil War photographs are examples of straight photography, as are Atget's pictures of Paris. But is this definition still applicable to Edward Weston's work, which is dodged during contact printing? Furthermore, is an unfiltered photograph necessarily more honest as a picture than a filtered shot although it shows, for example, the sky empty and white whereas in reality it was blue and dotted with clouds? And should the picture of a racing car streaking down the track be sharp or blurred, or appear to be standing still or in motion? And, if the use of dodging and filters is acceptable to the purist, why is the use of blur or perspective controls not acceptable, or of film grain, or halation and flare? Where should one draw the line between reporting and faking?

pp. 73, 170

pp. 226–227

How meaningless such squabbles are becomes apparent in considering a situation like the following: Two photographers record a boxing match. One is an amateur who uses a simple camera with a relatively slow lens and shoots by available light; the other is a professional who uses a press camera in conjunction with synchronized electronic flash. The pictures of the first are blurred and suggest action. Those of the second are sharply defined, the motion arrested. Let us suppose that the pictures of both, each set in its own way, report the event dramatically. Now, of the two sets of pictures so different from each other, can we say that only one is "pure" photography? And which of the two?

To me, both sets are potentially effective representations of the event, although each, of course, reflects a different approach. One has what the other lacks. The first, through blur, suggests the violence of action and dramatically illustrates the concept "fight." The second, through sharpness of rendition, shows that which could not have been seen in reality because it happened too fast: the impact of fist on chin and its effect upon the face. Either approach is legitimate. This example clearly indicates the need for planning and control if a photographer is to present in his pictures those aspects of a subject or event which he considers most important for effective characterization. To my mind, theorizing about straight versus controlled photography, experimental versus documentary approach, artistic intensification versus falsifying interference, and so forth, is a waste of time—indulged in by those who prefer talk to the more exacting task of making pictures. There are only *two* kinds of photographs and photographers: good and poor. The poor photographers, unimaginative and timid in their work, imitative rather than inventive, are enslaved by obsolete rules. In contrast, good photographers, continuously searching for new means of graphic expression, improve their craft through imaginative use of any means at hand.

p. 92

PHOTOGRAPHIC FINGER EXERCISES

It is axiomatic that the best way to learn to make good photographs is through practice. Reading about photography is necessary and recommended, and so is the study of the work of more accomplished photographers. But both are only preparatory to the work one hopes to do himself. And, no matter what a photographer may know about taking pictures, until he actually gets down to taking them, his theoretical knowledge is of little practical worth.

The purpose of this book is to encourage the reader to experiment and thus increase his scope. It is a thoroughly practical book, a new teaching technique. In a way, the series of comparative photographs which form its backbone can be likened to the finger exercises of the musician.

Normally, of course, no one would photograph the same subject through all the color filters from red to blue. But to be able to choose the most effective filter in a given case, a photographer must be familiar with the effect of every filter upon every color. The examples given on pp. 242–247 will help him to achieve this goal. The same can be said of all the other examples included here—the various methods and controls for the effective rendition of space, depth, motion, contrast, texture, light, and so forth. To get the full benefit from these examples, I recommend that the reader actually repeat each exercise by taking a series of photographs of a suitable subject in the various ways that are described later on; that he make complete and accurate notes concerning every step of each experiment; that he preserve all his negatives and prints whether they are successful or not; and that he mount them, together with their data, in an organized sequence which will be available for reference. The money, effort, and time spent upon this work will be the best investment a photographer can make in his future.

Lillinonah, April 1970 *Andreas Feininger*

PART 2

The Extent of Photographic Control

Practical considerations make it advisable to classify the various controls which a photographer has at his disposal as belonging to one of three stages in the making of a photograph:

Subject Selection
Subject Approach
Subject Rendition

To the uninitiated it may seem as if these stages were totally independent of one another, but, actually, precisely the opposite is true. Each forms an important link in a chain of events that begins with an idea in the photographer's mind and ends with a picture, the effect of which will be the stronger, the more the photographer was able to utilize the various photographic controls and integrate them into his master plan. Unless he can accomplish this, a mistake or an omission made earlier in the proceedings will invariably have its effect at a later stage, and no amount of skill and work can ever completely correct the resulting defect of the picture. This interdependence of the different steps and controls involved in the making of a photograph cannot be emphasized strongly enough; to understand it and act accordingly is a prerequisite for success.

The methods of photographic control described later in this book apply essentially to both color and black-and-white photography. Naturally, there are certain exceptions which are applicable *only* to color *or* to black-and-white photography, respectively. For example, some methods of contrast control based upon the use of color filters can be used only in black-and-white photography, whereas all controls dealing with the direct rendition of color (as opposed to translation of color into shades of gray) apply only to color photography. But barring such exceptions, the principles of control are as valid in color photography as they are in black-and-white. This is only to be expected since, of course, the problems of how to symbolize subject qualities such as three-dimensionality and depth, motion and change, the radiance of direct light, mood and "atmosphere," and so forth, are essentially the same, whether the picture is planned for execution in black-and-white or in color.

pp. 20–24

An important injunction that should be mentioned at the outset is that, for best results, a photograph must be planned beforehand for execution *either* in color *or* in black-and-white. From a purely technical point of view, most subjects can, of course, be photographed equally well in color and in black-and-white. Since not only the *techniques* of color and black-and-white photography are somewhat different from one another particularly in regard to problems of contrast range and illumination, and the *emotional effect* of a picture in color is different from that of one in black-and-white, it is usually *not* possible to photograph a subject in both media *under identical conditions* if optimal results are expected.

An example will clarify this point: in color photography, the most important picture element is color; in black-and-white, it is contrast, i.e., juxtaposition and interplay of light and dark, outline, and form. Now, let's assume that we must take two photographs: one, on a beach, of a girl in a red bathing suit seen against a deep blue sky; the other, in the studio, of a model in a dress of delicate shades of pastel colors that harmonize with one another. Each could be quite effective photographed in color, but very dull in an uncontrolled black-and-white photograph, because the colors which in reality differ in hue would be rendered as almost identical shades of gray; lack of separation of tone and form would result in a flat, insipid picture. For *effective* presentation of these subjects in black-and-white, a photographer would have to illuminate each one quite differently to create the necessary contrast for adequate tonal and spatial differentiation. This, of course, would require a different approach, for instead of featuring color, the photographer would have to base the graphic effect of his picture upon contrast, line, and form. Therefore, whereas the color shots would probably demand frontal illumination, a black-and-white rendition, in addition to appropriate filtration, might require sidelight or backlight. In the outdoor picture, this would doubtlessly necessitate a change in camera position, and, in the studio shot, a rearrangement of the lights.

PART 3

Control in Regard to Subject Selection

Experienced photographers know that it is of practical advantage to assign photographic subjects to one of two groups: those which possess what are popularly known as photogenic qualities, and those which lack these characteristics. Photogenic subjects have qualities which make them particularly well suited to rendition with typically photographic means. Unphotogenic subjects, which lack such qualities, make notoriously disappointing pictures.

Below are listed what I consider the ten most important photogenic qualities. The more of these qualities a subject possesses, the greater the probability that it will appear effective in a photograph. On the other hand, the fewer of these qualities it has, the greater is the likelihood that it will make a disappointing picture:

Clarity and simplicity of organization, outline, and form.
Contrast, i.e., satisfactory differentiation in regard to color, tonal shades, and spatial elements.
Forms that are clean-cut, interesting, and bold.
Outline that is typical of the subject, powerful, or unusual, including pure silhouettes.
Graphic design, i.e., artistically effective arrangement in regard to lines, forms, and distribution of light and dark picture elements.
Depth suggested by receding lines, objects situated in different planes, or aerial perspective.
Texture that characterizes and enlivens the subject's surface.
Detail that is meaningful and crisp.
Pattern, i.e., rhythm and repetition of significant, related forms.
Spontaneity and motion indicative of action and life.

Subjects that either lack the characteristics listed above or have the following unphotogenic qualities are likely to appear disappointing in picture form, no matter how much they may appeal to the eye. However, occasionally, even subjects which have some of these normally undesirable characteristics can make interesting pictures when competently handled by an imaginative photographer.

pp. 100–107 **Complexity and disorder,** usually the result of an attempt on the part of the photographer to include too much subject matter in a single photograph instead of presenting it in the form of several pictures. Overcrowding a picture with too much detail by shooting from too far away is a common mistake of the beginner.

pp. 222–241 **Lack of contrast** (this applies only to black-and-white photography) that prevents a graphically effective separation of the various picture elements through translation of color into different shades of gray.

pp. 242–247 **Significant coloration** (this applies only to black-and-white photography). If color is the outstanding quality of a subject (for example, food, fruit, flowers, birds, butterflies, and so on), even the best possible translation of color into shades of gray will fail to characterize such subjects effectively. A color photograph is then essential.

pp. 114–119 **Absence of spatial definition and scale,** i.e., subjects in which space is not defined in terms of receding lines, objects situated in different planes, aerial perspective, or scale. A typical example of this is a wide-open view without foreground matter. Though pleasing to the eye, such a view almost invariably makes a disappointing picture.

pp. 122–127 **Unsuitable background,** one which is so similar in tone or texture to the subject proper of the picture that it blends with it, or one that detracts too much because it is too aggressive or dominating in color or design.

Since subjects that possess photogenic qualities invariably make better pictures than subjects that lack such qualities, a knowledgeable photographer will, as far as possible, select the former and reject the latter. Evaluated in this way, subject selection—the possibility of choice on the part of the photographer to select or reject—becomes an important means of photographic control that can be exercised far in advance of the actual production of the picture.

The importance of subject selection on the basis of photogenic qualities cannot be overemphasized. It greatly increases a photographer's chances for succeeding in his task because it gives him the invaluable advantage of a good start. Actually, of course, this is nothing new. Any craftsman who makes sure that his raw material is not only perfect but also suitable for the job at hand before he spends (and possibly wastes) time and energy on it, practices, in effect, subject selection. Similarly, any commercial photographer, fashion editor, or art director who, prior to a photographic session, screens a number of prospective models before he chooses one as most suitable for the intended task, exerts control over the final appearance of his picture through subject control.

Subject control through selection is possible in virtually any field of photography. Granted—it is easiest in cases in which the number of potential subjects is large, as, for example, in travel and landscape photography. It becomes progressively more difficult the more clearly defined the subject is, as in documentary or architectural photography. And it can be a real challenge to the photographer's resourcefulness and ingenuity if the assignment is very specific, as in portraiture, product, and scientific photography. However, even under such limiting conditions, a knowledgeable and imaginative photographer will usually be able to avoid those hopeless shots that a less competent photographer might attempt, only to deplore when he sees the result.

To be more specific, I'd like to illustrate the problem of subject selection by describing an actual experience. A few years ago, *Life* decided to try for a cover shot of a big rocket seen against the rising moon. To minimize the chances of failure through bad weather, two photographers were assigned to two widely separated locations—Ralph Crane to California, I to Huntsville, Alabama. As far as the editors knew, both of us were going to shoot under identical conditions. In both areas, the Army had promised full cooperation. In both cases, the subject was the same, a giant rocket and the moon. But there the similarity ended because, actually, conditions on location were so different that in one case they led to success and in the other to failure.

The California location was perfect. The rocket stood in a very photogenic gantry, studded with glittering worklights, silhouetted against the sky. In front, the ground stretched perfectly level for a considerable distance, far enough for Crane to back up and shoot the picture with a super-telephoto lens of a focal length sufficiently long to render the moon in impressive scale. The timing, too, was right, since everything was ready by the time the moon was full and the sky at moonrise was still light enough to register well in color. As a result of these photogenic conditions, Crane was able to make a set of very striking pictures.

In contrast, at Huntsville, the missile was set up at the edge of the Army's airstrip, not in a gantry, but on a low, circular launching table of the kind that would be used under actual field conditions. Practical—yes; photogenic—decidedly not, for it left the rocket standing unadorned and naked. Unfortunately, also, Huntsville is surrounded by mountains, and the farther back I stepped to bring my big telephoto lens into position, the more the mountains appeared to rise, covering just that part of the sky where the moon was scheduled to appear. But worse still, the airfield was not level. It was located on the bulldozed top of a hill and had the shape of an inverted saucer. The farther back I stepped, the lower my point of view became, and the more the ground between my camera and the rocket rose, gradually cutting off the launching table and the bottom of the missile and threatening to obscure the men who were pretending to fuel the rocket. As a result, shooting distance between the camera and the rocket was severely restricted and much too short to use a telephoto lens with a focal length long enough to render the moon sufficiently large. To compound the misery, the Army had been unable to set the missile up in time, as a result of which I was unable to shoot until two days after the full moon. As far as the picture of the moon itself was concerned, this made no difference; but it made the difference between success and failure in regard to rendition of the sky. Each night the moonrise progresses by approximately one hour, and although at the time of the rise of the full moon the sky had still been quite light, two days later it was ink-black, and graphic separation of earth and sky became impossible. As a consequence of these unphotogenic conditions, I ended up with what *Life's* picture editor rightly described as a "rather undistinguished picture."

However, important as subject selection in accordance with photogenic principles is, this kind of control covers only the first phase in the making of a successful picture. For, as many a photographer has found out to his sorrow, the picture of a beautiful girl is not necessarily a beautiful picture. Unless knowledge of what to look for in a subject is coupled with knowledge of how to approach and render it, all these preliminary efforts will have been in vain.

PART 4

Control in Regard to Subject Approach

Having chosen from a number of potential subjects the most photogenic one—the one most likely to be effective in picture form—a photographer must next decide how to present it. This involves two phases: p. 15

Subject Approach
Subject Rendition

Each of these is open to a large number of controls that can be used to influence the appearance of the picture and make it more effective than it might have been otherwise. The first phase, subject approach, which is discussed in the following, takes place in the photographer's mind. The second phase, subject rendition, of which more will be said later, concerns the physical implementation of the picture. p. 35

IMAGINATION AND INTEREST

Any subject can be photographed in many different ways, some of which, of course, will be more effective than others. Actually, no two photographers covering the same subject ever come up with identical pictures. And the more creative and imaginative a photographer is, the more different in concept and execution his pictures are likely to be from the run of the mill kind. Such differences, which make for more enjoyable, interesting, and informative pictures, are primarily the result of a different subject approach.

A photographer reveals his personality, talent, and interest by the way in which he approaches his subject. An original subject approach, reflected in a new and more revealing way of seeing, is a sign of imagination, interest in the subject, or both. Conversely, if his approach is dull and his pictures uninspired, one can be quite sure that the photographer either lacked imagination or his subject left him cold. Imagination is a quality that one does or does not have. It cannot be taught but, if latent, can be developed. It is a priceless asset in the making of good photographs. And interest in the subject provides the indispensable driving force without which no photographer can do his best.

COLOR VERSUS BLACK-AND-WHITE

The first decision in regard to subject approach that a photographer must make is whether to take the picture in black-and-white or in color.

Any subject can, of course, be photographed either in black-and-white or in color. Although each medium has its distinct characteristics, neither is by itself superior to the other; they are merely different. Consequently, the choice between black-and-white and color cannot be made on the basis of superiority of one form of rendition over the other, but only on the basis of suitability. To determine which of these two media is more suitable as far as a specific case is concerned, a photographer must consider two aspects, one artistic, the other practical.

Artistic considerations

The choice between rendition in color and in black-and-white is essentially a choice between a more naturalistic and a more abstract form of representation. Since neither is inherently superior and thus preferable to the other, to compare the two is pointless unless the comparison is made in relation to a specific problem. Any such comparison must take into consideration the following three questions:

1. Is color the most important subject quality?

If the answer is affirmative, then rendition in color is probably preferable (unless cancelled by one of the subsequently discussed considerations), since a rendition in black-and-white would be less complete. In such a case, the use of color is not only justified but mandatory for the most effective rendition. Particularly typical subjects of this kind are brilliantly colored flowers, birds, and butterflies; flaming sunset skies; women's fashions; food arrangements; paintings; modern interiors; and many landscape and outdoor scenes. In such subjects, color is too important to be omitted without seriously impairing the informative and aesthetic values of the picture.

On the other hand, if color is not of great importance—if the subject might just as well have been of another color, or if form, spatial aspects, or illumination effects are more important to the characterization of the subject than color—then, of course, rendition in black-and-white is probably preferable because its more abstract nature permits the photographer to work with bolder graphic means and to create artistically more powerful effects.

2. Is a more realistic or a more abstract rendition preferable?

In my experience, it is normally easier to produce artistically satisfactory photographs in black-and-white than in color. Also, whereas a poor black-and-white shot can be overlooked, a poor color picture, because of its more pretentious character, is often aggressively offensive. So, when in doubt, a rendition in black-and-white is normally preferable to one in color.

There is a solid reason behind this fact. We have been so thoroughly conditioned by more than 100 years of black-and-white photography that normally the absence of color in a photograph does not make the subject less recognizable. As a matter of fact, the opposite may occasionally be the case. A good portrait in black-and-white, for example, gives a better and more natural impression of a person than one in color in which the skin tones are discolored toward green, red, or blue, as is so often the case. Similarly, a bold and "graphic" black-and-white rendition of a landscape usually makes a stronger impression than a color shot which, although more naturalistic, may for this very reason appear insipid and trite.

Furthermore, because of its more abstract nature as well as for phototechnical reasons, a black-and-white photograph is easier to control than one in color. Consequently, the photographer can to a higher degree shape his picture to express his concepts of the subject. For black-and-white photography offers a photographer the choice of a larger number of different controls and therefore a greater variety of different forms of rendition, thereby tending to make this medium more stimulating to the creative mind.

p. 25 The purpose of a photograph can be either illustrative or interpretive. If illustrative, its main function is to show the subject as accurately and objectively as possible, complete in all its qualities, color, of course, included. In such a case, color would obviously be preferable to black-and-white.

On the other hand, if the emphasis is on interpretation of a subject's intangible qualities rather than on rendition of its more superficial aspects, a black-and-white photograph is often preferable to one in color. The abstract effect of black-and-white gives a photographer greater freedom for creative-subjective interpretation of qualities that must be indicated in symbolic form because they cannot be depicted directly—qualities such as power and strength, loneliness, sadness and tragedy, pleasure and joy.

The subject proper of a picture is either a concrete thing: a person, an object; or an intangible concept: a mood, a feeling, or a state of mind. In the first case, the basically realistic character of the subject usually makes it more suitable for rendition in color, the more realistic medium of photographic expression. In the latter case, the content of the picture is often better expressed through the more abstract medium of black-and-white photography.

The same subject can, of course, be conceived either as a concrete thing or as an intangible concept. A particular landscape, for example, may inspire a photographer to render it in the form of a "portrait"—the documentary approach—in which case a realistic treatment in color would probably be preferable. Alternatively, he may consider the landscape merely as a vehicle by means of which he can express, in symbolic form, feelings of vastness, loneliness, the grandeur of nature, or the insignificance of man. If this is the case, a black-and-white rendition is usually more likely to produce the strongest effect.

3. Is color likely to turn out technically good or bad?

Even in cases in which other considerations point to color as the more suitable medium of rendition, a treatment in black-and-white may occasionally produce the better result. This is true because no "perfect" color film exists as yet, and satisfactory color rendition can only be expected if certain conditions are fulfilled. And, as was pointed out earlier, a rendition in distorted color (unless deliberately produced and controlled by the photographer as a means to create a specific effect) is generally less satisfactory than a good rendition in black-and-white. Distorted color is most likely to occur under the following conditions:

If the spectral composition of the illumination differs from that for which the color film is balanced
If subject contrast is abnormally high
If subject color is desaturated, i. e., if pastel shades predominate

When any of these conditions exist, it may be advisable, in addition to photographing the subject in color, to photograph it also in black-and-white as a safeguard in case the color shot turns out unsatisfactory.

Sometimes, the choice between color and black-and-white can be made on the basis of the nature of the subject. It usually is relatively safe to photograph *manmade* objects in color because most such objects (works of art, of course, excepted) could be of any color or shade, and therefore even a fairly high degree of color distortion is usually accepted by the observer of the picture who, unfamiliar with the specific subject, could not possibly know whether or not the colors of the rendition were true. On the other hand, most *objects of nature* such as green foliage, flowers, sky and clouds, sea and sand, and common animals and birds, are so familiar to almost anyone that even slight deviations from natural color are immediately detected, causing the photograph to be rejected as unnatural. Most critical in this respect are color photographs of people, particularly portraits in color, in which even the slightest color deviations from normal skin tones appear objectionable. If subjects of this kind must be rendered in color, a photographer should take particular care and make sure that his color is true.

Practical considerations

People who take photographs exclusively for their own pleasure have only to worry about whether they have the necessary know-how to get good color photographs; whether they are willing to pay the higher price of color film; or whether they would be better off to play it safe and be satisfied with the simpler, less expensive black-and-white type of picture. Everyone, of course, must answer such questions for himself. Photographers, however, who expect to sell their work, must also consider *the purpose of their pictures* before they decide whether to take them in color or in black-and-white. In this respect, they must consider the following:

Black-and-white photographs are considerably simpler and cheaper to produce than color photographs. Furthermore, any number of "originals" can be printed easily and inexpensively from a black-and-white negative whereas duplicating a color shot, whether made on reversal or negative color film, is both complicated and costly. In addition, color transparencies are originals and unique; once they are damaged or lost, they are gone forever. On the other hand, in black-and-white photography, the valuable and unique master record, the negative, never has to leave the hands of the photographer who only sends out expendable prints.

Black-and-white photographs still have a larger market than color photographs. If a picture is intended for newspaper or rotogravure reproduction, for illustration of a book or pamphlet printed only in black-and-white, for distribution by Wirephoto service, or for use as a photomural, obviously only black-and-white will do. Also, magazines still use a considerably larger number of editorial illustrations in black-and-white than in color, although this may soon no longer be true. On the other hand, prices paid for black-and-white photographs are generally much lower than those for color work.

Color photographs, because they are more difficult and costly to produce, bring considerably higher prices than pictures in black-and-white. A few days of color work will frequently be as remunerative as an entire month devoted to black-and-white photography.

Color photographs are primarily in demand for advertisements and publicity promotion; magazine covers; feature articles and editorial illustrations in better-class, nationally distributed magazines; record album covers; book jackets; and, in the form of 35mm slides, for educational purposes, training, and lecturing.

ILLUSTRATION VERSUS INTERPRETATION

Choice between an illustrative and an interpretive subject approach is, in my opinion, one of the most consequential controls a photographer has for determining the effect of his picture. The difference between the two is a difference of attitude.

The illustrative approach is objective and factual, honest in the sense that its aim is to show the subject in such a way that it can be recognized immediately by anyone. It is a documentary approach—the approach of a reporter or a scientist, direct, unbiased, and objective inasmuch as the photographer tries to suppress his own opinion. It is an attempt at representing something in picture form as factually as possible, leaving it to the observer of the photograph to draw his own conclusions. p. 98

The interpretive approach is subjective, a deliberate attempt on the part of the photographer to express his personal opinion of the subject. This kind of approach is less concerned with facts than with feelings. Instead of limiting himself to a graphic description of the physical aspects of his subject, an interpretive photographer tries to include in his picture, and convey to the observer, something of what he felt and thought in response to it. This is a much more difficult approach, but potentially ever so much more rewarding because the picture, if successful, instead of being merely descriptive, will, in addition, show the subject to the observer in a new light. p. 99

At its best, an illustrative photograph is interesting and informative; but an interpretive photograph at its best is not only interesting and informative, but also stimulating to the mind.

However, an interpretive approach is not necessarily better than an illustrative one. As with the choice between color and black-and-white, neither is superior to the other; they are merely different. Consequently, the decision must always be made in accordance with the requirements of the particular case. Obviously, it would be foolish to use an interpretive approach when factual accuracy is of prime importance, as in scientific and catalog photography. And besides, a factual approach does not necessarily need to be stereotyped and dull. Even a strictly factual photograph can be made pictorially attractive through imagination and photo-technical resourcefulness. Such a photograph can even be enlivened by the incorporation of certain interpretive touches without forfeit of accuracy. On the other hand, an interpretive photograph need not necessarily be abstract to the point where the subject is unrecognizable; it can very well include factual features without losing its stimulating character.

PHYSICAL ASPECTS OF APPROACH

Most photographs are concerned with the rendition of three-dimensional subjects located in three-dimensional space. From this, it follows that, at least theoretically, a photographer has an infinite number of viewpoints or camera positions from which to choose the one that will enable him to present his subject in the most effective form.

Once again, creative control is essentially a process of rejection and selection: reject the obviously undesirable and unattainable camera positions and, from the remainder, select the best. This problem of selection may sound difficult but immediately becomes relatively simple if the photographer considers its two phases separately: subject distance and direction of view.

Subject distance

Appropriate choice of subject distance is a valuable though often unrealized means of photographic control because this factor determines two important picture aspects:

The scale of subject rendition
The relationship of foreground to background

The scale of subject rendition. The image of the subject on the film will be the larger, the shorter the subject-to-camera distance and/or the longer the focal length of the lens, and vice versa. The two extremes are the close-up and the overall view.

p. 282

pp. 100–109

THE CLOSE-UP. A common fault of many photographs is that they contain too much subject matter. This overabundance of subject matter, being squeezed into too small a format, is then rendered in such a small scale that it is graphically ineffective. Typical examples are photographs of people taken in full figure in which the identifying factor, the face, is so tiny that it is virtually unrecognizable. This undesirable effect is due to the fact that the distance between subject and camera was too great or that the picture was made with a lens of insufficiently long focal length.

This habit of shooting from too far away probably results from the unconscious wish to reproduce a subject or event exactly as it appeared to the eye. Few amateur photographers realize that, for reasons already mentioned, a literal translation of reality into picture form is usually impossible, and that any attempt to make such a translation is likely to fail as far as picture impact is concerned. On the other hand, with the aid of the appropriate controls, it is entirely possible to produce photographs that show aspects of the subject that the observer had not noticed in reality, and thus to create even stronger impressions than those made by the actual scene. One such control is the close-up.

A close-up is either a photograph taken from a relatively short subject-to-camera distance, or one made with a lens of longer than standard focal length. As far as impact is concerned, close-ups generally score higher than the average type of photograph for the following reasons:

pp. 108, 109
pp. 104–107

A close-up is a highly concentrated form of rendition containing fewer unimportant or distracting picture elements than average views. It shows the subject in a more tightly edited version, often limiting itself to showing only its most significant part. As a result, it is a particularly clear form of pictorial statement, and, as we learned before, clarity ranks high among the photogenic qualities.

Because close-ups show the subject in larger scale than average pictures, they show it with clearer rendition of surface texture and fine detail. As a result, they often show aspects which the observer had been unable to see in reality, thereby giving a stronger impression of the subject and contributing to the viewer's knowledge.

Finally, because most photographs are taken at relatively great subject-to-camera distances, close-ups are comparatively rare, and the rare automatically commands more attention than the common.

THE OVERALL VIEW is the opposite of the close-up, a photograph

pp. 100, 106

either taken from a greater-than-average distance between subject and camera, or with a wide-angle lens. Whereas a close-up shows the subject in a highly concentrated form, an overall view presents it in the context of its surroundings. The purpose of an overall view is usually to provide an impression of the entire subject-complex: for example, to prepare the reader of a magazine for the more specific views that will follow as the picture story unfolds.

p. 152

If circumstances prevent a photographer from increasing the distance between subject and camera sufficiently to take an overall shot with a lens of standard focal length, a wide-angle lens will usually enable him to get the desired panoramic effect. However, although the area included in the picture may be the same in a wide-angle shot taken from nearby as in a shot made with a lens of standard focal length from farther away, the relative proportions of the individual picture components to one another will be quite different in the two views. This brings us to the second role which subject distance plays in regard to the effect of the picture:

The relationship of foreground to background. It is a fallacious but extremely persistent idea, not only among beginners and amateurs but even among many professional photographers, that wide-angle lenses cause perspective distortion and telephoto lenses produce pictures in which space is "compressed." This is, strictly speaking, not true. These phenomena, although real enough, are *not* caused by faults inherent in these lenses; they are solely the product of subject-to-camera distance. This anyone can find out for himself by performing the following experiment.

p. 282

Take your camera to a place that offers a good overall view of your town. Without changing the camera position in any way (best, mount your camera on a tripod), take three photographs: the first with a lens of standard focal length, the second with a wide-angle lens, the third with a telephoto lens. To simplify later comparison of the three shots, be sure that a prominent building, tower, or other kind of landmark appears in the center of all three. Develop your films and make two sets of enlargements in accordance with the following instructions:

THE FIRST SET. Make one enlargement of each of the three negatives *on the same size paper* (for example, 5 x 7 in.). In each case, be sure to enlarge the entire negative without cropping, using the same degree of magnification for each.

As you might have anticipated (see page 282), the picture taken with the lens of standard focal length will appear normal; the wide-angle shot will seem distorted because foreground matter will appear too large and prominent in comparison to the more distant buildings of the town; and in the telephotograph, space will seem compressed because buildings actually remote will appear unfamiliarly near. However, as you will see in a moment, these seeming abnormalities are only optical illusions.

THE SECOND SET. Make one enlargement of each of the three negatives on the same size paper that you used before. However, this time enlarge each negative *to the same image* (NOT negative!) *scale*, using the scale of the telephoto shot as the standard. Begin with the telephoto shot and enlarge the full negative to 5 x 7 in. (if this is the paper size you used for your first set of prints). Next, on 5 x 7 in. paper, enlarge the negative taken with the lens of standard focal length *to the exact scale of the telephoto print*, a process which necessitates raising the enlarger head to obtain the necessary higher degree of magnification. Finally, on 5 x 7 in. paper, enlarge the negative taken with the wide-angle lens *to the exact scale of the telephoto print*, once more adjusting the enlarger to give the required degree of magnification. Naturally, in making the last two prints, you will print only that section of the negative which corresponds to the subject area covered by the telephoto shot.

EVALUATION OF THE EXPERIMENT. Place the three prints of your second set side by side and compare them. Apart from differences in graininess and definition caused by the differences in degree of magnification, you will find that, as far as perspective, presence or absence of distortion, or compression of space are concerned, *there will be absolutely no difference among the three prints.* THEY WILL BE IDENTICAL, despite the fact that they were made from negatives taken with lenses of three different focal lengths. Why is this so? Because all three photographs were taken from the identical camera position (and therefore subject-to-camera distance), and *it is the subject-to-camera distance alone which determines the perspective of a picture.*

pp. 288–289

Now, return for a moment to the first set of prints and compare them.

Each print, of course, produces a different effect. But actually, this difference is *not* a difference of perspective, but only a difference in scale and angle of view: an optical illusion. The wide-angle shot, encompassing a wider-than-normal angle of view rendered in relatively small scale, shows a greater area than the picture taken with the lens of standard focal length, which includes a somewhat narrower angle of view rendered in somewhat larger scale. And the picture taken with the telephoto lens takes in a still smaller area rendered in still larger scale. But, although they differ in regard to angle of view and image scale, within comparable picture areas, *the proportions of the individual picture components to one another as well as the effects of overlapping and relative diminution are identical in all three prints,* a fact which is only natural, since the three pictures were taken from the identical point of view.

pp. 283–285 A SECOND EXPERIMENT. In case you want additional proof of the fact that it is subject-to-camera distance and *not* the focal length of the lens that is responsible for the perspective and possible "distortion" of your pictures, try this second highly instructive experiment:

p. 284 Photograph a person against an easily identifiable background of buildings, trees, and so forth, which are neither too close to the person nor too far away. Take three photographs with different lenses, one with a lens of standard focal length, one with a wide-angle lens, and one with a telephoto lens. Select your subject distance so that *the image of the person depicted will be identical in scale in each picture,* for example, exactly the height of the negative, regardless of the type of lens used. To do this, of course, you must take the wide-angle shot from a relatively short distance, the shot with the lens of standard focal length from somewhat farther away, and the telephoto picture from a still greater distance. The main thing is that the model be rendered in exactly the same image size on all three negatives. To simplify later comparison, keep the angle of view constant in all three shots, selecting a point of reference in line with, but far behind, your subject—a specific building or a particular tree—and be sure that it occupies the same position in each shot. Develop your films, make 5x7 in. enlargements of the full negatives, and compare the differences in "perspective."

Although the scale of rendition of the subject proper, that is the figure, will be the same in all three photographs, the spatial effect of each shot will be different. In the picture made with the lens of standard focal length, space will appear normal. In the wide-angle shot, distance between subject and background will appear greater than it appeared to the eye, and space will appear extended: the buildings, trees, and such in the background will be rendered disproportionately small. Conversely, in the telephotograph, distance between subject and background will appear smaller than it appeared to the eye, space will appear less extensive (compressed), and background objects will seem to loom up unnaturally large and close.

Now, you may perhaps think that these are exactly the effects which you noticed in the first set of prints from your first experiment, in which space also appeared normal, exaggerated, and compressed, respectively. But in this you would be wrong. In your first set of pictures, the different spatial impressions were caused by an optical illusion as was proved by appropriate enlarging, which produced a set of prints that, although made from negatives taken with lenses of different focal lengths, were identical in regard to perspective and, if superimposed, would register down to the smallest detail.

However, no matter how you enlarge this last set of negatives, you will never be able to produce prints which match with regard to perspective. And, no matter how hard you try, you cannot equalize the different spatial impressions produced by the three photographs because, in this case, *these differences are real.*

Why is this so? Because in your first experiment the distance between subject and camera was always the same, which resulted in a set of pictures in which perspective was the same, too. But in the second experiment, the three comparison pictures were shot at different subject-to-camera distances, as a result of which the perspective is different in each.

CONCLUSION. A photographer has far-reaching control over the spatial effect of his pictures in regard to scale of rendition, perspective, the relative proportions of the individual picture components to one another, and the extent of the encompassed angle of view. This control is effected through appropriate selection of the distance between subject and camera in conjunction with selection of a lens of appropriate focal length and covering power (angle of view). As a result, a good photographer can render space in his pictures exactly as he experiences it.

Direction of view

Only a beginner will be satisfied with the first view of his subject and photograph it accordingly. An experienced photographer knows that the first view is not necessarily the best; that the most obvious view is likely to result in a picture that "has been done before"; and that any three-dimensional subject can be approached from a virtually unlimited number of different angles. Accordingly, as far as conditions permit, he will study his subject from all sides: front and back, right and left, above and below, before he commits it to film, taking full advantage of his privilege of choice, and select his camera position and direction of view under consideration of the following factors:

p. 110

The nature of the subject
The nature of the background
The angle of the illumination
The purpose of the picture

The nature of the subject. Some subjects, such as a man, a dog, or a car, have definite front, side, rear, and top views. Others, a landscape, a street, or a tree, lack these characteristics, although they may appear very different when approached from different directions. Naturally, it makes a difference whether a picture shows a subject in frontal instead of side view, or perhaps seen from above or below, although it must be understood that, for example, a frontal view is not necessarily more beautiful, important, or informative than a view from a different direction. A prize-winning photograph of John F. Kennedy, for instance, shows the late president silhouetted against a window with his back toward the camera.

pp. 110–111

Furthermore, thought must be given to the perspective of the future picture, specifically to foreshortening, diminution, overlapping, and distortion. Seen from one direction, a subject may appear "distorted," particularly if subject-to-camera distance is relatively short and the shot is to be made with a wide-angle lens; or it may appear confused because of an unfortunate overlapping of some of its components. A change in the direction of view usually avoids such undesirable effects.

pp. 268–272, 312–315

pp. 122–127

The nature of the background. The very word "background" seems to imply something unimportant, something not worth wasting one's time on, something that can be disregarded. And disregarded the background of the subject often is, very much to the detriment of the photograph. For an unsuitable background can ruin the effect of any picture, a reason why the background should get as much attention on the part of the photographer as the subject itself. Graphically speaking, a good background is one which is unobtrusive enough not to distract the observer's attention from the subject of the picture but which, at the same time, emphasizes the subject, making it more prominent with regard to color and design by contrasting it with its own muted subordination.

Now, whereas it is usually very simple to change the appearance of an unsuitable background if the subject is movable (a person, a small object), if the subject is stationary (a monument, a tree), controlling the background may require some patience, time, and ingenuity. In such a case, the three most effective background controls are: (1) approaching the subject from a different angle to show it against a different background; (2) taking the picture with a relatively large diaphragm stop to throw the background out of focus and, by rendering it unsharp, make it less obtrusive; and (3) making the shot at a different time of day or under different atmospheric conditions in order to tone down the background by means of shadow or haze. If none of these controls can be applied, an unsuitable background is, in my opinion, reason enough to abstain from making the picture.

pp. 154–157, 316

The angle of the illumination. If neither the subject nor the source of illumination is movable (otherwise, there would be no problem), selection of the most effective direction of view must take place with due consideration to the angle of the incident light. Photographing a monument, for example, a photographer may find that the best direction of view, as far as the subject itself is concerned (i.e., in regard to angle of view, foreshortening, overlapping of individual forms, and so forth) is unfortunately, unsatisfactory as far as the illumination is concerned (the angle of the incident light). If this is the case, he has the choice of several possibilities. He can wait until the sun has moved into a more suitable position, resulting in a better distribution of light and shadow (which may require his returning some other time); he can come back when the sky is overcast and the light more evenly diffused; he can make the shot at night by artificial light (street lights or, if the job is important enough and he has the necessary authority and means, flash); or he can decide to forego the picture. For, in the last analysis, rejection is as much a means of photographic control as selection.

The purpose of the picture. It obviously makes a difference whether a photograph is made, say, to illustrate a textbook or to convey an emotional experience. In the first case, only a strictly factual, i.e., illustrative, subject approach can lead to success, whereas in the second case, an imaginative, i.e., interpretive, approach is most likely to produce the desired result. In terms of subject approach this means that in the first case a matter-of-fact direction of view (perhaps head-on), which avoids the danger of perspective distortion and thereby shows the subject in an easily "readable" form, is preferable, whereas in the latter case an unusual and even distorting direction of view, which leads to a subject rendition in a more attention-commanding manner, is more likely to produce the desired effect.

pp. 25, 98–99

For example, if the subject is a skyscraper, a photographer could approach it in one of two ways: if the picture is intended as a technical illustration for an architectural journal, a horizontal direction of view (camera held level, lens raised, see p. 280), which would produce a picture in which the walls of the building are rendered parallel, is probably more appropriate. On the other hand, if the purpose of the picture is to create a feeling of the soaring power of a new addition to the skyline of a city featured in a general magazine, an oblique direction of view (camera tilted upward), which would produce a picture in which the walls of the building appear to converge toward the sky, will probably convey a stronger impression of height and would therefore be preferable. Here, too, a photographer has a choice, and whether he succeeds or fails in his task depends to a very large extent on the degree to which he is able to exert control.

PART 5

Control in Regard to Subject Rendition

As mentioned before, photographic control can be applied at three different levels, each set of controls operating within its own specific sphere. The first two sets of control, pertaining to subject selection and subject approach, which have already been discussed, are of a preparatory nature. The third set of controls, pertaining to subject rendition, is concerned with the actual implementation of a photograph by physical means. For practical reasons, it is advisable to subdivide this third set of controls into four different groups:

p. 13

pp. 15, 19

Equipment and material
Methods and techniques
Modifiable picture aspects
Timing the moment of exposure

Before discussing the multitudinous controls belonging to this aspect of picture-making, I wish to point out the following: Not only can each of the respective controls be varied to a greater or lesser degree, but each of these variations in turn can be combined with each of the variations of any of the other controls. As a result, the number of different possibilities for rendering a given subject is truly astronomical, giving a knowledgeable and imaginative photographer virtually unlimited control over the final appearance of his picture.

EQUIPMENT AND MATERIAL

As far as the graphic effect of a photograph upon the observer of the print or transparency is concerned, it can make a great difference whether or not the rendition was deliberately controlled by the photographer (whether the shot was made: with a 35mm or a 4x5 in. camera; with a standard, wide-angle, or telephoto lens; at 1/10 sec. at *f*/25 or pp. 226–227 1/1000 sec. at f/2.5; with or without a corrective filter; on this kind of film or on that). Although such subtleties may seem trifling to the tyro, to the exacting photographer as well as the discriminate, visually educated observer they can make the difference between an effective and an ineffective presentation of the subject. For it is often the way in which he handles delicate controls like these which makes the difference between success and failure, which decides whether a photographer is able to effectively render surface texture and important fine detail; create illusions of depth and space with two-dimensional means; translate colorful reality into suggestive shades of gray; utilize the potentialities of sharpness, unsharpness, and directional blur as a means for symbolizing movement and "life."

The most important of the means and methods which enable a photographer to exert this kind of control are briefly discussed in the following:

The camera

The overwhelming popularity of the 35mm single-lens reflex camera followed by indiscriminate use has, in my opinion, led to a general deterioration of photographic standards, both technical and artistic. Granted, there isn't a subject that somehow cannot be photographed with a 35mm camera. But this doesn't imply that a 35mm camera is the most suitable instrument for making every kind of picture regardless of the nature of the subject and the purpose of the photograph. Like any other tool, a camera produces best results only if it is used for the specific purpose for which it was designed.

Artists and artisans alike know that not every kind of brush, chisel, hammer, or knife is equally suited to every job for which a brush, chisel, hammer, or knife is normally used; hunters are very careful to choose their guns in accordance with the kind of game they intend to kill; workers in wood distinguish between a great many different kinds of saw. Only amateur photographers seem to believe that a camera is a camera is a camera, and that the 35mm is king. That this is a fallacy is proven by a veritable deluge of unsharp, blurry, grainy pictures, photographs that clearly show that something is wrong. What is wrong is absence of control. For selecting his camera in accordance with the nature of the subject, the purpose of the picture, and the requirements of the job is one of the most consequential controls which a photographer has at his disposal.

Apart from differences in quality, cameras differ from one another in two main respects: design and size. Here is a brief run-down of their differences in regard to size, type, and purpose:

Camera size. Most camera designs are available in two or more different sizes for use in conjunction with different sizes of film. Generally speaking, *small cameras* have over large ones the advantages of lightness, inconspicuousness, and higher speed with lower cost of operation, and are therefore particularly suitable for photographing *dynamic subjects*: people, action, fast-breaking events.

pp. 146, 345

On the other hand, *large cameras*, although relatively cumbersome and slow, yield pictures of potentially much higher technical quality and produce better results in cases in which speed of operation is not essential, that is, when photographing *static subjects* that hold still.

Detailed information on the advantages and disadvantages of different film sizes will be given later.

pp. 56–57

The single-lens reflex camera. This design is primarily intended for photographing people and action; it is also particularly well suited for close-up and telephotography and is the only design which permits the use of zoom lenses.

p. 148

Especially valuable characteristics are: freedom from parallax (the image seen in the viewfinder coincides in every respect with the image on the film); a viewfinder image as large as the negative size (which facilitates image control in regard to sharpness and composition); direct visual control of the extent of sharpness in depth; adaptability to virtually any kind of lens of any focal length; the possibility of using different kinds of viewfinders in accordance with the special requirements of the job; freedom from dependence on accessory viewfinders for lenses of different focal lengths or reflex housings for close-up and telephotography.

Drawbacks are: unless the camera is equipped with a semi- or fully automatic diaphragm and an instant-return mirror, the image appears progressively darker the more the lens is stopped down, and blacks out completely during and after exposure. Wide-angle photography requires relatively large and costly lenses of retrofocus design. Great mechanical complexity, high noise level, and possibility of "mirror shock" that can lead to blurred pictures. No, or only very limited, provisions for perspective control.

The twin-lens reflex camera. This is an excellent design for all-around photography of average subjects and, in my opinion, unsurpassed for the beginner. However, its usefulness for close-up photography is limited, and, unless interchangeability of lenses is provided, it cannot be used for wide-angle and telephotography.

The greatest asset of the twin-lens reflex design is its large, negative-size viewfinder image which is bright and visible at all times, even during and immediately after the exposure. Noise level is very low, and, since the mirror is stationary, there is no possibility of mirror shock.

Drawbacks are: parallax, i.e., the images formed by the viewfinder lens and the lens that takes the picture do not exactly coincide, the less so, the closer the subject; to correct this discrepancy, most twin-lens cameras feature some kind of parallax compensation device. Lens interchangeability is normally not provided for (exceptions exist). Construction is considerably heavier and bulkier than that of other camera designs which produce negatives in the same size. Extent of sharpness in depth cannot be checked visually but only with the aid of a depth-of-field scale.

p. 146 **The lens-coupled rangefinder camera.** This is the most compact and fastest focusing of all camera designs intended for hand-held shooting. However, it is steadily losing ground to the single-lens reflex design because of certain inherent inconveniences and limitations: the small size of the viewfinder image makes composing difficult; the extent of sharpness in depth cannot be determined visually but only with the aid of a depth-of-field scale; parallax (usually controlled with the aid of a built-in parallax compensator); unsuitability to close-ups and telephotography unless equipped with an accessory reflex housing; dependence upon lenses specifically designed for use with the respective camera unless a reflex housing is used; dependence for sharp focusing on the rangefinder which might get out of order without the photographer becoming aware of it until the damage has been done.

The view camera. Characteristic for this design is relatively large size (standard is 4x5 in.), absence of a special viewfinder, and restriction to a single focusing and viewing control, the negative-size groundglass. As a result, view cameras cannot be used for hand-held shooting but must be mounted on a tripod.

p. 144

View cameras are unsurpassed for photographing anything that holds still: objects of any kind, landscapes, interiors, architectural subjects, commercial products, machinery, works of art, and so on. They can be fitted with any shutter-equipped lens of any design and focal length, and represent the only camera design which can be (and usually is) equipped with individually adjustable front and back movements for complete perspective control.

pp. 49, 67, 278–280

Press cameras are view-type designs equipped with lens-coupled rangefinders. In my opinion, they are obsolete and superseded by cameras of more modern design such as the Graflex XL, the Linhof 220 and Technika Press, and the Koni-Omega.

Polaroid Land cameras are limited-purpose cameras which have the unique advantage that finished pictures in color or black-and-white are available within minutes of the exposure. Their main drawback is restriction to the special films provided by Polaroid, most of which don't produce a usable negative; as a result, duplicates or enlargements can be made only via a copy negative. Lens interchangeability is, at least for the present, not provided for; wide-angle and telephotography are therefore impossible. Although the regular models are unsuited to close-up photography, special close-up and photomicrography cameras are available.

Amateurs like Polaroid cameras for obvious reasons; professionals, because they are eminently suitable for instant illumination and exposure checks under difficult lighting conditions and because they enable a photographer to create good will and show his appreciation by rewarding those who were of help to him with immediately available snapshots. Self-contained Polaroid Land backs are also available for use in conjunction with most 4x5 in. cameras.

Wide-angle cameras are highly specialized instruments suitable only to extreme wide-angle photography and for the creation of pictures in

p. 152

which perspective is deliberately distorted. Typical representatives are the Hasselblad Super Wide and the Plaubel Veriwide; both cover angles of view of approximately 100°; perspective is rectilinear.

pp 276–277, 294

pp. 302–305

Panoramic cameras are extreme wide-angle cameras equipped with lenses that swing through an arc during exposure. Typical representatives are the Panon, Panox, and Widelux. They cover angles of view of 140° and produce pictures in which perspective is cylindrical.

p. 295

The lens

Cameras come equipped with either a permanently attached lens or a detachable lens that can be interchanged with lenses having other characteristics. Whereas the usefulness of the first camera type is severely restricted, the second offers almost unlimited possibilities for creative control, particularly in regard to space rendition and perspective.

The suitability of a lens for a given task depends on its characteristics in regard to four qualities common to all lenses:

Focal length
Relative aperture
Covering power
Performance

p. 1

Although, as mentioned in the beginning, it is assumed that the reader is familiar with basic photographic concepts and techniques, because of their importance as means of creative control, these qualities are briefly reviewed in the following:

Focal length, measured in millimeters, centimeters, or inches and engraved on the mount of any photographic lens, controls the scale of the image on the film. The longer the focal length, the larger the image, and vice versa. Focal length and image size are directly proportional: a lens with a focal length twice as long as that of another lens produces an image that shows the subject twice as large if both pictures are taken from the identical camera position. From this it follows that, by using a lens of appropriate focal length, a photographer has full control over the scale of his picture. How extensive this control is should be apparent from the fact that, merely for 35mm cameras, lenses with focal lengths ranging from 8 to 1000mm and more are available.

For practical reasons, lenses are often referred to as standard, short-focus, and long-focus lenses. Standard lenses, which produce pictures in which perspective manifests itself more or less as it appears in reality to the eye, have focal lengths approximately equal to the diagonal of the negative size for which they are intended. In other words, a standard lens intended for 35mm photography has a focal length somewhere between 45 and 55mm, one designed to cover a 4x5 in. negative has a focal length of approximately 6 in. The term short-focus lens is popularly equivalent with wide-angle lens, the term long-focus lens with telephoto lens. The first type, in addition to wide-angle photography, is also suitable to the production of pictures in which space appears extended and perspective "exaggerated"; the second, in addition to telephotography, is suitable to the creation of photographs in which space appears "compressed" and objects particularly "distortion-free."

p. 153

p. 105

Relative aperture is the measure of the maximum light-transmission of a lens; it is expressed in the form of an *f*/number engraved on the lens mount. The "*faster*" the lens (and the higher its "speed"), the *smaller* the corresponding *f*/number: an *f*/2 is twice as "fast" as an *f*/2.8 lens and four times as "fast" as an *f*/4 lens.

Relative aperture controls two important aspects of picture-making: maximum shutter speed and minimum extent of the sharply rendered zone in depth. The higher the "speed" of a lens, i.e., the larger its relative aperture and the smaller its *f*/number, other factors being equal, the higher the shortest applicable shutter speed and the shallower the sharply rendered zone in depth. Practically, this means that a high-speed lens enables a photographer to "freeze" a subject in motion more effectively than a lens of slower speed; it also offers him the possibility of keeping the sharply rendered zone in depth shallower than if he had used a slower lens, thereby creating a stronger impression of "depth." And in those cases in which a longer exposure time or an increase in the extent of the sharply rendered zone in depth is desirable, a fast lens can always be stopped down to achieve these results and is therefore potentially a more versatile means of creative control than a slower lens.

pp. 320, 324

pp. 274, 316

Covering power is "potential angle of view" and determines the largest negative size that a specific lens can cover sharply from corner to corner. Covering power has very little to do with focal length. A lens of very long focal length may have very little covering power, and vice versa. For example, certain 500mm (20 in.) telephoto lenses designed for use in conjunction with small roll-film cameras have only sufficient power to cover the comparatively small negative size of 2¼x2¼ in. In contrast, a Goerz Hypergon wide-angle lens of only 75mm (3 in.) focal length covers the relatively enormous negative size of 8x10 in.

pp. 278–280

Covering power becomes an important factor if a lens is used in conjunction with a swing-equipped view camera for perspective control. Unless the covering power of such a lens is adequate, the special adjustments of the view camera cannot be used to full advantage, because parts of the negative would fall outside the area covered by the lens and appear either unsharp or blank. To avoid this possibility, experienced photographers working with, say, a 4x5 in. view camera, instead of using an ordinary standard lens with a focal length of 6 in., use a 6 in. wide-angle lens designed to cover sharply the next larger negative size of 5x7 in. Since the focal lengths of both lenses are the same, the perspective will likewise be the same. But whereas the standard lens, because of insufficient covering power, would be unable to cover the perspective-controlled negative sharply from corner to corner, the wide-angle lens will do this with ease.

Performance. As far as their performance is concerned, lenses can differ in regard to five main characteristics:

Sharpness
Color correction
Internal reflection
Light distribution
Distortion

SHARPNESS. Basically, lenses computed for use in small cameras are inherently sharper than lenses designed for larger cameras (small negatives must be able to stand higher degrees of magnification than larger ones); high-speed lenses are usually not quite as sharp as lenses of more moderate apertures; and expensive lenses are, as a rule though not always, sharper than less expensive ones of comparable focal length and speed.

The sharpness of rendition of most lenses increases with stopping down the diaphragm and usually reaches its optimum two or three stops beyond maximum aperture. Further stopping down, of course, increases the extent of the sharply covered zone in depth but may impair rather than improve the sharpness of the rendition.

Occasionally, sharpness is not a desirable picture quality because a softer form of rendition may seem more appropriate for the characterization of a specific subject. If this is the case, special soft-focus lenses or soft-focus devices (which adapt to the front of the regular lens) can be used to produce the desired effect.

pp. 207, 212

Most photographic lenses are computed to give maximum sharpness of rendition if used to photograph average subjects at average distances (which means somewhere between 10 and 100 feet); if used for extreme close-ups (subject distance measured in inches rather than in feet), their performance may be unsatisfactory. In such cases, special close-up or true macro lenses should be used, or the "normal" lens should be used in reversed position, with its front element facing the film (for some cameras, special adapters are available for this purpose).

COLOR CORRECTION. Except for lenses found only on the cheapest cameras, all modern lenses are sufficiently color-corrected to satisfy normal demands. Basically, however, as far as color correction is concerned, two main types of lenses must be distinguished:

Achromatic lenses are corrected for two colors: blue and green. To this type belong the overwhelming majority of all photographic lenses which, as experience has shown, are perfectly satisfactory for everyday color photography.

Apochromatic lenses are corrected for three colors: blue, green, and red. Their performance is somewhat superior to that of achromatic lenses, a fact which, however, matters only in cases in which demands are exceptionally high as, for example, in top-quality, large-camera, commercial photography; when making high-magnification color enlargements; or in the production of color separation negatives for photomechanical reproduction. Lenses of this kind are made only in a limited number of focal lengths, most of which are designed for use with larger cameras, and are correspondingly expensive.

INTERNAL REFLECTION. Unfortunately, only part of the light collected by the lens reaches the film in the form of a usable image. A certain percentage—how much, depends upon the design of the respective lens—is reflected by the surfaces of the lens elements, the inner surfaces of the lens mount, and the internal parts of the camera, bounces back and forth, is scattered, and eventually reaches the film in the form of fog or flare. Occasionally, however, flare can be used creatively and become a means for symbolizing the radiance of direct light.

pp. 214–215

Fog is undesirable because it reduces the contrast of the image; flare manifests itself in the form of light spots which can have almost any shape but are most frequently fan- or crescent-like, circular, or repeating the form of the diaphragm. Both phenomena are most likely to occur in backlit shots if direct light is permitted to strike the lens, which, of course, is quite unavoidable if the light source itself forms part of the picture.

As a rule, internal reflection is most likely to occur in lenses that are very complex in design (having a great many individual elements), that possess a large number of glass-to-air surfaces, that have a strongly curved front surface. Relatively simple lenses with moderately curved surfaces and cemented instead of air-spaced elements are usually less prone to internal reflection, which even the best "coating" can never completely eliminate. But only testing can reveal the actual extent to which a lens is subject to fog and flare.

LIGHT DISTRIBUTION. To a greater or lesser extent, any lens delivers proportionately more light to the center of the film than to its edges and corners. Although normally negligible, this phenomenon, i.e., uneven light distribution, can occasionally amount to a "control in reverse," adversely affecting the impression of the picture instead of improving it. Such occasions are most likely to occur if photographs, and particulary color pictures, are taken with one of the more extreme wide-angle lenses.

Since color film has a narrower contrast range than black-and-white film, it reacts more strongly to unevenness of light distribution; and since unevenness of light distribution increases with increases in the angle of view of a lens, wide-angle lenses display this fault to a higher degree than standard or telephoto lenses. Before they acquire one of the more extreme wide-angle lenses, color photographers are therefore advised to test it in conjunction with color film to find out whether or not its performance is acceptable to them.

DISTORTION. Photographers must distinguish between four different types, only one of which, however, is the fault of the lens. This particular type of distortion manifests itself by rendering actually straight lines as curves and is increasingly pronounced toward the edges of the picture. Depending on whether such lines curve outward or inward, it is called barrel or pincushion distortion, respectively. Lenses most likely to be afflicted with this fault are wide-angle and zoom lenses. This fault is, of course, noticeable only if the photograph contains straight lines near the edges of the picture and, if photo-technical requirements are high, makes the thus afflicted lens unsuitable for architectural and interior photography.

pp. 120–121

Perspective distortion, for example, hands and feet extended toward the camera which in the picture appear unnaturally large, is not due to a lens fault but is the fault of the photographer who made the mistake of photographing a subject with great extension in depth, with a lens of relatively short focal length, from a distance that was too short. Using a lens of longer focal length and increasing the distance accordingly would have prevented this fault.

p. 153

Unnaturally elongated heads near the edges of the picture in extreme wide-angle shots are the unavoidable result of projecting a spherical or cylindrical form on a flat surface (the film) at a relatively sharp angle. Again, this phenomenon is not the fault of the lens, but that of the photographer who arranged his subject badly.

p. 120

The more-or-less curved rendition of actually straight lines typical of photographs made with panoramic cameras or cameras equipped with fish-eye lenses is not the result of a lens fault, but an inherent characteristic of the respective camera or lens design.

pp. 302–309

Diaphragm and shutter

As any photographer knows, the diaphragm controls the amount of light allowed to pass through the lens, while the shutter controls the time during which this amount of light is permitted to affect the film. Consequently, in conjunction, diaphragm aperture and shutter speed control the exposure. And since a correct exposure is an indispensable prerequisite for a technically satisfactory negative or color transparency, appropriate adjustment of diaphragm aperture and shutter speed is in effect one of the most important photographic controls.

Exposure control. The data for setting diaphragm aperture and shutter speed should preferably be determined with the aid of a dependable exposure meter, since the eye is a notoriously unreliable judge of brightness values, and memory and previous experience are deceptive. For the sake of argument, let's assume that, in a specific case, such an exposure meter reading should yield the following data (corresponding to an Exposure Value number of 14):

Shutter speed	1/30	1/60	1/125	1/250	1/500	1/1000	sec.
Diaphragm aperture	*f/22*	*f/16*	*f/11*	*f/8*	*f/5.6*	*f/4*	*f/stop*

Each of these six combinations of shutter speed and diaphragm aperture would lead to a perfect exposure and yield a negative (or color transparency) that, in regard to density (or color), would be identical with the other five. But this is where the similarity between the six negatives (or color transparencies) would end. For although identical as far as the exposure is concerned, they would vary considerably in regard to such important picture aspects as depth of field, motion rendition, and possibly sharpness also. In other words, appropriate adjustment of diaphragm aperture and shutter speed allows a photographer to control not only *one*, but *four* different aspects of picture-making. To be able to use this opportunity to best advantage and select the most favorable of the applicable exposure data, he must consider the following:

pp. 162–163, 326–327

Depth-of-field control. When a lens is critically focused on a specific subject, objects closer to the camera or farther away from it will be rendered more or less unsharp, increasingly so, the farther they are from the actual plane of focus. However, the translation from sharp to unsharp is not abrupt but gradual, as a result of which there is a zone immediately in front of and behind the sharply focused plane in which blur is too insignificant to be noticeable. This zone of apparent sharpness is called the depth of field.

The extent of the depth of field varies with three factors: distance between subject and camera, focal length of the lens, and diaphragm aperture. Depth of field will be the more extensive, the greater the subject distance, the shorter the focal length, and the smaller the diaphragm aperture; and vice versa. Hence, each of these three factors represents an important picture control.

pp. 156–157

In this connection, a half-truth must be reviewed—the popular belief that, equality of diaphragm aperture provided, short-focus (or wide-angle) lenses have greater depth of field than long-focus (or telephoto) lenses. This is true only if both lenses are used at the same subject distance. However, at equal subject distances, the short-focus lens renders the subject in proportionately smaller scale than the long-focus lens; an increase in depth of field is gained at the expense of a loss in image size. If, on the other hand, the subject-to-camera distances are adjusted in such a way that the scale of rendition (the image size) is identical in both pictures, the one taken with the short-focus lens and the one taken with the long-focus lens (which, of course, would necessitate using the short-focus lens at a correspondingly shorter subject distance than the long-focus lens), depth of field at identical diaphragm apertures will be identical in both pictures.

In practice, the simplest way to increase the zone of sharpness in depth is, of course, by means of stopping down the diaphragm. Naturally, in order to avoid underexposure of the film, any decrease in diaphragm aperture from the data supplied by the exposure meter must be offset by a corresponding decrease in shutter speed. But despite the fact that, as we saw above, as far as exposure is concerned, identical results will be achieved whether the film is exposed 1/30 sec. at *f*/22 or 1/1000 sec. at *f*/4, the two photographs would appear very different in regard to the extent of the sharply rendered zone in depth (depth of field) and, as we'll see in a moment, rendition of motion. Which one of these extremes, or, more likely, of the intermediate combinations of *f*/stop and shutter speed a photographer should use depends, of course, on the requirements of the specific task. What is important here is for the reader to realize that he has a choice, a choice which is tantamount to control of some of the most important factors which determine the outcome of his picture.

pp. 156–157, 161–163

Motion control. As will be shown later, motion can be indicated in a still photograph in many ways, two of which, "freezing" and directional

pp. 320–341

p. 324 blur, are directly controlled by the shutter speed: to "freeze" a subject in motion, the photograph must be made with a relatively high shutter pp. 326, 333 speed; to indicate motion through blur, a relatively low shutter speed must be used. How high or how low the shutter speed should be depends on the speed of the subject and the intentions of the photographer and has been fully discussed in THE COMPLETE PHOTOGRAPHER and THE COLOR PHOTO BOOK by this author.

What is important here is that the reader realize that, normally, small pp. 162–163 diaphragm aperture (equivalent to great depth of field) and high shutter speed (equivalent to great motion-stopping ability) are mutually exclusive. Under ordinary shooting conditions, a photographer can have either one, or the other, but not both (exceptions: photography under unusually bright light conditions or with flash). However, he always has a choice, which means he must make a decision as to which is more important, extensive sharpness in depth or power to stop motion, and select his diaphragm aperture and shutter speed accordingly.

Sharpness control. Experienced photographers distinguish between three different kinds of sharpness:

Sharpness of rendition (within the plane of focus) is "two-dimensional pp. 42, 154 sharpness"; it is controlled by lens performance, accuracy of focus, and, to some extent, the sharpness of the film.

Sharpness in depth (depth of field) is "three-dimensional sharpness"; as pp. 46, 156–157 explained before, it is controlled by the diaphragm aperture in conjunction with subject distance and focal length of the lens.

Sharpness of motion is absence of blur (directional unsharpness) due to movement at the moment of exposure of either the subject or the camera; pp. 326–327 it is controlled by the shutter speed (and, unless a tripod is used, the ability of the photographer to hold the camera perfectly still during the exposure).

In practice, demands for highest possible sharpness usually require that the photographer find the best compromise between the smallest practicable diaphragm aperture (for greatest feasible sharpness in depth) and highest practicable shutter speed (for greatest feasible sharpness of motion.) For what good is the most extensive sharpness in depth if the entire picture is blurred because the corresponding shutter speed was so low that the photographer was unable to hold the camera motionless during the exposure?

In this respect, experience has shown that very few people can hold a camera still enough to get sharp pictures at shutter speeds slower than 1/60 sec.; for most, 1/125 sec. is the slowest hand-held shutter speed that is reasonably safe. Furthermore, these data apply only if the shot is made with a lens of standard focal length or shorter. Long-focus and telephoto lenses magnify not only the subject, but also its motion and any accidental camera movement, and require correspondingly higher shutter speeds to yield motion-sharp pictures. For photographs with extreme types of telephoto lenses, still higher shutter speeds or use of a gunstock or tripod is strongly recommended.

View camera swings and tilts

As mentioned before, among the unique features of view cameras are their individual front and back adjustments: the swings, tilts, and slides, which give a photographer a high degree of control over the rendition of horizontal and vertical lines, allow him either to avoid or deliberately create perspective distortion, and, in certain types of angle shots, greatly extend the zone of sharpness in depth. In this respect, three groups of camera adjustments, each with its own specific functions, must be distinguished:

pp. 278–280
pp. 158–159

The swings and tilts of the camera back enable a photographer to control the perspective of his rendition, to make lines that in reality are parallel (horizontals and verticals) appear parallel in the picture instead of converging, and to avoid or create distortion. In addition, in certain types of angle shots in which a slight degree of perspective distortion is not objectionable, appropriate use of the back adjustments allows a photographer to extend considerably in depth the sharply rendered zone without the need for resorting to impractically small diaphragm apertures.

pp. 278–280
pp. 158–160

The swings and tilts of the camera front control the overall sharpness of the picture and frequently enable a photographer to increase markedly the extent of the sharply rendered zone in depth *without* reducing the

pp. 158–160

diaphragm aperture to any great extent and *without* incurring perspective distortion.

The vertical and lateral sliding adjustments of the camera front and back control the position of the image on the film and make it possible to shift the image in any direction, without changing either the position of the camera or the direction in which the lens is pointed; without this feature, meaningful perspective control is impossible.

Application of these camera adjustments is subject to the following principles and considerations:

Whereas it is impossible in a photograph to render any three-dimensional subject with the exception of a sphere *completely* distortion-free, any flat, two-dimensional subject or plane can be rendered free from perspective distortion. What this implies is best explained by discussing a concrete example, for instance, the photographic rendition of a cube.

pp. 278–279

To make a cube appear three-dimensional in a picture, three of its sides must be visible. Why this is so is demonstrated by the following sketches:

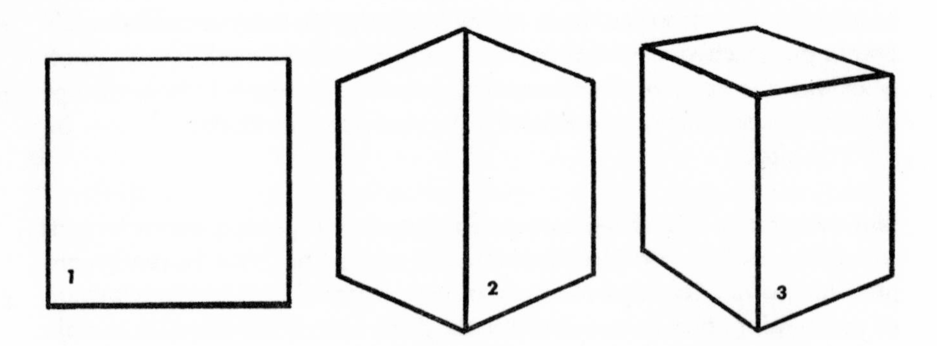

Rendered in the form of a head-on view with only one of its sides apparent (1), the photographic image of a cube would be indistinguishable from the picture of a square piece of paper. Similarly, a corner view, showing only two of its sides (2), would fail to convey the impression of a cube because it might just as well be a picture of a piece of cardboard bent at an angle of 90°. The only way to make a cube look like a cube, i.e., like a three-dimensional object, is by showing three of its sides simultaneously (3).

However, no matter how hard a photographer may try, he will never be able to show more than one of the cube's six sides distortion-free, i.e., with both vertical edges of equal length and parallel, both horizontal edges of equal length and parallel, and each of the four angles 90°. The other two visible sides must always appear "in perspective," i.e., distorted, their actually parallel edges converging, and their angles no longer 90° as in actuality, but either acute or obtuse.

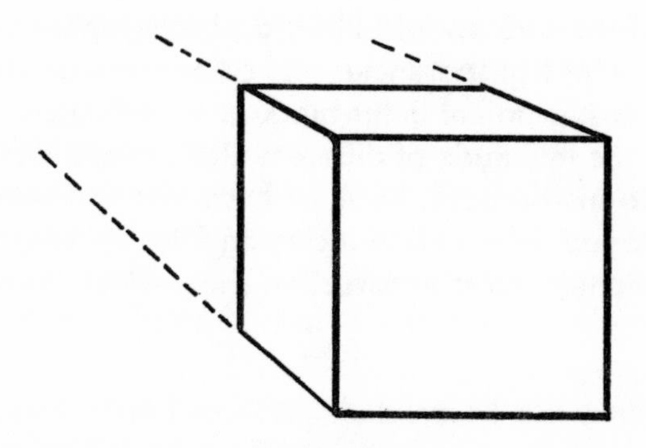

Luckily, *as long as one side is rendered distortion-free,* a cube, or any other three-dimensional object, will appear "undistorted" to the eye, which is so accustomed to perspective distortion that it often does not even recognize this phenomenon when confronted with it.

Therefore, the only way to photograph a three-dimensional object so that it *appears* undistorted is to photograph it in such a way that *one* of its sides is rendered distortion-free. To accomplish this, the photographer must adjust his camera so that the plane of the film and the side of the subject that must be rendered distortion-free are parallel to each other. Unless such parallelism is achieved, perspective distortion through foreshortening and diminution is unavoidable.

In our example, to achieve parallelism between the film and one side of the cube, the simplest way would be to place the camera so that the lens faces the cube head-on. Unfortunately, in this position, only one side of the cube would show in the picture, the cube would appear indistinguishable from a square, and the feeling of three-dimensionality would be nonexistent. This can only be avoided by placing the camera in such a way that the lens simultaneously "sees" three sides of the cube. But then, of course, the film would no longer be parallel to one of the sides of the cube, and perspective distortion would result. To avoid this, a view camera must be used, for its swings, tilts, and slides provide the only means for adjusting the film plane independently from that of the lens.

pp. 278–279

Filters

pp. 226–227, 242–247, 253

With the aid of the appropriate filter, a photographer can control the color rendition in his transparencies and color prints and the tonal separation and contrast gradient in his black-and-white pictures. To be able to choose from the multitude of different filters available to him the one most suitable to his purpose, he must know the following basic facts. (For specific product information including filter factors, consult the respective filter manufacturer's instruction sheet which accompanies each filter.)

Photographic filters can be divided into three major groups:

Filters intended for color photography
Filters intended for black-and-white photography
Filters suitable to both black-and-white and color

Filters for color photography can be divided into three subgroups, each of which serves a specific purpose. Detailed instructions for their use are given in THE COLOR PHOTO BOOK by this author.

COLOR CONVERSION FILTERS. With their aid, in an emergency, a color photographer can use a daylight-type color film in conjunction with tungsten illumination, or a tungsten-type color film in conjunction with daylight, a procedure which otherwise would produce normally unacceptable results. Use of the appropriate Kodak Filter Series 80 converts a daylight-type color film into a film suitable for photography by tungsten light. Conversely, the appropriate Kodak Filter Series 85 makes a tungsten-type color film suitable for photography in daylight.

p. 253

LIGHT BALANCING FILTERS. With their aid, a color photographer can in effect change the color of daylight or tungsten light so that it conforms to the color of the light for which a specific type of color film is balanced, thereby achieving the most faithful color rendition possible. For example, daylight-type color film is balanced for use with standard daylight, a combination of direct sunlight and light reflected from a clear blue sky with a few white clouds, from approximately two hours after sunrise to two hours before sunset. Earlier or later in the day, however, in the shade, or under a hazy or overcast sky, the color of the light is different from that of "standard daylight," with the result that unfiltered color photographs taken under such conditions would have a color cast. This kind of color degradation can be prevented with the aid of the appropriate light-balancing filter. Typical representatives are the Kodak Filter Series 81 (yellowish) and 82 (bluish).

COLOR COMPENSATING FILTERS. With their aid, a photographer can control his transparencies or prints in regard to overall color balance, making them, for example, either more, or less, reddish, greenish, bluish, and so on. Occasions for this kind of control are manifold: to compensate for the undesirable color characteristics of a specific film emulsion; to correct possible color deviations in abnormally long (time) or abnormally short (speedlight) exposures; to improve the color rendition of transparencies taken with unusual light sources like fluorescent light; to compensate for color deficiencies in pictures taken under water or through tinted window glass; or simply, to deliberately change the color balance of a transparency or print in order to give it a special mood. Typical representatives of this kind of filter are the Kodak CC Filters which are available in different densities in the colors red, yellow, green, blue, magenta, and cyan.

Filters for black-and-white photography, most of which are much stronger in color than those intended for color photography, change the response of the film emulsion to color and can be divided into the following three subgroups, each of which has its own specific purpose. Detailed instructions for their use are given in THE COMPLETE PHOTOGRAPHER by this author.

CORRECTION FILTERS enable a photographer to translate the colors of the subject into gray shades of corresponding brightness values. This can become necessary because all black-and-white films are excessively sensitive to blue-violet and ultraviolet, and some panchromatic films are overly sensitive to red. As a result, translated into shades of gray, in comparison with, for example, green, the colors blue, violet, and red may be rendered too light in the photograph. This tonal imbalance can be rectified with the aid of color correction filters, for instance, the Kodak Filters K2 (light yellow) and X1 (yellowish green), which are intended for use with panchromatic films, the first in conjunction with daylight, the second in conjunction with photoflood illumination.

pp. 226–227, 242–247

CONTRAST FILTERS enable a photographer to lighten or darken selectively specific colors of the subject for improved tonal separation. For example, translated into shades of gray, a red and a green of similar brightness may be rendered as identical tones, thus merging with one another and producing a dull and monotonous picture. To avoid this, to translate color contrast into brightness contrast, and to restore the tonal separation of the original, a photographer can control his color translation with the aid of the appropriate contrast filter: a red filter would render red lighter than green; a green filter would render green lighter than red.

Selection of the appropriate contrast filter takes place in accordance with a simple rule: to make a color appear lighter in black-and-white rendition than it would have appeared in an unfiltered shot, a filter in the same color must be used; to make it appear darker, a filter in the complementary color must be used. Complementary color pairs are:

red—blue-green
orange—blue
yellow—purple-blue
green—red-purple
blue—orange

Examples of what can be done in this respect are given on pp. 226–227 and 242–247.

INFRARED FILTERS appear black to the eye, transmit infrared radiation while absorbing virtually all visible light, and, in conjunction with infrared films, *must* be used in order to achieve the typical infrared effect. Without such a filter, infrared film renders a subject very much like ordinary panchromatic film.

However, when making hand-held shots on infrared film with a single-lens reflex camera, an ordinary red filter (Kodak Wratten A or F) can often be used. It has the advantage that the photographer can still see an indication of an image in the viewfinder of his camera, whereas true infrared filters, being black, result in total blackout. The effect produced by the red filter, although slightly different from that of a true infrared filter, is sufficiently similar to it to justify its use in most cases in which infrared film is used for pictorial rather than scientific purposes.

Filters suitable to both black-and-white and color photography are listed below. Detailed instructions for their use are given in THE COMPLETE PHOTOGRAPHER by this author.

ULTRAVIOLET (OR HAZE) FILTERS absorb ultraviolet radiation. Their purpose is to improve the rendition of long-distance outdoor shots, particularly those taken at relatively high altitudes, in the mountains, or from the air, by strengthening contrast in black-and-white and reducing excess blue in color photographs.

POLARIZERS are special kinds of filters which mitigate and, under certain conditions, eliminate glare and reflections from shiny surfaces other than metallic ones: glass, water, asphalt, varnish, glossy paint and paper, polished wood, and so on. In color photography, furthermore, they are the only means by which a pale blue sky can be somewhat darkened.

pp. 264–267

NEUTRAL DENSITY FILTERS are primarily used for reducing the exposure when pictures must be made on high-speed film in very bright light and the highest practical shutter speed in conjunction with the smallest diaphragm aperture would still result in overexposure. Alternately, they enable a photographer to work with relatively large apertures and/or slow shutter speeds (for the creation of special effects) even though he uses a fast film in bright light. Neutral density filters are supplied by Kodak in different densities, transmitting from 90 to 1/100 per cent of the incident light.

Film

Discriminating photographers have the choice of a fairly large number of different films with sometimes very different characteristics, each of them potentially a controlling factor in the final appearance of the picture. Here is a run-down of those factors which apply equally to black-and-white and color films.

Film size. Apart from the obvious fact that the film must fit the camera in which it is to be used, the *best* film size is normally the *largest* size that still enables a photographer to do a *perfect* job. Specifically, photographers having the choice of several cameras, or considering the purchase of a camera, should keep in mind the following:

LARGE FILM SIZES (the standard is 4x5 in.) have the following advantages over smaller ones: photo-technical quality of the print or transparency is potentially higher because a lesser degree of magnification is involved; to make, say, an 11x14 in. print, a 4x5 in. negative must be enlarged less than three times linear, a 35mm negative more than ten times. As a result, the tonal quality of prints made from larger negatives is generally richer, sharpness superior, and film grain less noticeable or entirely absent. And because of their much greater eye appeal, large color transparencies are commercially more in demand than small ones.

Large-sized films are, of course, used in conjunction with large-sized cameras that have large-sized groundglasses, which in turn make evaluation of the future picture much easier than small ones: detail (both desirable and objectionable ones) stands out more clearly; distribution of sharpness and unsharpness, light and shadow, can be checked with ease; organization of the subject along compositionally satisfactory lines is simplified. And, if necessary, relatively small sections of large negatives can be enlarged to full-sized prints without objectionable graininess or serious loss of definition, a handy substitute for a missing telephoto lens and always a good means for tightening up the composition.

Disadvantages of large-sized films over smaller ones are: considerably higher cost per exposure; much greater bulkiness (a single 4x5 in. film holder containing only two sheets of film takes more space and is heavier than film for more than 100 pictures contained in three 35mm cartridges); and the fact that the respective cameras are relatively heavy, clumsy, conspicuous, and slow in regard to lens speed and operation.

Consequently, large film sizes are recommended to the slow and careful worker, the perfectionist. They are particularly suitable to the rendition of static subjects that hold still, for use at home and in the studio, and are indispensable in all cases in which photo-technical excellence takes precedence over convenience.

SMALL FILM SIZES (the standard is 35mm) have the following advantages over larger ones: highest portability (film for more than 100 exposures takes less space than a pack of cigarettes) which, in conjunction with relatively low cost per exposure, is conducive to more thorough photographic coverage of a subject and reduces the danger of missing important shots. Furthermore, the respective cameras are comparatively light, small, and inconspicuous, extremely fast in operation, and can be equipped with lenses of much higher speed than are available for larger cameras. Kodachrome color film, the film with the highest resolution, is, except in the form of movie film, available only in 35mm size, the worldwide standard for color slides.

Disadvantages of small-sized films over larger ones are: general inferior photo-technical quality of the prints in regard to sharpness, tonal gradation, and graininess; indiscriminate shooting resulting from low cost and ease of operation; processing is rather critical since, due to the required high degree of magnification, even minute scratches and specks of dust stand out glaringly in the print. Also, many commercial users of color photographs still refuse to buy 35mm transparencies.

Consequently, small film sizes are recommended to the fast and impulsive worker, the man who has to travel light, the photographer who is more interested in capturing "life" than in photo-technical excellence. They are particularly suitable to the rendition of dynamic subjects: people, action, animals, and they can save the job in all cases in which a technically not quite perfect picture is still preferable to no picture at all.

MEDIUM FILM SIZES (the standard is 2¼x2¼ in.) combine, to a proportionately lesser degree, the advantages and disadvantages of larger and smaller films. They are recommended to those photographers who wish to use the same camera for photographing static as well as dynamic subjects; to professionals working with live models, particularly in the fields of advertising and fashion photography; to those who prefer color prints on paper to transparencies; and to serious beginners.

Film type. The question whether roll film or sheet film is more advantageous must be answered on the basis of the following considerations:

ROLL FILM (including 35mm film) is the most convenient type of film. Cameras can be loaded and unloaded in daylight (though never in direct sunlight; if necessary, use the shadow cast by your own body); shooting with roll film is faster than shooting with sheet film or film pack; and processing is more convenient than processing any other type of film.

Disadvantages are: impossibility of switching film type in the middle of a roll (for example, from black-and-white to color) without sacrificing the unexposed part unless the camera is equipped with interchangeable film magazines; individual shots cannot be processed individually, which makes it inadvisable to shoot pictures under very different light conditions on the same roll; results can be seen only after the entire roll has been exposed.

SHEET FILM has the advantage over roll film that each exposure can be processed individually, and that during a shooting session a changeover from black-and-white to color or vice versa is possible at any time without the need for sacrificing any film.

Disadvantages are the necessity for loading and unloading each film holder individually in the darkroom (or a darkened room) and, indirectly, the bulkiness and weight of the film holders.

FILM PACK has the advantage that it can be loaded and unloaded in daylight; that switching from black-and-white film pack to color sheet film is possible at any time; that a limited number of individual shots can be processed immediately after shooting since up to six exposed sheets can be taken from the pack without endangering the rest; and that 16 sheets of film inside a film pack adapter take hardly any more space than two sheets of sheet film in their holder.

Disadvantages are: a relatively thin film base which makes the individual sheets more susceptible to buckling out of the film plane or, unless glass pressure plates are used, in the enlarger; much higher cost per exposure than for sheet film of the same size; and the fact that, up to now, only black-and-white film is available in the form of film pack.

Film speed. Although a fast film may seem more advantageous per se than a slow one, this is not necessarily true. Almost without exception, in color as well as in black-and-white, fast films are more grainy than slow films. Practically speaking, this means that unless grain is to be used as a creative device, as far as speed is concerned, the *best* film is generally the *slowest* film that still permits a photographer to do a *perfect* job.

pp. 216–217

Color films

The problems connected with the question, whether to photograph a specific subject in color or in black-and-white, have already been discussed. If the decision is for color, a photographer must consider the following:

pp. 20–24

Positive or negative color film? A photographer who wishes to make transparencies (slides) suitable for projection (or reproduction by photo-mechanical means) must work with positive (reversal) color film. If he wishes to enjoy his color shots in the form of color prints on paper (which are equally suitable for reproduction by photo-mechanical means), he must work with negative (nonreversal) color film.

Whereas negative color film can be used either with daylight, tungsten light, or flash, positive color film (unless the appropriate color conversion filter is used) *must* be used in conjunction with the type of light for which it is intended ("balanced"). Otherwise, the colors of the transparency will not correspond to those of the subject. Three types of positive color film are available:

p. 52

Daylight-type color film is intended for use with standard daylight, blue flashbulbs, and electronic flash (speedlight).

Type A color film is intended for use with photoflood illumination (color temperature, 3400° K).

Type B color film is intended for use with professional tungsten illumination (color temperature, 3200° K).

As far as selection of a specific brand or variety of color film within the appropriate type-group is concerned, a color photographer faces problems which are different from those that confront a worker in black-and-white. There, film speed, contrast gradient, and degree of graininess are important factors; here, the overriding question is: what are the characteristics in regard to color rendition of the different, potentially suitable films? For variations in color rendition can be so great among the different brands of color film that a choice can be made only on the basis of personal preference. How to make the necessary tests is described in THE COLOR PHOTO BOOK by this author.

Black-and-white films

Modern black-and-white films can be classified as belonging to one of the following four groups, each of which has its own characteristics which determine its purpose:

Thin-emulsion films, which are available only in the form of 35mm film, are characterized by very low speeds (ASA 16–64), exceptionally fine grain, extraordinary definition, fairly steep contrast gradient, and very narrow exposure latitude. Provided great care is taken in their exposure (which has to be accurate within one *f*/stop) and development (which requires the use of special "compensating" developers), they are capable of yielding 16x20 in. prints that still are astonishingly sharp and all but grainless. However, in the hands of a careless or inexperienced worker, they are an invitation to disaster.

General-purpose films are characterized by medium-high speeds (ASA 125–400), reasonably fine grain, average contrast gradient, and generous exposure latitude that makes these films very forgiving in regard to over- and underexposure. Unless demands for film speed or absence of visible film grain are exceptionally stringent, this is the group from which experienced photographers choose their "workhorse" film.

High-speed films are characterized by very high speeds (ASA 500–1600), relatively coarse grain with correspondingly poor definition, low contrast gradient, and very low tolerance to overexposure that result in negatives that are so "flat" and contrastless as to be virtually useless. Films belonging to this group are totally unsuited to general photography and particularly to photography in bright light. However, they can save the job under lighting conditions under which general-purpose films fail because of insufficient speed and, in the hands of experts, yield very interesting results.

Special-purpose films. Because they are unsuited to general photography, a whole group of black-and-white films exist of which the average photographer knows almost nothing. Although only intended for specific limited purposes, when imaginatively used, these films are capable of producing very interesting results in other fields, also, and should be of interest to experimentally inclined photographers in search of new means of graphic expression. The following types of film deserve particular attention: Infrared sensitized films; document copy films; Kodak Fine Grain Positive film; Kodak Direct Positive Pan film; fluoroscope recording films; Kodalith Film. Interested readers are advised to request specific information concerning these films from their dealer or directly from the Educational Service Bureau of the Eastman Kodak Company.

Contrast gradient and grain. Contrast gradient and graininess are inherent characteristics of any photographic emulsion; some films are "harder" or "softer" (i.e., more or less contrasty) and more or less "grainy" than others, as indicated in the above survey. However, these characteristics are not unalterable qualities, and photographers wishing to utilize them as means of graphic control should know the following:

Overexposure by up to three *f*/stops, in conjunction with a proportionately shortened time of development, produces *negatives of correspondingly lower contrast gradient* than would have been normal for the respective film.

pp. 232–233

Underexposure by one or two *f*/stops, in conjunction with a 25–50 per cent increase in the time of development, produces *negatives of correspondingly higher contrast gradient* than would have been normal for the respective film.

pp. 232–233

Overexposure tends to produce negatives in which grain is more pronounced than in correctly exposed negatives while sharpness of rendition declines.

To keep graininess down to a minimum, start with a fine-grain film, expose "right on the button," use a fine-grain developer suitable for the specific type of film (consult the manufacturer's recommendations), rigidly avoid overdevelopment, and print the negative on a paper of comparatively soft gradation.

pp. 216–217 *To produce maximum film grain,* start with a high-speed film, expose on the short side, use a rapid developer, slightly increase the time of development above normal, and print on paper of hard gradation.

Film developers

The greatest favor a photographer can do himself is to develop his films in strict adherence to the manufacturer's recommendations in regard to type and temperature of the developer and time of development. However, although contrast gradient and grain structure are inherent characteristics of any specific photographic emulsion, as mentioned above, they are not unalterable qualities but can be controlled within certain limits through variations in exposure in conjunction with deviations from normal development. Still greater changes in the character of the negative can be brought about by adding another variable, the type of developer. Experimentally inclined photographers searching for unusual graphic effects may want to explore these possibilities. The following survey of the different types of film developers should aid them in this quest:

pp. 232–233

Standard developers act fast and thoroughly, utilizing the full inherent speed of a film, and produce negatives of average contrast and moderately fine grain. They are particularly well suited for the development of negatives from 2¼x2¼ in. on up and will normally produce the most satisfactory results. Typical example: Kodak Developer D-76.

Rapid developers are somewhat more energetic than standard developers. They work faster and produce negatives with somewhat higher contrast and slightly larger grain. They are particularly well suited for developing 4x5 in. sheet film and film pack negatives of low-contrast subjects and for getting the utmost out of underexposed films. Typical example: Kodak Developer DK-60a.

High-contrast developers, originally designed for the development of black-and-white reproductions of line drawings, printed pages, and so on, produce negatives of extremely high contrast. They offer creative possibilities to photographers who wish to explore the graphic potential of pure, abstract black-and-white. Typical example: Kodak Developer D-8.

Fine-grain developers produce negatives with somewhat finer grain structure than standard developers. They are specifically intended for the development of 35mm films but can also be used for larger sizes. Most fine-grain developers require a certain exposure increase, the factor depending on the respective make. Typical example: Kodak Microdol-X.

Ultra-fine-grain developers produce negatives with still finer grain structure than fine-grain developers, usually at the price of still higher losses in film speed. Unfortunately, the whole field of ultra-fine-grain development is somewhat muddled by the frequent appearance of "bigger and better" ultra-fine-grain developers heralded by often fantastic claims. Photographers interested in this subject are advised to make their own tests and draw their own conclusions.

Photographic papers

The simplest, although not necessarily the best, way of controlling the contrast gradient of a photograph is through printing the negative on a paper of appropriate gradation. This control may become necessary for one of two reasons:

To correct a technical mistake, that is, to produce a print of satisfactory gradation from a negative of unsatisfactory gradation.

For artistic-creative purposes, that is, to produce, from negatives of normal gradation, prints in which contrast has been increased or decreased, respectively, in order to bring about specific effects.

A photographer has the choice of a variety of sensitized papers in four or more different gradations with the following three different characteristics.

pp. 234–235

Papers of normal gradation more or less preserve in the print the contrast gradient of the negative.

Papers of soft gradation produce prints that have less contrast than the negatives from which they were made.

Papers of hard gradation produce prints that are more contrasty than the negatives from which they were made.

METHODS AND TECHNIQUES

Every photograph is the combined result of four (transparencies) or five (prints) separate operations:

Aiming
Focusing
Exposing
Developing
Printing

Each of these operations can be controlled, i.e., executed in different ways involving different means and methods, each modification resulting in a correspondingly different picture. Photographers who are not satisfied with chance results can do no better than to study these possibilities for control, which are discussed in the following, and to use them to their advantage.

Aiming

An aiming control, a finder, is as indispensable to the efficient operation of a camera as the sights are to the operation of a rifle. And just as there are different types of rifle sights: open sights, peep sights, telescopic sights, so there are different types of camera finders, each of which has certain advantages over the others. In this respect, a photographer has the choice of the following devices:

Combination rangefinder–viewfinder. The image is *not* formed by the lens that takes the picture but by a separate lens. Potentially, i.e., if the subject contains distinct edges or lines on which the rangefinder can be focused, this is the fastest of all aiming devices, making the so-equipped camera particularly suited to photography of people and other dynamic, moving, constantly changing subjects. However, since the finder image is *not* formed by the lens that takes the picture, but by a separate lens which "sees" the subject from a slightly different angle, a discrepancy exists between the subject as seen and the subject as photographed. This discrepancy, called parallax, increases with increasing nearness of the subject; it is usually corrected with the aid of a built-in parallax compensating device that, however, ceases to function when subject distance is shorter than approximately 3 ft., making close-ups impossible. Other drawbacks of rangefinder–viewfinders are that they cannot be used in conjunction with telephoto lenses of more than moderate focal lengths; that they don't permit direct, visual control of the extent of the depth of field; that they are not easy to use if the subject does not contain any sharply defined forms; and that the finder image is always relatively small, making its evaluation in regard to compositional respects difficult.

Groundglass finder. The image *is* formed by the lens that takes the picture. This device has several advantages: complete freedom from parallax (see above) at any focusing distance; suitability to close-up and telephotography; direct, visual control of the extent of the depth of field; and a large, negative-sized finder image that facilitates composition.

Groundglass finders come in two versions, i.e., with the groundglass either in vertical or in horizontal position when the camera is held level. The first type, typical of view cameras, has the advantage of greatest mechanical simplicity (and hence reliability and low cost) and the disadvantage that the so-equipped camera (unless fitted with another viewfinder) cannot be used hand-held but only mounted on a tripod; the second, typical of reflex cameras, involves mechanical complexity but, on the other hand, makes the so-equipped camera suitable to hand-held shooting.

p. 39

pp. 37–38

A vertical groundglass finder (panel) is eminently suited to photography of all static subjects that hold still but totally useless when it comes to photographing dynamic subjects and for hand-held shots. In the form of a reflex finder, a horizontal groundglass is eminently suited to photography of dynamic subjects and for hand-held shots but, because of mechanical problems, is restricted to relatively small cameras. Large reflex cameras in sizes of up to 5x7 in. exist, but they are inordinately big and heavy.

Eye-level versus waist-level finder. The difference between these two types of aiming devices is that the photographer looks *through* an eye-level finder and looks *down into* a waist-level finder. Combination rangefinder–viewfinders, pentaprism-equipped reflex finders, and vertical groundglass panels are eye-level finders. Reflex finders of 2¼x 2¼ in. single-lens reflex cameras, reflex finders of twin-lens reflex cameras, and many reflex housings of 35mm cameras are waist-level finders.

Usually, photographs made with a camera equipped with an eye-level finder are taken from a slightly greater height than photographs made with a camera equipped with a waist-level finder, as a result of which, other factors being equal, there is a slight difference in the perspective of the respective pictures. The latter show more of a "worm's-eye view" than the former. Of greater practical consequence, however, is the fact that occasionally one finder has definite advantages over the other. For example, when the distance between subject and camera is severely restricted, a reflex camera equipped with a waist-level finder can be set up with its back touching a wall and its aim and focus checked from above, thereby giving the photographer a little more distance than he would have if he used a camera equipped with an eye-level finder. The latter would compel him to move the camera forward so that he could get his head between it and the wall in order to check aim and focus. Furthermore, if necessary, a photographer can hold a camera equipped with a waist-level finder high above his head in upside-down position, checking aim and focus from below, and thus shoot pictures over the top of a wall, or over the heads of people standing in front of him who otherwise would have blocked his camera's view. Whenever photographs have to be taken very close to the ground (as often in nature photography), a camera equipped with a waist-level finder is much more comfortable to operate than a camera equipped with an eye-level finder, which compels the photographer to work prone. Some cameras offer a choice of several, interchangeable types of viewfinder or permit the use of auxiliary viewing devices such as pentaprisms, super-wide-angle finders, right-angle finders for "sneak shots," etc.

Focusing

Theoretically, a lens can only be focused upon a plane located at a specific distance from the camera, and objects in front of and behind this plane will appear increasingly unsharp the farther they are from it. Practically, however, such a plane is never a true plane but rather a zone with a certain depth. Objects situated within this zone, the depth of field, appear sharp; those in front of or behind it appear increasingly unsharp, the farther away they are. The depth of this sharply rendered picture zone can be controlled by two means:

pp. 46–47

The diaphragm. The smaller its aperture (i.e., the larger its *f*/number), the more extensive the depth of the sharply rendered zone in the picture, and vice versa.

pp. 156–157

The "swings" of a view camera. Normally, the plane of focus is located at a certain distance from the lens *at right angles to the optical axis* (i.e., parallel with the film). However, the front or back adjustments of a view camera make it possible either to tilt the plane of focus around an imaginary horizontal axis, or to swing it laterally around an imaginary vertical axis, or to do both simultaneously. Therefore, *in certain kinds of angle shots,* the plane of focus can be tilted so that it coincides with the principal plane of the (inclined) subject, as a result of which depth of field will increase considerably even though the diaphragm aperture remains the same.

pp. 39, 49

To make the plane of focus coincide with the principal plane of the (inclined) subject in an oblique view, tilt the lens slightly toward that plane or, as an alternative, tilt the back of the camera slightly away from that plane. Correct adjustment is achieved if imaginary lines drawn through the planes of subject, lens, and film meet at a common point. The difference between the two procedures is that tilting the lens forward does *not* affect the perspective of the rendition (but may have other disadvantages), whereas tilting the back backward produces a certain degree of perspective distortion (which may, or may not, be objectionable). Since both adjustments are rather critical (the lens adjustment even more than the back adjustment), their effects must be watched carefully on the groundglass. Detailed instructions are given in THE COLOR PHOTO BOOK by this author.

pp. 158–159

Exposing

In black-and-white photography, through appropriate exposure, a photographer can gain a certain amount of control in regard to the following aspects of his negatives:

pp. 164–165

Density and shadow detail. Basically, within reasonable limits, the longer the exposure, the denser the negative and the more detailed the shadows, and vice versa. For example, in night photography, due to the light-accumulating property of photographic emulsions, sufficiently long exposure will reveal detail where nothing but apparently impenetrable black met the eye.

pp. 166–167

pp. 232–233

The contrast gradient of the negative. Through appropriate exposure in conjunction with special development, other factors being equal, negatives of normal, high, or low contrast can be produced at will, a valuable control for producing printable negatives even though the respective subject was abnormally contrastless (many telephotographs) or overly contrasty (close-ups shot in bright sunlight). A shorter than normal exposure in conjunction with longer than normal development produces more contrasty negatives. Conversely, a longer than normal exposure in conjunction with shorter than normal development produces negatives of lower than normal contrast.

Sharpness of rendition. Other factors being equal, an overexposed negative, due to light scattering in the excessively dense areas, is always less sharp than a correctly exposed negative.

Graininess of rendition. Other factors being equal, an overexposed negative is usually more grainy than a negative that is correctly exposed.

pp. 326–327

Rendition of subject motion. The slower the shutter speed relative to the velocity of the subject, the more blurred the rendition and the stronger the feeling of speed. Conversely, to "freeze" a moving subject in the picture, the exposure must be made with a sufficiently high shutter speed. Detailed instructions are given in THE COMPLETE PHOTOGRAPHER by this author.

Exposure controls. Normally, exposure is controlled by the combined action of two factors, diaphragm aperture and shutter speed, the functions of which have already been discussed. However, in cases in which the subject is illuminated with electronic flash (speedlight), a third control comes into play, the duration of the illuminating flash. Then, duration of the exposure is no longer determined by the shutter speed, but by the speed of the much shorter flash which, because of its very short duration, enables a photographer to "stop" even extremely rapid events.

pp. 45–46

pp. 324–325

Exposure factors. The data determined with the aid of an exposure meter furnish the raw material from which a photographer must select that combination of diaphragm aperture and shutter speed that, in a given case, is most likely to yield the best result. However, even such specific data often require further refinement, a refinement that always amounts to an increase in exposure that can be accomplished either by opening up the diaphragm, using a slower shutter speed, or a combination of both. Such exposure increases are required whenever one or more of the following factors are involved in the making of a photograph: a color filter or a light-balancing filter; a polarizer; a fine-grain developer (black-and-white film only); abnormal subject brightness; a subject-to-lens distance equal to, or less than, eight times the focal length of the lens; an abnormally long exposure time (reciprocity failure). The values of the first three factors must be established with the aid of the respective manufacturer's instruction sheet that accompanies his product. The values of the last three factors depend on the nature of the subject or the circumstances connected with the exposure; they are fully discussed in THE COMPLETE PHOTOGRAPHER by this author.

Developing

Through appropriate development, a photographer can exert a fair amount of control over the following qualities of his black-and-white negatives:

Density. Up to a certain limit, the longer a film is developed, the more the negative increases in density, and vice versa.

Contrast. Up to a certain limit, the longer a film is developed, the more contrasty the negative becomes, and vice versa. Furthermore, other factors being equal, some developers produce negatives with less contrast (softer gradation) than others. As a rule, correctly used, fine-grain

pp. 232–233

developers produce negatives of softer gradation than standard developers, which in turn produce less contrasty negatives than rapid developers. Contrast developers produce the most contrasty negatives.

Contour sharpness (acutance). Other factors being equal, prints made from overdeveloped negatives are always less sharp than prints made from correctly developed negatives. This loss of sharpness becomes particularly pronounced if the negative is also overexposed.

pp. 216–217

Graininess. Up to a certain limit, the longer a film is developed, the coarser its grain structure becomes. Rapid and standard developers produce negatives with noticeably coarser grain structure than fine-grain developers.

Graininess and sharpness are not necessarily incompatible. As a matter of fact, under certain conditions, a fine-grain image can appear less sharp than an image in which grain structure is more pronounced. This may happen when fine-grain, thin-emulsion films are processed in a fine-grain developer of the type which alleviates graininess by dissolving a portion of the image-forming, metallic silver deposited during development. As a result, a mottled grain pattern is produced that adversely affects the contour sharpness (acutance) of the image. Thin-emulsion films should therefore not be developed in fine-grain developers which contain silver-dissolving chemicals.

Film speed. Under certain conditions, by means of appropriate prolongation of development, the rated speed of a black-and-white film can be increased (boosted) by a factor of two or more. But since prolongation of development also increases the contrast gradient of the negative, satisfactory results can be expected only if subject contrast is relatively low and the film has an inherently soft gradation. Best suited to boosting are films with exposure indices around 400. Less suited, because boosting would produce excessive graininess, are high-speed films with exposure indices of 500 and higher. Totally unsuited, because boosting would result in undesirably high contrast and no worthwhile increase in speed, are all slow and fine-grain films.

The speed of certain color films can be increased by one or two stops through appropriate changes in the mode of development; instructions for this are given in THE COLOR PHOTO BOOK by this author.

Printing

Technically, the making of a print parallels the taking of a photograph. Here, too, four separate stages can be distinguished, each subject to specific controls, each offering the photographer a choice of several possibilities for presenting his ideas. Elementary technical aspects involved in contact-printing and enlarging have already been discussed in THE COMPLETE PHOTOGRAPHER by this author to which the interested reader is referred. The following contains a run-down of the different controls available at each stage.

First, however, a word of advice: The technically most satisfactory print is always a print made from a technically faultless negative. Although a skillful printer can, to a greater or lesser extent, correct many aspects of an unsatisfactory negative, particularly in regard to contrast, exposure, perspective, distribution of light and dark, composition, and image scale, still better results could have been achieved if the negative itself had been perfect in these respects. Therefore, an experienced photographer will go to great lengths to incorporate in his negatives, already, all those qualities that he expects to see in his prints, later, and regards corrections during enlarging as measures that are better avoided.

"Aiming" an enlarger can be compared to aiming a camera: in both cases, the purpose of this operation is the presentation of the subject in its most effective form in regard to cropping and composition. If the photographer has been successful in this respect while taking the picture, the negative can be enlarged in its entirety, in which case "aiming" the enlarger involves merely determination of the most suitable degree of magnification. More often, however, the "aim" of the photographer was only an approximation that requires further refinement if the subject is to appear to its best advantage: the negative must be "cropped" in the print, and to decide which areas should be cut off and where the new boundaries should be is an important part of that immensely consequential operation popularly known as composing. Composing with the aid of an enlarger can become necessary for several reasons:

The picture was made with a square camera, and the photographer is tired of seeing nothing but square prints. Successful conversion of a square negative into a rectangular print depends on the way in which it is cropped (what is cut off) and where the new boundaries are drawn.

The negative is too crowded with subject matter, much of it superfluous or distracting; or, the subject proper of the picture, for example, a face, appears too small to be effective. In either case, lopping off excess parts of the negative through judicious cropping during projection and enlarging only the important area of the film brings the subject "up to scale," tightens the composition, and enormously improves the effect of the print. (These corrections could have been avoided, if the shot had been made from a shorter distance between subject and camera, or with a lens of longer focal length. Either way, the subject proper would have been rendered in larger scale, less waste would have been included in the picture, and the resulting negative could have been enlarged in its entirety, requiring a lesser degree of magnification and therefore yielding a sharper print.)

"Perspective distortion" in the form of "converging verticals" is a common fault of many photographs of architectural subjects. This convergence of actually parallel lines can be corrected during enlarging, and verticals (and other parallel lines) made to appear parallel again in the print, by correspondingly tilting toward each other the negative in the enlarger and the sensitized paper on the easel. Specific instructions are given in THE COMPLETE PHOTOGRAPHER by this author. (A simpler method of preserving the parallelism of actually parallel lines in oblique shots is by means of the "swings" of a view camera; see instructions on p. 280).

p. 281

Focusing the enlarger lens is best done with the aid of one of the special enlarging magnifiers that enable a photographer to achieve critical sharpness by focusing directly on the film grain. This, in my experience, is the best way to assure perfect sharpness of the print. To maintain this sharpness over the entire paper surface, I made it a habit to avoid glassless negative carriers, working instead with the remarkable anti-Newton-ring glass pressure plates offered by Simmon-Omega, Inc., of W. Woodside, N.Y. For maximum sharpness, the enlarger lens should be stopped down at least two stops.

p. 168

Exposing the sensitized paper for a shorter or longer time results in correspondingly lighter or darker prints, a valuable control by means of which a photographer can produce from the same negative normal, high-key, or low-key renditions and thereby control the mood of his picture – the lighter, the gayer; the darker, the more somber.

Frequently, even a negative of otherwise satisfactory gradation contains certain areas which, if printed "straight," would appear either too light or too dark. The most common faults of this kind are highlights that are too dense and therefore print too light, and shadows that are too thin and therefore print too black. Such unsatisfactory negative gradation of a limited extent can usually be corrected in the print through "dodging" —application of local contrast control—a technique based on the principle: to make a particular area darker, it must receive more exposure during enlarging than the rest of the picture; conversely, to make it lighter, it must receive less exposure during enlarging than the rest of the picture. Dodging, which requires a considerable amount of skill, is discussed more thoroughly in THE COMPLETE PHOTOGRAPHER by this author.

pp. 170–171

How to control the overall contrast of a print through selection of a paper of the appropriate gradation and thereby, if necessary, produce relatively contrasty prints from contrastless negatives, and vice versa, has already been discussed.

pp. 63, 234

To bring out the full, rich gradation inherent in a sensitized paper, the exposure, whether "straight" or "dodged," must be timed so that the print can be left in the developer a minimum of 1½ min. or, better still, 2 min. Prints that turn too dark before this time are overexposed and, if yanked prematurely, fixed, and dried, will appear mottled, "dirty," and "flat." Prints that are still too light after 2 min. in the developer are underexposed and, if development is continued in an effort to make them darker, will only turn out harsh and chalky and possibly have yellow or brownish stains.

Developing. For reasons explained above, photographic papers should normally be exposed so that the print looks just right after having been developed for not less than 1½ and not more than 2–2½ min. However, some papers have greater exposure latitude than others. Such papers can, if necessary, be exposed somewhat longer than normal and developed somewhat shorter than normal, and thereby made to yield prints in which contrast is slightly lower than it would have been if exposure and development had been normal. This control permits a photographer to produce prints with contrast gradients about half-way between the paper he used and the one with the next softer gradation – a bonus for the photographic perfectionist.

As a rule, a wrongly exposed print is a total loss and belongs in the waste can. However, if only part of it is too light or too dark, particularly if this area is not too large, it can be worth the effort to try to save the print, especially if it is large or was difficult to make because of extensive dodging. In such a case, the area that appears too light can be darkened to some extent by treating it either with hot water, or with concentrated developer; and the area that appears too dark can be lightened with the aid of a potassium ferricyanide solution (Farmer's reducer). Explicit instructions are given in THE COMPLETE PHOTOGRAPHER by this author.

MODIFIABLE PICTURE ASPECTS

The purpose of this book is to help the reader become a better photographer by showing him that every subject can be rendered in a multitude of different ways, some of them resulting in more effective pictures than others; by proving to him that he has the possibility of choice and control in regard to subject selection and approach, equipment and material, methods and techniques; and by teaching him in words and pictures how to make the best of these opportunities.

The preceding chapters dealt with control in regard to equipment and technique, a subject which can be taught in the form of words. However, when it comes to demonstrating the actual changes that can be brought about through appropriate modification of the various aspects of the picture itself in regard to light and shadow, contrast, color, sharpness, blur, perspective, depth, film grain, rendition of texture or motion, mood, and so on, words alone are inadequate and specific photographs must be used. Accordingly, I have devoted the main part of this book to illustrations. Beginning on page 81, in the form of 380 individual pictures, the reader will find examples of the many different controls which an experienced photographer has at his command. I trust he will find the collection informative.

TIMING THE MOMENT OF EXPOSURE

No matter how suitable the equipment of a photographer or how accomplished his technique, unless his timing is right, his pictures are bound to miss. On the other hand, no matter how much valid criticism a photograph may invite because of inadequate technique, as long as the subject is provocative and the timing right, it will never fail completely to arouse interest because most people don't know very much about phototechnique and care even less, but they care a great deal whether a photograph bores or pleases them. In this sense, timing the precise moment of exposure must be considered a more important factor than "technique," an indispensable control which can decide the fate of the picture.

Timing is particularly important in regard to the following aspects:

The psychological moment
The motion of subject or photographer
Light and atmospheric conditions

The psychological moment

Every event has its climax, i.e., the moment when tension reaches a peak, the unexpected happens, tempers explode, collapse sets in—the dramatic highlight, the instant of victory or defeat. These are the moments which give an action picture meaning and validity, but to capture them requires split-second timing.

A climax is not always violent or spectacular. Often its poignancy is subtle, making it all the more difficult to anticipate and capture on film. Yet once the psychological moment has passed, the chance for a significant picture has been lost.

A good example in point is Paul Schutzer's classic news shot of the then Vice-President Nixon angrily pointing his finger at a heckler. This event may not have lasted more than a second, but a photographer with hair-trigger reflexes timed it right and came up with one of the great news pictures of our time. In another instant, the decisive moment may be less

pp. 344–345

obvious yet no less meaningful, for example, the series of perfectly timed close-ups taken during a congressional investigation into labor racketeering that, by capturing the momentarily unguarded expressions on the defendants' faces, revealed the true character of these men, their hidden ruthlessness and greed.

One of the most difficult things to time correctly is a smile. Everybody has seen the toothy grins shot by commercial photographers at the command "Say cheese"; there is no real pleasure or joy in them, they are clichés, meaningless and embarrassing. In their phoniness they are the perfect complement to the exaggerated claims and paid testimonials of the advertisements that they illustrate. A genuine smile is a very different thing, a spontaneous emotional response to a humorous or tender situation that reflects in the eyes and can light up the entire face. Unfortunately, it is gone almost as soon as it begins and can be captured only by perfect timing.

The motion of subject or photographer

We live in a world of constant change and motion: people and animals, automobiles and airplanes, trains and ships; trees and flowers swaying with the wind; clouds moving in the sky; the waves of the sea, the currents of a river, the ripples made by a frog in a pond. And even when things are static and still, the photographer himself moves, and with every step he takes, with every mile he drives, he sees his subjects from a different angle, in different apparent size, and in a different relationship to their surroundings. No wonder that success or failure often depends on which phase of motion a photographer selects, which moment he chooses to arrest, how he times his shots.

Movement of the subject or of the photographer can influence the appearance of the picture in many ways. Movement that results in a change of distance between subject and camera, for example, causes a change in the apparent size of the subject and, in the photograph, a change in the scale of rendition. This change in image size must be considered whenever a subject moves toward or away from the photographer and also, of course, whenever a photographer moves toward or away from his subject. In practice, this situation is particularly common in sports photography.

Another result of motion a photographer must consider when timing a shot is the relative position of the various picture components. To give a simple example: let us suppose that a famous personality taking a constitutional has to be photographed. He passes people and cars, trees and buildings, is at one time clearly visible in front of a wall, the next moment half-hidden by a bush. Obviously, it makes a great difference how a photographer times such a shot—whether the person is seen in front of and blending with a busy background, half-hidden behind some obstruction, or clearly defined against a suitable setting. In each case, the subject (the person taking a walk) is the same, but the many pictures that could be made of him would be vastly different, their effectiveness decided by timing.

This example may represent a very simple case, but nevertheless it contains all the elements of more complex situations. The important picture aspects, the aspects that are the combined result of subject motion, movement on the part of the photographer, and timing, are differences in contrast and color, clarity of subject presentation, and overlapping and juxtaposition of forms. What is the momentary relationship between the subject and the other picture elements: foreground matter, background, people, buildings, trees? In what way do these various picture elements affect one another in respect to the effect and clarity of the rendition? Does one component cover, obscure, compete, or blend with some of the others in an undesirable way? How do they affect one another in regard to composition? Do the main masses of the picture balance one another harmoniously? What is the distribution of light and dark?

Another aspect of motion that requires consideration is the fact that most living things, and also certain objects, change in appearance from moment to moment as they move. As an example, take a series of photographs in rapid succession of a person walking. No doubt, in some of these pictures the subject will look as if he were about to fall over his own feet, while in others he will appear to move along with a free and easy stride. Depending on their timing, some of the pictures will appear grotesque while others will seem to have captured the essence of rhythmically flowing motion.

Similar considerations apply, of course, to almost any subject in motion. Take the simplest example, the photograph of a hand gesturing in accompaniment to a spirited discussion. Whether the gesture appears awkward or expressive will depend entirely upon timing. Or consider the movements of a flag in a gentle breeze: at one moment limp, scarcely moving; at another, ponderously flapping or briskly rippling, constantly changing form. The stage at which it is photographed determines whether it looks like an unimpressive rag or the proud symbol of the nation it represents.

p. 256 Timing can even make a difference in photographing landscapes on days when rifts in the clouds let through occasional sunlight, and shadows move across the land. If a photographer has sufficient time and patience, he may eventually get a distribution of light and shadow, with the focal point of his composition emphasized by rays of light, as perfectly balanced as if he had illuminated the landscape with studio lamps, another instance in which proper timing can enhance a picture.

Light and atmospheric conditions

One of the most frustrating aspects of working as a photographer on a picture magazine is that usually everything must be done in a hurry. The effect of this constant rush is felt most acutely on outdoor assignments of the "feature" type in which the impact of a picture often depends almost entirely on presenting the subject in the right kind of light and mood. I have done many stories of this kind for *Life*, but rarely have I suffered more from the restrictions imposed upon my work by lack of time than when I did the story of the Hudson River.

For its effect, almost every picture in this essay depended on "mood": the right combination of weather and light. As a result, many otherwise suitable subjects could not be photographed, the light and weather conditions were never right during the allotted time. Naturally, when close to 100 different photographs have to be taken along some 300 miles of river, it is not always possible to wait for the light or the weather to change.

That the story came off at all is due to the fact that I never made a picture unless I had the right kind of weather and light. If I felt a scene should p. 258 be shot in early morning mist (like the opening picture), I shot it thus, or not at all. The narrows along the Storm King Highway, I felt, had to be photographed during a storm. I was fortunate enough to have that kind of weather; if I hadn't been able to shoot under a sultry, thunderous sky, I would not have taken the picture. Showing this wild and dramatic part of the river in peaceful sunshine would have negated the character of the landscape.

To be at their effective best, all outdoor photographs must be timed in accordance with the particular light and weather which the subject demands. For outdoor portraits, for example, the best light is usually light from a hazy or thinly overcast sky, or the diffused light of open shade. In direct sunlight everyone feels uncomfortable, and this discomfort is reflected in squinting eyes and distorted features. Excessive contrast, for example, burned-out highlights and ink-black shadows, further aggravate the poor impression made by such ill-timed pictures. Specifically, in timing his outdoor shots, in addition to the effects of motion, a photographer must consider the following factors:

The quality of the light. A photographer has the choice of direct sunlight, hazy sun, and light in the shade or from a more or less overcast sky. Furthermore, early morning and late afternoon light have completely different qualities from light around noon.

Differences in the quality of daylight are differences in brightness, contrast, and color. The less the sun is obstructed by haze or clouds, the brighter and more contrasty the illumination, and vice versa. And the color of daylight changes rapidly and often drastically with changes in the atmospheric conditions and the time of day, a fact which is of particular importance to color photographers.

pp. 249, 254–257

The direction of the light. A photographer has the choice of frontlight, different degrees of sidelight, and different degrees of backlight. Low-slanting morning and evening light, because of the extensive and greatly elongated shadows which they cast, have a totally different effect from that of light around noon, which is more or less overhead light that casts comparatively short shadows or no shadows at all (except, of course, beneath the subject, where they are usually invisible.)

pp. 190–201

Atmospheric conditions. A photographer has the choice of weather as different as sunshine, rain, and snow; haze, mist, and fog; calm, windy, and stormy. The same landscape, photographed in early morning mist,

pp, 202, 258

will look totally different when photographed in harsh sunlight at noon, or on a stormy, overcast day. One picture may be nothing more than a "calendar shot" a photographic cliché, whereas another may be a revelation.

THE CONTROLS APPLIED

The following illustrations demonstrate in picture form most of the various and often highly diversified controls which are at the disposal of any photographer who cares to avail himself of them. The need for such control will be obvious to anyone who considers the following.

Any subject can be rendered graphically in many different forms. Some of these, of course, are more effective, i. e., more eye-catching, informative, mood-inducing, or esthetically pleasing, than others. Only those photographers who are aware of such differences in subject approach and rendition — in other words, only those who are familiar with the various means of photographic control — will be able to select and apply the means suitable to produce the best results.

It is impossible to render directly three of most subjects' most important characteristics in a black-and-white photograph: color, depth (three-dimensionality), and motion. Therefore, these qualities must be indicated symbolically through gray-shade, contrast, perspective, blur, etc. Each can be symbolized in many different forms. To be able to choose and apply the form which will be the most effective, a photographer must be familiar with them all.

The eye and the lens "see" differently. For this reason, if one wishes to capture and convey the "feeling" of a subject in a photograph, it is usually not possible to achieve this simply by pointing the camera and snapping the picture. Only if a photographer makes allowances for these differences in "seeing" — that is, if he exercises control — will he be able to translate reality into effective photographs.

Differences in "seeing" between eye and lens

The eye, guided by the brain and influenced by memory and emotion, sees subjectively. The lens, controlled by rigid optical laws, sees objectively.

In effect, this means that, as a rule, we see things not as they are but as we think they ought to be. For example, if someone is seen under a tree, the greenish cast on the face caused by the filter effect of the leaves wouldn't be noticed, but the lens and film would record it in an uncontrolled color photograph.

The eye sees selectively, focusing only on what interests us and what we wish to see, overlooking everything else. The uncontrolled lens, however, "sees" indiscriminately, rendering both the important and the unimportant in a photograph. Thus, in reality, we probably would not "see" the crooked tree in the background which, in an uncontrolled photograph, to our surprise and dismay may seem to grow out of the subject's head.

We know that the walls of buildings are parallel. As a result, we always "see" them thus, even when looking up toward the roof. But the uncontrolled lens renders them in picture-form as converging, which makes them appear about to collapse.

The eye can follow an object in motion, seeing it sharply defined, and yet convey to the brain the fact that the object moves. On the other hand, the lens, in rendering a moving object sharply, usually produces pictures which give the impression that the object was at rest. This can easily be verified by looking at photographs of automobile races in which the sharply rendered cars, doing perhaps a hundred miles an hour, appear at a standstill.

In looking at an object that has considerable extension in depth, the eye instantly corrects focus for points located at different distances, thus "scanning" depth and orienting itself in space; whereas the uncontrolled lens often produces an effect popularly known as "perspective distortion." This can easily be confirmed by looking at photographs showing objects of considerable depth taken at close range with a wide-angle lens.

The brain-controlled eye rapidly adapts to changes in brightness, thus, in effect, minimizing differences between shadow and light so that we can distinguish detail in both. However, in uncontrolled photographs, the objective rendering of the actual contrast range of a scene often results in detail-less patches of black and white side by side.

On the following spread, four pairs of pictures which demonstrate differences between controlled and uncontrolled photographs show how the same subject appeared in the form of "controlled" photographs to the "subjective" eye, and how it appeared to the "objective" uncontrolled lens.

Differences in "seeing" between the eye and the lens

The eye sees this:

Walls appear vertical and parallel.

The lens "sees" this:

Walls converge as if about to collapse.

An automobile in motion appears sharp.

An automobile in motion is rendered blurred.

he eye sees this:

The lens "sees" this:

he hand appears smaller than the head.

The hand is rendered grotesquely large.

hadows appear transparent and full of detail.

Shadows are detail-less areas of solid black.

"Positive camera lies"

The old adage, "The camera does not lie," is not true. Actually, the vast majority of photographs are "camera lies" in that they don't conform to reality — for example: two-dimensional pictures of three-dimensional subjects; black-and-white renditions of colorful things; motion studies in the form of "stills."

However, let's accept the fact that most photographs "lie" and make the best of it. For "lying" in the sense it is used here does not necessarily suggest a negative quality. It simply implies that a difference exists between a photograph and the subject it depicts. In most uncontrolled photographs this difference, of course, becomes a negative factor, for the uncontrolled photograph usually creates a lesser impression of what was apparent to the eye.

However, once one understands the difference between what the eye sees and what the camera records, it is possible to exploit this difference to advantage. For although the lens (and the entire photographic process) is in some respects inferior to the eye, in others it is superior. Uncontrolled photographs show only its inferiority. But if a photographer knows how to control his medium, he can utilize its superior qualities to impart through his photographs more than an observer would have been able to see in the subject itself. Skillfully used, photography becomes a means for discovery and the camera an instrument for widening the range of our visual experience.

The following pages show examples of such "positive camera lies."

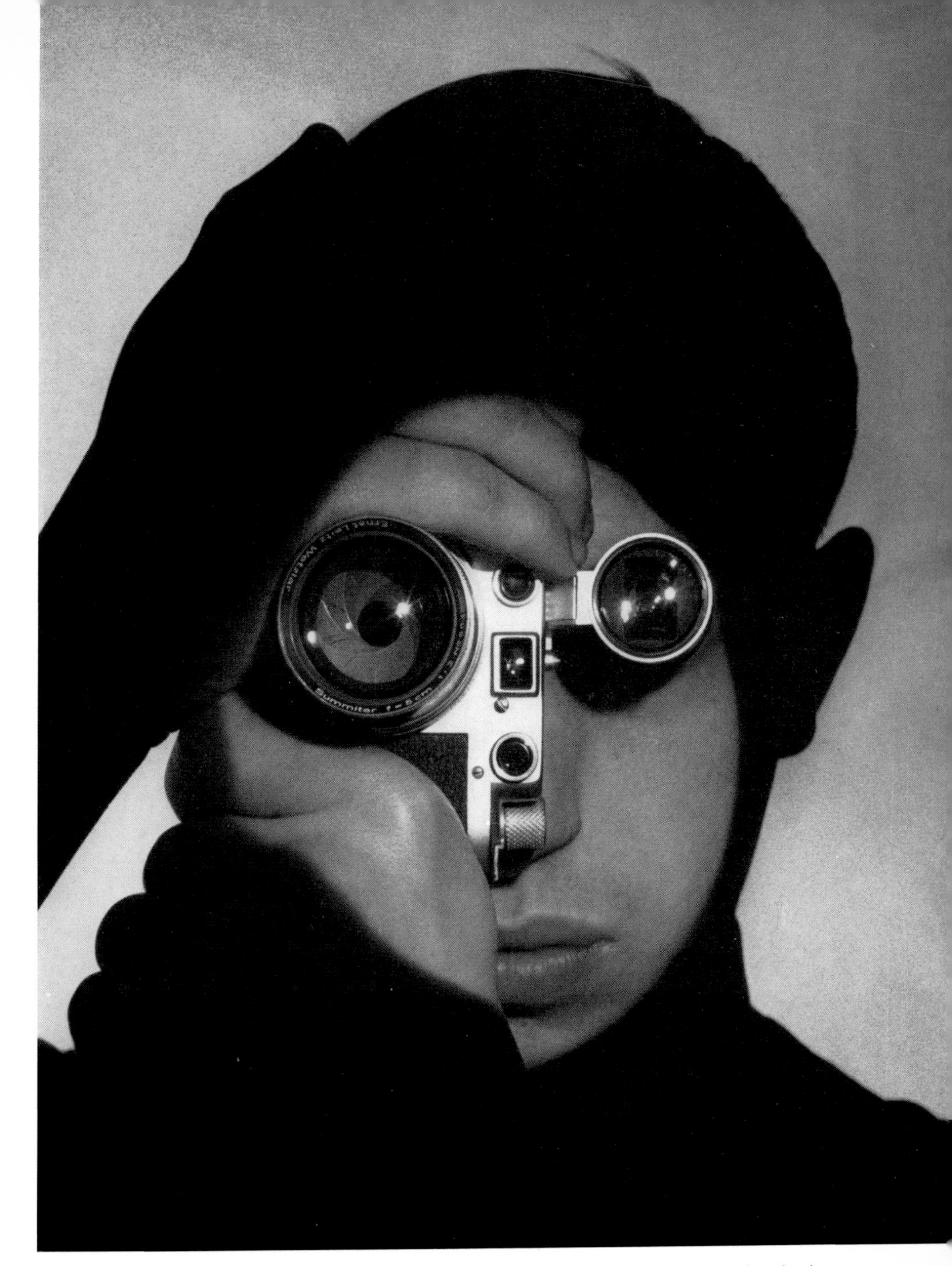

Graphic expression of a concept: the photo-journalist. Normally, no photographer looks like this. But the conceptual image of a photo-reporter whose camera becomes an extension of his own vision can be reduced to these three essentials: the viewfinder, the lens, and the brain. This carefully controlled photograph, which was conceived as a cover for Live Magazine, represents an attempt to express this concept in graphic form.

The eye cannot translate color into shades of black-and-white. But through using filters and sensitized paper of suitable gradation, a photographer can change even the most uninteresting colors into graphically powerful, pictorially effective shades of gray as well as black and white as demonstrated by this photograph of the Matterhorn made by G. E. Kidder Smith.

The eye cannot resolve objects beyond a certain distance. But with the aid of telephoto lenses a photographer can conquer distance and show even far away objects in large size and full detail. The small picture (left) shows the scene as it appeared to the eye, including the camera with which this photograph of the New York waterfront was made.

The angle of acute vision of the human eye is restricted to less than twenty degrees, but photographic lenses exist which can sharply cover angles of view of 90 degrees and greater. The greatest coverage is provided by the Nikon "Fish-eye lens" which covers an angle of 180 degrees. The photograph above of the cockpit of a commercial airliner was made with such a lens.

Naturally, the perspective of such wide-angle shots seems strange at first. But once one has become used to it and learned to "interpret" it correctly, one sees the enormous advantages of such pictures: subjects which otherwise would require a whole series of photographs can now be shown in a single integrated picture.

The human eye cannot resolve objects located at distances shorter than approximately eight inches, but no such restriction exists for the photographic lens. With a camera that has sufficient bellows extension, a photographer can sharply render objects at distances as close as fractions of an inch, thereby opening the heretofore closed world of the nearest and smallest and delighting us with such fantastic things as the rear view of a trapdoor spider, shown here in ten times natural size.

The eye sees objects in very rapid motion as more or less blurred or it cannot perceive them at all. But through use of high shutter speeds or electronic flash, photographers can produce tack-sharp pictures of objects moving so fast that they appear only as a blur and depict events of durations so short that they were invisible to the eye — for example, the effect of the impact of a fighter's fist on his opponent's face which is shown in the picture above.

If sharply rendered, two images of the same subject, one photographed in motion, the other at rest, are often alike. As a result, a person who looks at such pictures may not be able to tell whether the depicted object (for example, an automobile) moved or stood still. This confusion can be avoided if the photographer uses a relatively slow shutter speed to create a degree of blur in the picture that will suggest the motion but will not make the subject unrecognizable. In the photograph above, shot through the windshield of a moving car, a carefully controlled amount of blur in the trees graphically symbolizes "speed."

The eye cannot retain an image for any length of time, nor can it superimpose the different images produced by a sequence of events; the camera, of course, can. The picture above shows a merry-go-round at night, a graph of space and motion produced through a time-exposure of its revolving lights. On the opposite page, a photograph by Gjon Mili demonstrates how different aspects of an occurrence can be superimposed with the aid of multiple electronic flash to show at one glance many phases of an event.

Dynamic and static subjects

For reasons relating to subject approach and rendition, it is practical to classify photographic subjects in two groups: dynamic subjects and static subjects.

Dynamic subjects are ever-changing, never the same twice. In this group are people and animals, street scenes, the sea and the sky and other dynamic manifestations of nature.

Dynamic subjects, because of their innumerable different aspects, offer a photographer unending opportunities for original solutions. Success or failure in photographing such subjects depends almost entirely upon the photographer's approach and his ability to "see" them in new and interesting ways. Timing is particularly important. Usually, a small, inconspicuous, mobile camera (35 mm) gives the best results.

Static subjects do not move or change appearance except under the influence of external agencies. In this group are most objects, works of art (like the African fetish shown here), architectural subjects including interiors, most landscapes, and many objects of nature such as flowers, crystals, shells, etc.

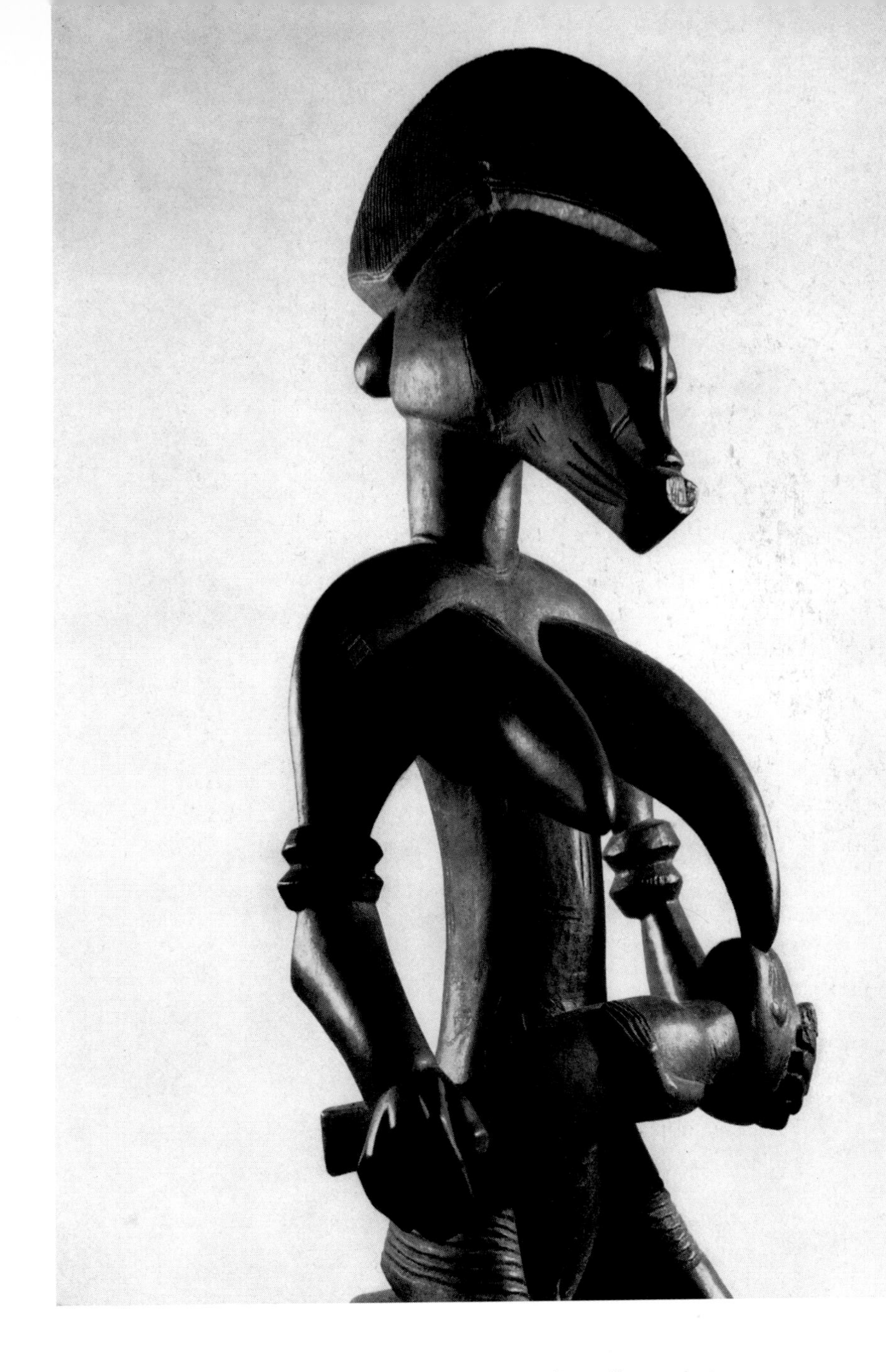

Most static subjects, because of their inherent rigidity, offer a photographer less scope for imaginative treatment than dynamic subjects. Subject approach, viewpoint, and illumination are particularly important. Usually, a large camera (4" × 5") gives the best results.

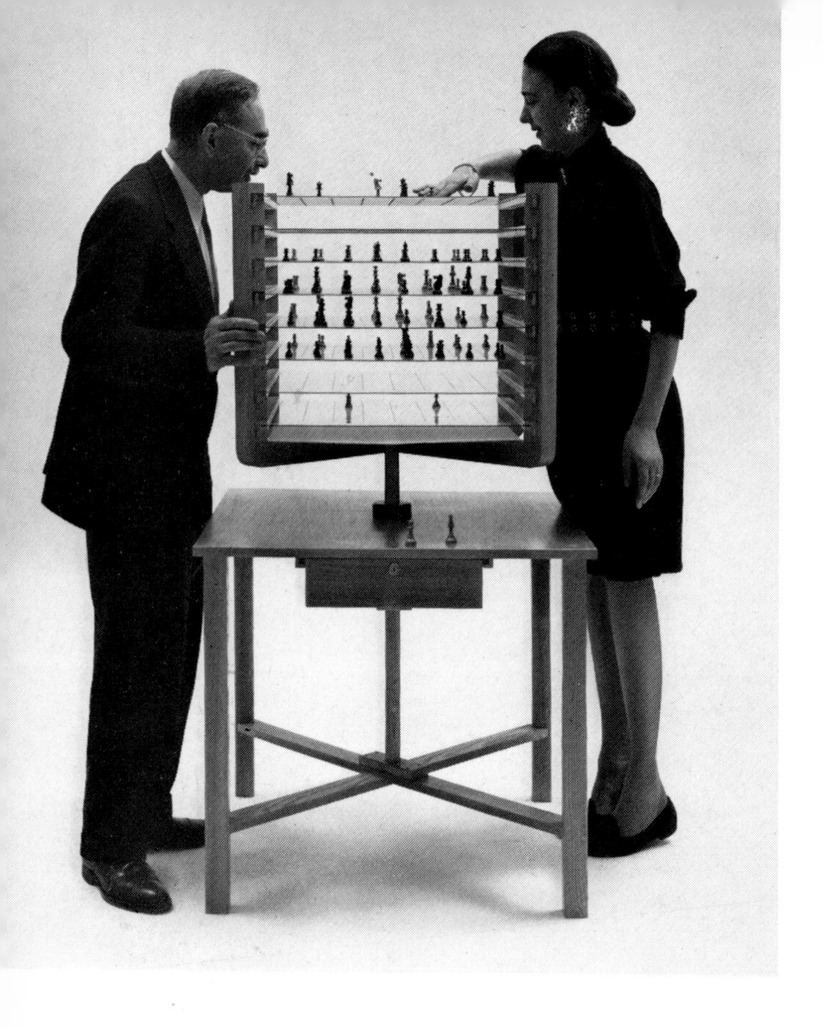

Objective or subjective approach

Basically, a photographer has the choice of an objective or a subjective approach to his subjects.

Objective approach. This is the approach of the documentarian or scientist, characterized by a conscious effort to report objectively without bias or expression of personal opinion. Clarity of rendition is particularly important. Imagination may be a hindrance rather than an aid, although objectivity in photo-reporting should never become an excuse for dull or hackneyed work.

The picture above by Yale Joel, showing a three-dimensional game of chess, can be said to typify the objective approach.

Subjective approach. This is the approach of the creative photographer or artist which is characterized by a deliberate effort to express in picture-form a personal opinion or an experience which the photographer wished to share with others. Imagination and genuine feeling for the subject are particularly important.

Subjective photographs, because they are the result of thought, feeling, and personal experience, generally are more interesting and stimulating than objective pictures. At their best, they give the observer something new, something he had not seen, or thought of, before, a new awareness or experience in the field of graphic expression.

The picture above shows Yale Joel's imaginative, subjective approach to three-dimensional chess.

Subject approach: from over-all view to close-up

In regard to subject distance and scale, a photographer has the choice of over-all views, medium-long shots, and close-ups.

The over-all view shows the subject in relation to its environment. Its purpose is to orient the observer and enable him to correlate and see in their proper relationship subsequent medium-long shots and close-ups. Over-all views are usually taken from relatively far away with a lens of standard focal length. If sufficient distance is lacking, they are taken with a wide-angle lens.

The medium-long shot shows the subject proper in its entirety while excluding most of its surroundings. It already contains a certain amount of detail and enables the observer to correlate subsequent close-ups of important areas of the subject. Normally, medium-long shots are best taken with a standard lens or, if subject-to-camera distance is great, with a moderate telephoto lens.

The close-up shows important areas of the subject in large size and with emphasis on detail. Close-ups are supplementary views whose purpose is to give the observer a detailed understanding of his subject. Depending upon the subject-to-camera distance, they can be taken with either a standard, a telephoto, or a wide-angle lens. The subject proper of this sequence of pictures is the young woman shown in the last photograph. However, it could also be argued that the subject of the first picture is a garden shown in a medium-long shot, that of the second a group of people in a medium-long shot, and that of the last two photographs, a girl shown in the form of a medium-long shot and a close-up, respectively.

Subject approach: from over-all view to close-up

The choice of an over-all view, a medium-long shot, or a close-up applies whether one photographs outdoors or indoors.

This sequence, the individual components of which complement one another, shows the sculptor Cecil Howard at work. The over-all view represents the scene of action, the medium-long shot is a portrait of the artist, and the close-up gives a detailed view of the work.

Technically, the transition from over-all view to close-up can be accomplished in one of two ways: either by gradually decreasing the distance between subject and camera, or by using lenses of increasingly longer focal lengths.

Subject approach: the telephoto close-up

Frequently, considerations of space-rendition make it undesirable to decrease the camera-to-subject distance sufficiently for a close-up shot to be taken with a lens of standard focal length.

If a similar picture of the Manhattan skyline had been photographed from a boat and a standard lens had been used, "perspective distortion" would have resulted — nearby ships would have appeared unproportionally large in the picture, and the far away buildings unproportionally small or entirely hidden behind the nearby structures. To avoid this kind of distortion, both the over-all and the close-up views were made from the same camera position, the first with a lens of standard focal length, the latter with an extreme telephoto lens.

Similar considerations, of course, apply in portrait photography in which insufficient subject distance always entails the danger of "distortion" (see photographs on p. 121).

WELCOME
HOME

Subject approach: the picture within the picture

Most photographs show "too much." This fault may be corrected by enlarging only the most interesting section of the negative. However, for phototechnical reasons, it is preferable to photograph the subject proper with a lens of sufficiently long focal length which restricts the angle of view, and thereby eliminates distracting marginal picture elements.

The photograph above shows a rather dreary view of a New York City street as it appears to the eye. However, within this view, another, more dramatic picture was contained — the human-interest shot of a poor housewife hanging up her laundry in the desert of brick and steel shown at right. A long-focus telephoto lens was needed to produce this picture. If a sectional enlargement of an "ordinary" negative had been used, the film grain would have obscured the fine, editorially important texture of the bricks.

M.P.
31679
NE
SHELL

Subject approach: the close-up

One of the most powerful means for intensified seeing is the super close-up — a photograph of a small subject rendered in more than natural size.

When human vision fails to see certain subjects because they are too small, the camera, equipped with short-focus lenses and long bellows extensions or extension tubes, shows us these things which otherwise we could not see. This is the realm of macrophotography — exploration through photographic means of the fascinating world of things that are too small to be seen in full detail but are not small enough to require the use of a microscope.

These pictures show examples of macrophotography: ice crystals on a window pane in 20 times linear magnification, and the head of a male Luna moth in five times natural size.

Subject approach: point of view

A good photographer studies his subject from every possible angle to be sure of showing it from the most effective point of view.

This must be taken quite literally: look at your subject from right and left, front and rear, above and below, before you decide from which position to shoot it. Any view is permissible — horizontal, diagonal, vertical — as long as it results in a better, clearer, more instructive, or more interesting picture.

The accompanying photographs show two ordinary subjects seen from unordinary points of view: a stand of young Black Birches taken from below, and a crowd photographed from directly above. In each case, the unusual camera point of view was deliberately chosen as the one most likely to produce the most informative and pictorially interesting picture.

Subject approach: there is always a choice . . .

Any subject can be photographed in many different ways, some of which, of course, are more effective than others. Sometimes, even slight changes in subject approach can produce entirely different pictures as is proved by these two pairs of comparison photographs.

New York harbor scene. Stepping back a few feet enabled the photographer to include in his picture the steel girders which "frame" the approaching railroad ferry and, through juxtaposition of near and far objects, to improve the illusion of depth in the photograph.

F i f t h A v e n u e , N e w Y o r k. A 90-degree turn of the camera, resulting in a change from frontlight to backlight, produced two very different renditions of the same scene. Of these, the backlit photograph, characterized by shadows falling toward the camera, gives the stronger depth effect. Both pictures were made from the same camera position within seconds of one another.

The importance of scale

To give an observer an idea of the actual dimensions of the subject depicted, a photograph must contain an indicator of scale.

Scale indicators are familiar objects whose dimensions are known, i. e., the human figure, a hand, windows, automobiles, etc., in relation to which the actual dimensions of the depicted subject can be gauged. If such scale indicators are lacking, no conclusions can be drawn regarding the actual size of the depicted subject.

Eroded highway embankment. This is a typical example of a scaleless picture. No one can be sure whether the depicted area was, in reality, inches wide or perhaps a thousand feet. On the other hand, the small comparison photograph has scale. The fence posts and trees in the background indicate that the depicted area was relatively small.

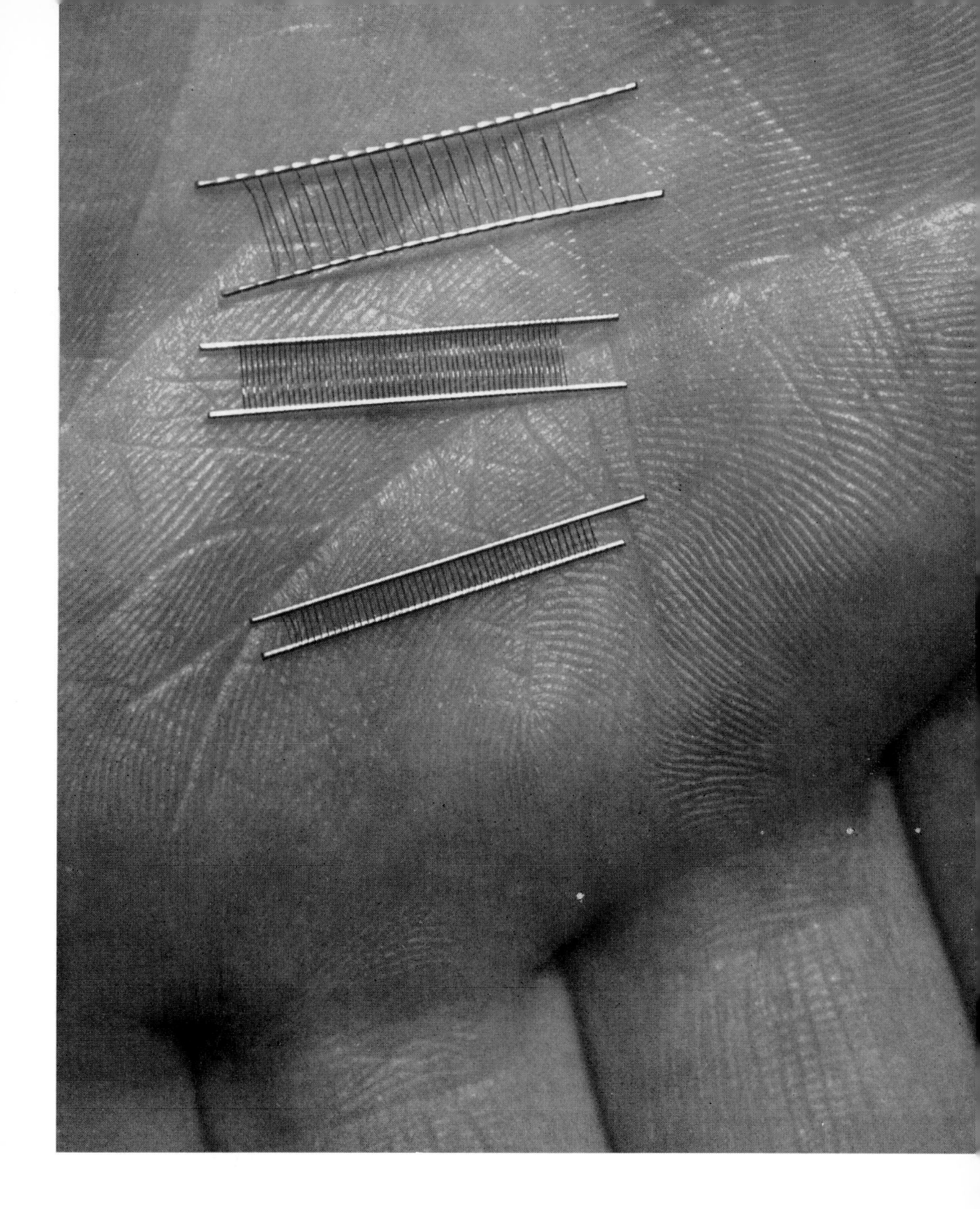

This close-up of electronic vacuum tube grids made by the Sonotone Corporation has scale which is provided by the palm and whorls of the hand on which the grids rest. Without an indicator of scale in a photograph of these grids, one could not know their actual size. Occasionally, of course, scalelessness in a photograph may be used to add suspense to a rendition by withholding an indication of size.

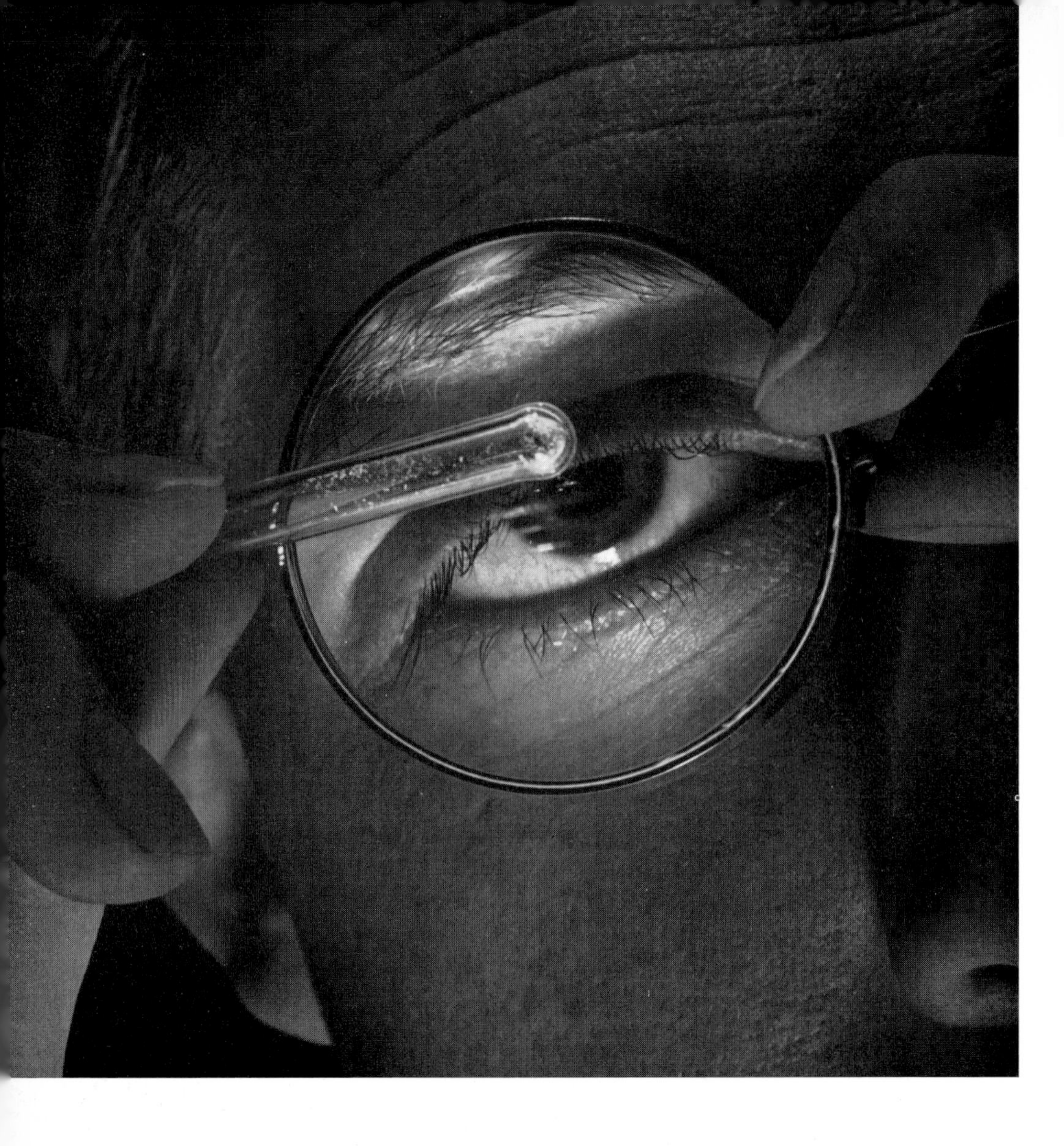

The importance of scale

Synthetic penicillin. An eye provides this photograph with scale, indicating in contrast to its own, well-known size, the minuteness of the first few grains of penicillin to be produced artificially.

Subminiature camera. To make the camera appear as small as possible, a man's big face and hands were deliberately chosen to provide the picture with scale. Contrasted to a girl's more delicate face and hands, the camera would have appeared much larger.

The importance of scale

One reason photographs of landscapes so often turn out disappointingly is that they lack scale.

Landscapes represent the largest of all photographic subjects. Reduced to a minute fraction of their true dimensions, they naturally appear unimpressive in picture form unless the observer is given an indication of their actual size. This can be done in one of two ways: either by enlarging the negative to mural size (which is seldom practical), or by providing the picture with scale.

The best indicator of scale in a landscape photograph is the human figure. However, in order to make the landscape appear large, the unit of scale — the figure — must appear small. Tiny figures far away in the background make a landscape appear wide and big; large figures in the foreground make it appear small. Thus a photographer, by placing his scale indicators at a suitable distance from the camera, can control the space impressions of his outdoor photographs.

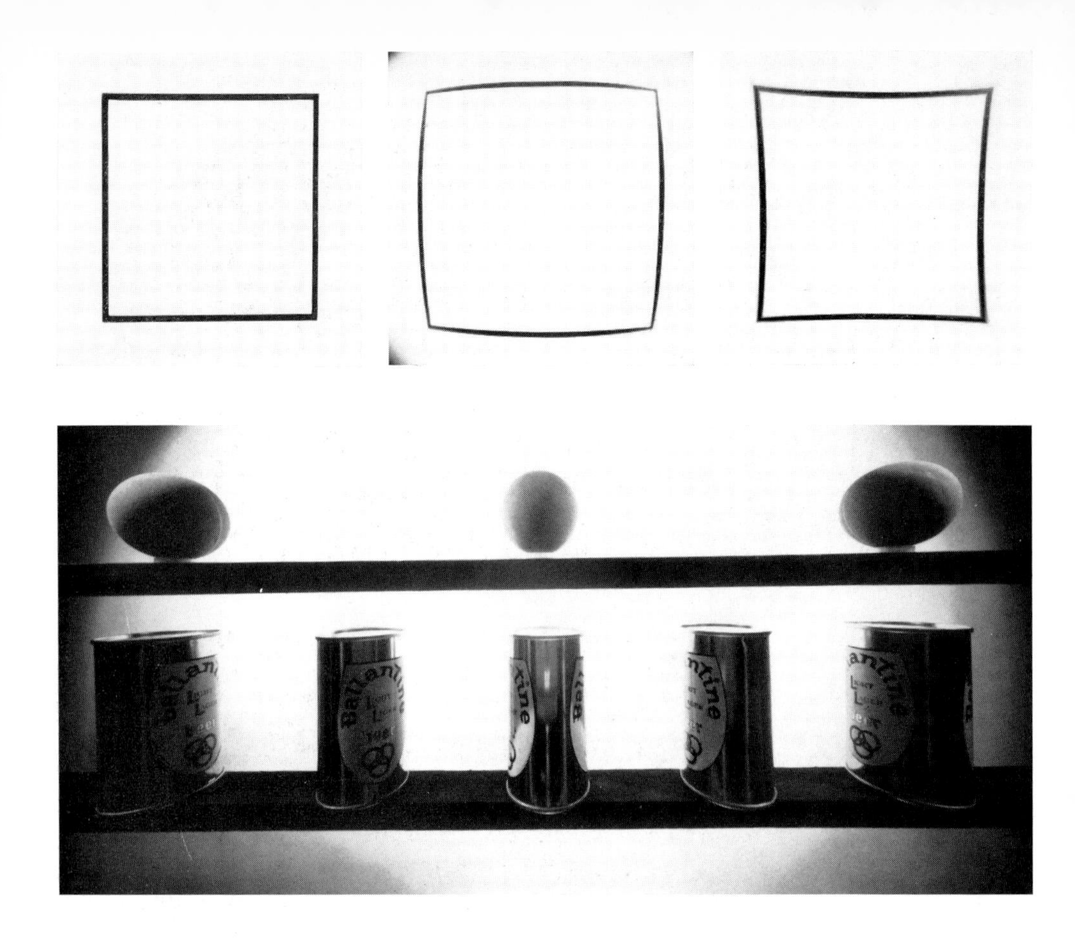

Distortion

There are two types of distortion: "true" distortion which is caused by shortcomings of the lens; and "pseudo" distortion which is a natural manifestation of perspective.

The top row of photographs shows a square photographed with three different lenses: left, an undistorted rendition; center, barrel distortion; right, pincushion distortion. The first was made with a well-corrected lens; the latter two, made with uncorrected meniscus lenses, are examples of "true" distortion.

The beer cans and rubber balls near the edges of the picture appear distorted because the photograph was taken at very close range with a super wide-angle lens. Depending on the angle of coverage of a lens, this phenomenon is to a greater or lesser degree produced by all wide-angle lenses and is the unavoidable result of the projection of three-dimensional objects onto the flat surface of the film.

The two faces represent the same girl photographed at very close ranges with a wide-angle lens, once from slightly below eye-level, once from slightly above. The resulting pseudo-distortion is a natural manifestation of perspective, which would have been apparent in reality if the photographer could have looked

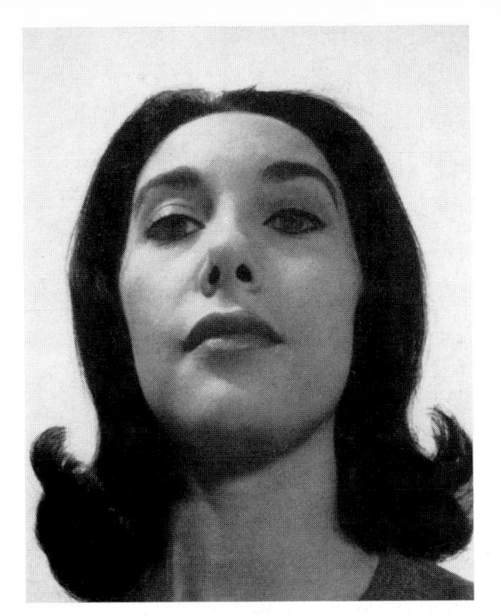

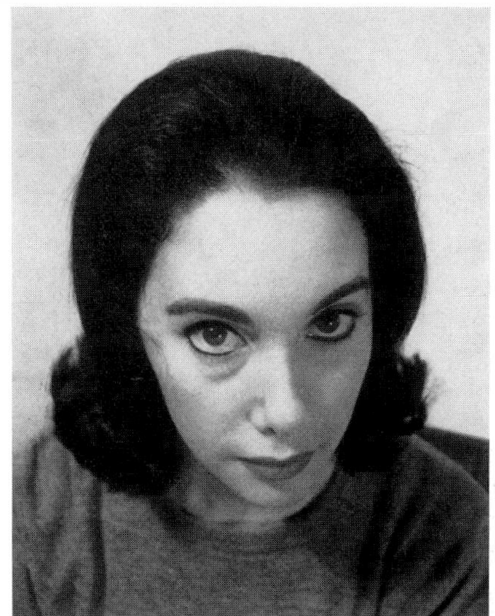

at the girl with his eyes in the same position as the lens, taking in the same wide angle of view (something which, unfortunately, is an impossibility for the human eye but not for certain fish and insect eyes). The only way this exaggerated perspective (which is, in fact, the graphic symbol of extreme closeness) can be avoided is to take the picture from a greater distance with a lens of longer focal length.

In the photograph of a building, the curving of the horizontals (which in actuality were straight) is due to the fact that the picture was taken with a panoramic camera, the lens of which swings through an arc in taking the picture. This view encompasses an angle of 140 degrees which closely corresponds to the impression one would get if one stood near the front of the building and turned one's head from side to side in order to see its entire expanse. An explanation of this type of "cylindrical" perspective is given on pp. 300–305.

The background

Normally, subject and background should be well differentiated from one another in regard to tone value, design, and degree of sharpness, to prevent undesirable blending of one with the other.

Although the background forms an integral and highly important part of most pictures, few photographers give it the proper attention. The effect of a confusing background is illustrated in the photograph above which shows how nature protects one of its creatures by giving it a pattern which blends with the pattern of the background (tree bark) on which it usually rests.

Normally, the simpler and less obtrusive the background, the stronger the impact of the subject. Small subjects can often be advantageously placed directly on a sheet of groundglass suspended a foot or two above a sheet of white paper (the Viking amulets at the top of the opposite page), or arranged well in front of a neutral background (right). In either case, the background itself must be evenly illuminated. The distance of the light from the background proper controls the tone value of the background in the photograph. This procedure results in photographs of unsurpassed clarity in which no shadows are cast by the subject upon the background to mar the graphic purity of the rendition.

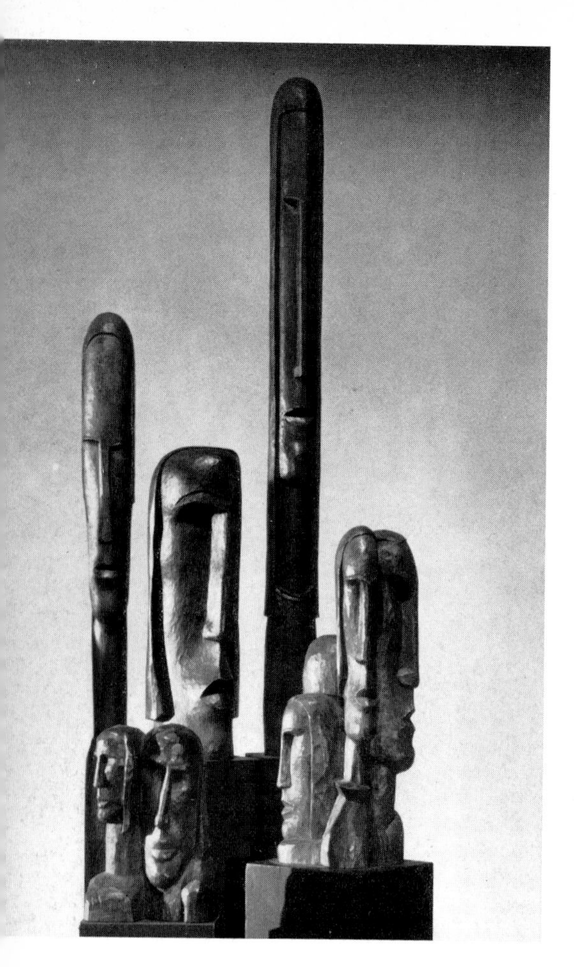

The background: variations on a theme

Three photographs of the same subject — sculptures by Nick Carpenko — illustrate how the impression of a picture can be influenced by the background.

A neutral background permits the sculpture to speak for itself.

Elongated shadows, integrated elements of the composition, repeat in muted form the dominant theme.

An arrangement photographed against the backdrop of New York suggests the influence which this skyline had upon Carpenko's work.

The background: outdoors

Outdoors, the best of all possible backgrounds is the unobstructed sky because it is neutral and yet delicately modulated, never dull and "dead."

Here, the blue sky was translated by a red filter into a shade of gray which is lighter than the dark, yet darker than the light side of the figure, providing perfect separation of tone.

And on the opposite page, a deep, natural shadow made just the right contrasting background for the lacy structure of this spiderweb. Only against such a simple background can a subject as complex and detailed as this appear effective.

The foreground

Evaluated in terms of pictorial rendition, the foreground symbolizes "nearness" and earthly qualities; the background, and particularly the sky, symbolize "distance" and spiritual qualities.

Consequently, by deliberately emphasizing one or the other in his picture, a photographer can stress at will either the earthly or the spiritual aspects or implications of his subject. Technically, this can be accomplished in one of two ways:

By tilting the camera downward or upward (or lowering or raising the lens), respectively, to include more or less foreground in the picture.
By using a wide-angle or a telephoto lens, respectively, to emphasize or minimize the foreground in the picture.

Juxtaposition of foreground and background matter creates the impression of "depth," and hence, it becomes a valuable means for symbolizing "space" within the two-dimensional plane of a picture. This type of space-impression can be controlled in three different ways:

Juxtaposition of near and far subject matter. In practice, this is most effectively accomplished by "framing," i. e., showing a distant subject through a "frame" provided by a foreground subject.

Juxtaposition of large (nearby) and small (far away) subject matter. This is a manifestation of perspective called diminution. It can be controlled through the combined effects of subject distance and focal length of the lens. The shorter the distance between the camera and the foreground subject and the wider the angle of the lens, the more pronounced the resulting diminution and vice versa.

Juxtaposition of light and dark. This is called "aerial perspective." The darker the rendition of the foreground and the lighter the far away subject matter, the stronger the feeling of "depth" and vice versa.

Predominance of foreground matter suggests earthy qualities, nearness, and intimacy. Here, tilting the camera downward produced a picture in which closeness of the ground resulted in good texture rendition, thereby enabling the viewer almost to "feel" the softness of the warm sand. Less foreground and more sky would have produced a totally different effect.

The foreground: juxtaposition of near and far subjects

Left: "Hands raised in welcome" by Terrence Spencer; right: astronauts' welcome parade (N. Y. Daily News Photo). In both shots, foreground matter was used as a device to create an illusion of depth. Note, however, that in both emphasis is still on the distant subjects — the crowds — which therefore are shown in sharp focus, while the depth-suggesting foreground matter can be rendered either sharp or unsharp without detracting attention from the subject proper of the picture.

WELCOME
ASTRONAUTS

The foreground: framing the subject

The French Quarter, New Orleans, La. "Framing" the church in one of the wrought-iron grills that are typical of New Orleans provided the picture with a heightened feeling of depth and made it unmistakably New Orleans.

Hulks of wooden ships in New York harbor. By "framing" the broken-down hulls in a piece of wreckage it was possible to take a close-up of the structure of such vessels and, through juxtaposition of near and far objects, to create a depth-effect in the picture.

The foreground: juxtaposition of dark and light

Control room in a freight-yard (above) and view across the Hudson River, New York. Aerial perspective — contrast of dark foreground and light background — accounts for the strong depth impressions of these pictures.

Aerial perspective can be controlled with the aid of filters and fill-in light. A blue filter increases, and a yellow or red filter decreases, aerial perspective in a photograph. If the foreground is lightened with the aid of auxiliary fill-in illumination, a common practice designed to improve the rendition of near-by shadow detail, contrast between near and far subjects is reduced and the effect of aerial perspective is weakened if not destroyed.

The horizon

If present in a photograph, the horizon is one of the most consequential picture elements.

The horizon divides a photograph into two sections–earth and sky–the proportions of which greatly affect the picture, making it either "heavy" or "light" (earthly or spiritual) by focusing attention either on the nearby foreground or on the distant sky.

A straight horizon suggests equilibrium, serenity, stability, and permanence.

A tilted horizon, by creating a feeling of instability in the composition, makes a picture dynamic, suggests change, and implies motion.

A wavy or jagged horizon suggests drama, violence, dynamic fluidity, and change.

The horizon

Beach on Cape Cod, Mass. Two views of the same subject demonstrate the great difference in impression which can be brought about merely by placing the horizon higher or lower in the picture.

The low horizon gives room to the sky — the distant view, air, clouds, and boundless space. The high horizon promotes the intimate view, the foreground, the soil, the detail. Neither position is "better" than the other, they are merely different. Which should be used, and when, depends upon the photographer's intentions and what he wishes to say.

The horizon

The ultimate two extremes: all sky and no sky at all. Significantly, the photograph of a Swiss village by G. E. Kidder Smith is dark whereas the picture of the hawk soaring in space is predominantly light — each in its own way symbolizing, respectively, the essence of earth and sky.

Devices and techniques

The production of a photograph is effected by the use of certain devices and techniques. Each device or technique can be modified or controlled to a greater or lesser extent; each modification will have a corresponding effect upon the outcome of the picture. Since any modification can be used either separately, or in combination with others, the number of variations in the rendition of almost any subject is tremendous, permitting a photographer to exert practically unlimited control over the appearance and effect of his pictures.

Here is a list of the principal devices and techniques that are suitable to modifications:

The camera. A photographer has the choice of several types which differ radically from one another in regard to construction. Most of these are available in different sizes for use in conjunction with different sizes and types of negative material (rollfilm, sheet film, filmpack). Each is a complex instrument consisting of a number of different components that in themselves, or in regard to their functions, are subject to modification: lens; diaphragm; shutter; the front and back adjustments of view cameras; aiming and focusing controls. For specific information, see pp. 36–40, 278–279.

Although almost any camera can, of course, produce a picture of almost any subject, certain types of camera will consistently produce not only *better* pictures of specific subjects or events than other cameras, but will also enable a photographer to make superior pictures faster and with greater ease. Consequently, the choosing of a camera that is best suited to a specific kind of work is an important photographic control.

The lens-coupled rangefinder camera. This is the fastest camera type, the camera *par excellence* for the photo-journalist, unsurpassed for photographing people and action.

The reflex camera. This is the best all-round camera type: 35 mm for color slides, 2¼ × 2¼ inch for color prints, both for black and white, equally well suited for amateurs and professionals. And single-lens reflex cameras are unsurpassed for close-up and telephotography.

The view camera. This camera type is unsurpassed for photographing static objects of any kind, architectural subjects, interiors, landscapes, still lifes, and reproductions. It is the only camera type which permits complete perspective control.

The wide-angle cameras. Available in three radically different types, these cameras are highly specialized tools, unsuited for anything except extreme wide-angle photography. The Hasselblad Super Wide

$2\frac{1}{4} \times 2\frac{1}{4}$ inch and the Plaubel Veriwide $2\frac{1}{4} \times 3\frac{1}{2}$ inch cameras both cover an angle of view close to 100 degrees, and the Goerz Hypergon lenses for large view cameras cover 130 degrees. All three produce pictures in which perspective is rectilinear (see explanation on p. 294).

Panoramic cameras, i.e., cameras with lenses that swing through an arc during exposure, like the 35 mm Panox and the $2\frac{1}{4} \times 4$ inch Panon, produce pictures in which perspective is "cylindrical" (see the photographs on pp. 302–305). They cover an angle of view of 140 degrees.

Cameras equipped with "fish-eye" lenses cover the fantastic angle of view of 180 degrees but produce pictures in which perspective is "spherical" (see the photographs on pp. 307–309).

The aerial cameras. These are ideal for aerial photography. However, their usually considerable bulk and weight, and the fact that their lenses are permanently fix-focused on infinity, make this type of camera unfit for any other branch of photography.

For more specific information on cameras and lenses see pp. 36–45.

Focusing. Appropriate use of the focusing controls (groundglass, rangefinder) in conjunction with suitable adjustments of the diaphragm and, if available, the camera's front and back adjustments, gives a photographer almost complete control over the degree and extent of sharpness or unsharpness. For specific information see pp. 67, 154–161.

Exposing. Appropriate use of the exposure controls (diaphragm and shutter) in conjunction with suitable negative development gives a photographer a very high degree of control over the density, contrast gradient, rendition of shadow detail, contour sharpness (acutance), and degree of graininess of his negative. In addition, it permits him the choice of rendering subjects in motion either sharply, or more or less blurred. For specific information, see pp. 68–69, 162–167.

Developing. Appropriate use of the developing controls (type of developer, temperature of the solution, duration of development) gives a photographer far-reaching control over the density, contrast gradient, contour sharpness (acutance), and degree of graininess of his negative. For specific information see pp. 69–70, 232–233.

Printing. Appropriate use of the printing controls (selection of a paper of suitable gradation, exposure for lighter or darker over-all tone, tone control on a local scale through "dodging," correction of "perspective distortion," sectional negative enlarging and "cropping") permits a photographer to correct many mistakes and to produce acceptable prints even from technically mediocre negatives. For specific information see pp. 71–73, 168–171, 234–241, 281.

The view camera

With its almost limitless adaptability to specific situations; its large and easily "readable" groundglass; its front and back adjustments; plus the fact that it can be equipped with practically any type of lens; and because of its inherent slowness of operation, this type of camera is best suited to photographing inanimate, static subjects such as architecture, interiors, works of art, and objects of any kind under conditions that make speed and time unimportant.

Above: the Capitol, Washington, D. C.; right: base of a chief's throne from the Belgian Congo.

The lens-coupled rangefinder camera

Equipped with a high-speed lens — fast, light, unobtrusive, and ready to shoot rapidly up to 36 pictures on a single roll of film — this is the ideal camera for the photo-journalist and reporter,

best suited to photographing people and action, and for "available light photography," i. e., under circumstances when illumination is marginal for instantaneous exposures. This photograph by Tony Triolo shows a group of people tensely watching a fire.

The single-lens reflex camera

This camera type, if necessary used in conjunction with auxiliary bellows or extension tubes, because it has groundglass focusing, freedom from parallax, and because the subject can be observed on the groundglass until the moment of exposure, is, besides being an excellent camera for all-round photography, best suited for close-ups and tele-photography.

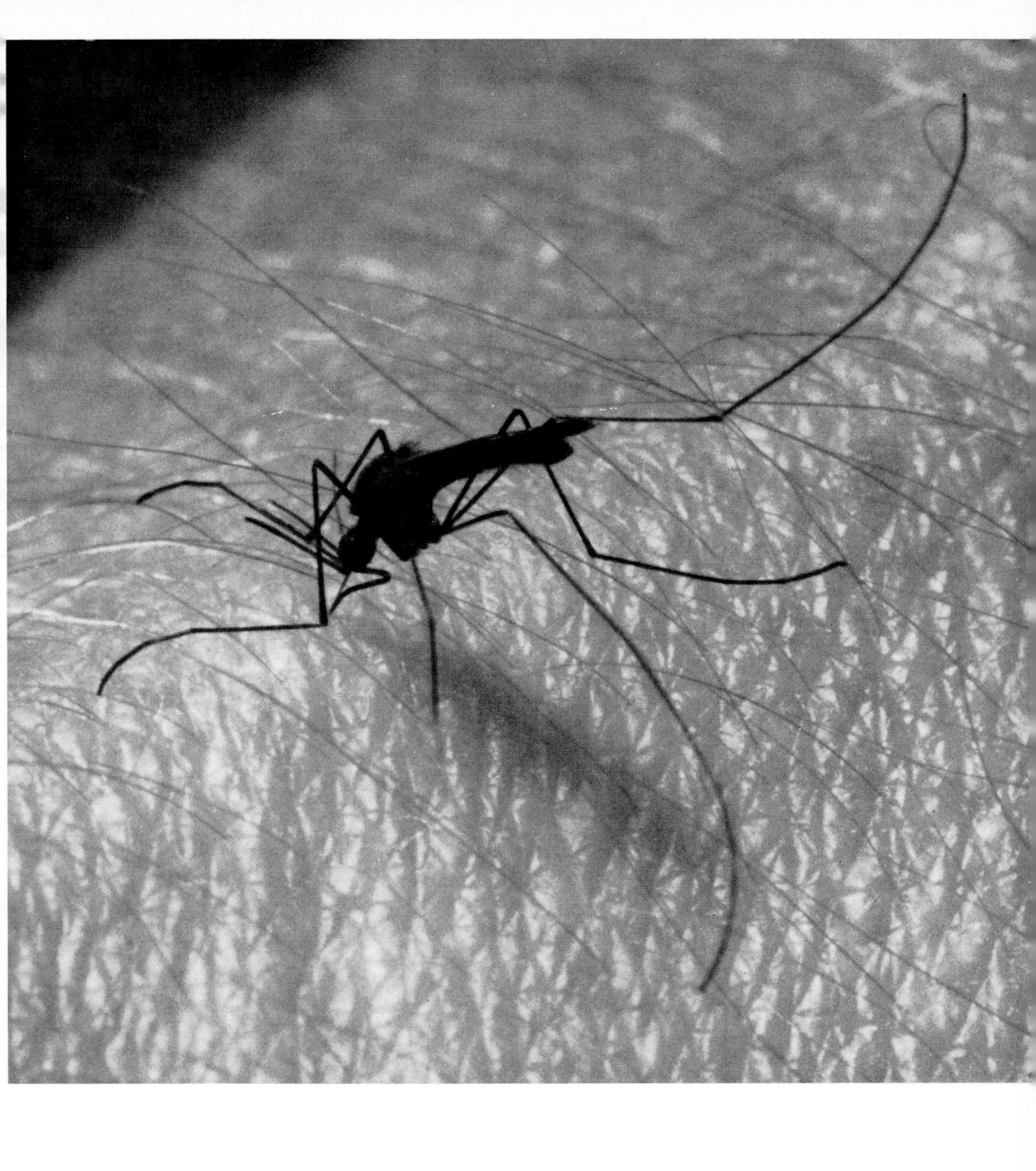

Left: a wolf spider feeding on a grasshopper; right: a mosquito sucking blood.

The aerial camera

Because of rigidity of construction and the fact that they take large film sizes suitable for photographing subjects rich in fine detail, aerial cameras are the only tools thoroughly suited to taking aerial photographs such as the ski slope, photographed by Robert Lackenbach, and the view of Midtown Manhattan (right), which was made by the U. S. Coast Guard and the U. S. Geodetic Survey.

The wide-angle camera

Because wide-angle cameras cover wider-than-normal angles of view, they are the only instruments which can produce satisfactory photographs when subject-to-camera distance is too short to permit the use of lenses of standard focal length.

The three pictures on this page were taken from the same camera position with three different cameras: a Rolleiflex and lens of standard focal length (top, left), a Hasselblad Super Wide (top, right), and a Panon which cover angles of view of 45, 90, and 140 degrees, respectively.

Wide-angle cameras and lenses tend to produce pictures in which perspective appears exaggerated: far objects appear too small and near objects appear disproportionally large. However, if this type of super-perspective is used with discrimination and understanding, it can be extremely effective, as in Grey Villet's photograph of Senator Kefauver "The Hand that shook the Democrats."

Focusing: selective focus

By focusing his lens upon a preselected, specific zone in depth, a photographer can single it out, emphasize, and render it sharply while allowing other zones to appear increasingly unsharp the farther they are from the plane of focus. The difference between sharp and unsharp will become more pronounced and the sharply rendered zone will become shallower, the larger the relative aperture and focal length of the lens and the shorter the subject-to-lens distance and vice versa.

To become familiar with the technique of selective focusing, it is suggested that the reader build a set consisting of three objects placed at different distances from the camera, similar to the setup shown in the photograph at the left; that he photograph it three times with the diaphragm wide open and the lens focused, respectively, on the background, middle ground, and foreground object (see photographs above); and that he study the resulting pictures, paying particular attention to the distribution and degree of sharpness and unsharpness in each.

Creation of sharpness in depth through stopping down the diaphragm

A photographer can either limit the extent of sharpness of rendition to a predetermined, more or less shallow zone in depth (see the pictures on the previous spread), or progressively extend it until it encompasses the entire depth of the subject. This is controlled by the diaphragm: the more it is stopped down, the greater the extent of sharpness in depth and vice versa.

The photographs above show the same setup that was used on the previous spread. However, in making these three pictures, the lens was focused on the middle ground (the statue). The first shot was made with the diaphragm wide open at f/3.5; the second with the diaphragm stopped down to f/12.5; and the third with the diaphragm stopped down to f/45.

Creation of sharpness in depth through use of camera "swings"

In making oblique angle shots of relatively flat subjects one can extend sharpness in depth from very close by to infinity with the aid of the "swings" of a view camera. To accomplish this, the plane of focus must be tilted until it coincides with the sharp image of the subject. In practice, the simplest way to achieve this is to tilt the lens toward the subject (or the back of the camera away from the subject), while checking the sharpness distribution of the image on the groundglass and readjusting the focus. If all adjustments are correctly made, very little stopping down of the diaphragm will be needed to bring the entire area covered by the lens into perfect focus (see opposite page, left).

The first picture of the series above was made with all the camera adjustments in neutral position, the diaphragm wide open at f/3.5, and the lens focused on the Hasselblad camera, which was placed at approximately one-third the depth of the picture. In the second photograph, the only change was that the diaphragm was stopped down to f/6.3. In the third picture, the lens was tilted forward (toward the subject) and the focus readjusted accordingly, but the diaphragm was still set at f/6.3; please observe that the sharpness extends over the entire depth of this picture. The fourth picture was made in a way identical to the third except that the statue was added, to show that in this technique sharpness is more or less limited to a two-dimensional plane (the base of the statue is sharp, the upper part unsharp). To extend sharpness in the third dimension, the diaphragm must be stopped down in the usual way.

Creation of sharpness from foreground to background

As valuable as the front and back adjustments of a view camera are for extending the zone of sharpness in depth without considerable stopping down of the diaphragm, they can be used only in oblique shots of subjects of a more or less two-dimensional nature, an example of which is the photograph above. In such a case, sharpness from foreground to background can be produced by tilting the lens forward (toward the subject), or the back of the camera backward (away from the subject), which, however, causes a certain amount of

perspective distortion, and stopping down the diaphragm only enough to extend sharpness in depth sufficiently to include those parts of the subject which protrude from the sharply focused, oblique plane (here, the people working on an aerial mapping problem).

However, if the subject is not primarily confined to one plane, the only way to extend sharpness from foreground to background is through use of the diaphragm. The boiler room shown above provides an example. To render it sharply from foreground to background, the lens had to be stopped down to f/32.

Exposing: interrelationship between diaphragm opening and shutter speed

Correct exposure is the result of correct adjustment of the diaphragm aperture in relation to the shutter speed (and, of course, the intensity of the illumination and the speed of the film). Negative density will be the same whether the diaphragm aperture is large and the shutter speed high, or the diaphragm aperture is small and the shutter speed low. However, two important aspects would be very different in these pictures: the extent in depth of the sharply rendered zone, and rendition of the subject's motion.

The four pictures in this series were exposed at, respectively, 1/1000 sec. at f/2.8; 1/250 sec. at f/5.6; 1/50 sec. at f/12.5; and 1/10 sec. f/29. The density of the four negatives was, of course, exactly the same. But the effect of these pictures in regard to sharpness in depth and rendition of motion is entirely different; as depth increases, the figures of the moving skaters appear increasingly blurred and vice versa. Which type of rendition is preferable must, of course, be left to the individual photographer to decide.

Exposing: the light-accumulating property of negative emulsions

The effect of light on any photographic emulsion is cumulative. Within certain limits, the longer the exposure, the denser the negative and vice versa. This property is useful if a photographer is confronted by a very dark subject. In the photograph above, left, for example, which was exposed according to meter reading, the shadow parts were rendered as unrelieved areas of black. In contrast, the picture at the right was exposed much longer. As a result, the shadows were rendered transparent and full of detail, although detail in the sunlit parts is largely lost through overexposure. However, with proper "dodging" during printing (see p. 170), this negative could be made to produce an acceptable print, whereas the other could not.

The four night photographs on the opposite page, exposed, respectively, 1, 10, 60, and 300 seconds, prove that even the darkest subject can be rendered with full shadow detail if exposed sufficiently long. The first of these pictures corresponds approximately to what the eye saw at the moment of exposure; the last is as detailed as a daylight shot would have been.

Exposure as a means of contrast control

It is a well-known fact that negatives given short exposure, particularly if they are developed somewhat longer than is normal, to compensate for underexposure, are more contrasty than negatives of the same subject that received a relatively long exposure, particularly if they are developed for a somewhat shorter time than is normal, to compensate for overexposure. Although, under normal conditions, best results are always achieved if exposure is correct, occasionally deliberate use of either under- or overexposure to increase or reduce, respectively, the

contrast gradient of a negative, can become a valuable means of photographic control. The pictures on this spread show the same subject photographed under identical conditions with the exception that the left shot was underexposed by two full stops and the right overexposed by four full stops. Both negatives were given normal development and printed on paper of normal gradation. The differences in contrast gradient and shadow rendition are truly astonishing. Of course, through adjustments of exposure, any intermediate contrasts can be produced.

Print controls: lighter or darker

Over-all tone control in the print can be effected through the time of exposure of the sensitized paper. Within certain limits, the longer the exposure, the darker the over-all tone of the print and vice versa. Basically, a light over-all tone (high key) suggests a light and gay, playful, or friendly mood, whereas a dark over-all tone (low key) suggests a serious, ominous, or tragic mood.

Print controls: dodging

Tone control on a local scale can be effected through "dodging". Ta make a specific negative area print lighter than it normally would, it must be given less exposure than the rest and vice versa. To shield an area of the sensitized paper during part of the exposure, use your hands or a round piece of cardboard at the end of a thin wire which serves as a handle. To give additional exposure to a dense negative area, shield the rest of the paper with your hands while "burning in" that particular area through

an opening formed by the fingers. To insure a smooth, unnoticeable transition from "dodged" to untreated print area, the "dodger" and the hands must be moved slightly during the entire process of "dodging."

Although it may seem incredible, both pictures on this spread were printed from the same negative. Careful study of the plumes of smoke, the position of the automobiles in the streets, and the ships in the distance reveal this. The haze is typical of New York.

Aspects of photographic rendition

If we, figuratively speaking, dissect a photograph and analyze point by point all the aspects of rendering reality in picture form, we find that, regardless of its subject matter and the circumstances under which it was made, a photograph is always the sum total of a number of specific, constantly recurring factors. Each of these factors can be subjected to often very diversified modifications; each can be controlled, often to a surprisingly high degree, by the photographer. The more important of these factors – individual aspects of photographic rendition – are listed in the following survey.

Illumination and light. Light, and its negative form, shadow, is perhaps the most influential of all the factors that determine the graphic effect of a photograph. Because of its importance, the first of the following chapters is devoted to the exploration and demonstration of the different qualities of light and their controls.
For additional information, see pp. 176–215.

Sharpness of rendition. Sharpness is relative – no photograph is really sharp. Seen under twenty times magnification even the sharpest picture assumes the texture of coarse sandpaper and the "sharpest" contour appears ragged. Unsharpness in a photograph, too, is relative, a matter of degree; some pictures are more unsharp than others. Furthermore, there are different types of unsharpness: the unsharpness of an out-of-focus photograph differs from that of a picture taken with a soft-focus lens, and both are different from the unsharpness produced by a "pinhole lens." Unsharpness of photographic rendition can be controlled by the photographer and used to achieve specific, predetermined effects. Two surprising examples are reproduced on pp. 220–221.

Graininess. Although it should normally be avoided, under certain conditions graininess can become an important graphic means for strengthening the impact of a picture. The degree of grain which appears in a photograph can be controlled with the aid of the following factors, each of which contributes to the presence or absence of film grain in the print: Type of negative emulsion (see p. 61); film exposure (see p. 68); negative developer (see p. 63); duration of negative development (see p. 70); gradation of the sensitized paper (the more contrasty, the more pronounced the film grain in the print); degree of negative enlargement (the higher the magnification, the more pronounced the negative grain in the print). The particular pictorial effect of negative grain is illustrated on pp. 216–217.

Contrast gradient. In black-and-white photography, every image is the direct result of contrast – the contrast between black and white and intermediate shades of gray. Without such contrast, there would be no picture, no differentiation of tone and form. Even the simplest line or silhouette is a manifestation of contrast – a juxtaposition of light and dark.

Contrast – one of the most important aspects of any picture – is subject to almost total control by the photographer. He has the choice of the following devices and techniques with which he can either preserve, increase, or decrease the natural contrast gradient of his subject in accordance with esthetic and editorial considerations: choice of film (see p. 60); choice of filter (see pp. 54, 226); choice of illumination (see pp. 228–231); choice of exposure (see p. 68); choice of developer (see p. 62); choice of duration of development (see p. 232); choice of the gradation of the sensitized paper (see pp. 234–235); "dodging" during printing and enlarging (see pp. 73 and 170). The extent to which application of these controls can influence the contrast gradient of the print is illustrated on pp. 222–223.

Color translation. In black-and-white photographs, color is translated into shades of gray. Photographed under normal conditions (in sunlight) on panchromatic film, most colors appear in the print as gray tones whose lightness or darkness more or less corresponds to the lightness or darkness of the colors as they appeared to the eye. ("More or less" because most films render blue somewhat too light. Many panchromatic films render red too light and green too dark. And all orthochromatic films render red much too dark or as black).

However, there are reasons why it is occasionally desirable to render a specific color in the form of a gray tone that is either lighter or darker than that particular color would normally be. For example: a red and a blue of equal brightness appear side by side in a subject. Translated into their equivalent gray tone values, they would appear as identical shades of gray and would blend one into another, with the result that separation of tone and form would be lost. Furthermore, the emotional value of red is "aggressive," whereas blue appears "receding" and "passive." Now, in the sphere of graphic black-and-white, white (or lightness) is aggressive and black (or darkness) is passive and receding, whereas gray is somewhere in between. Consequently, to characterize the emotional qualities of these colors in a black-and-white photograph, red must be rendered lighter than it would "normally" be and blue darker. This would apply even if each color existed alone in the subject, and problems of tonal separation were not involved.

The gray tone in which a particular color appears in the print can be controlled through appropriate choice of negative emulsion (orthochromatic or panchromatic) and color filter (see p. 53), examples of the effects of which are shown on pp. 226–227, 242–247.

Glare and reflections. In the form of highlights, glare (specular reflection) often enlivens a photograph. Occasionally, however, glare may obscure important subject matter as, for example, in cases in which reflections in a pane of glass (a shop window, the glass protecting a painting) make it impossible to see clearly the subject behind it. If this is the case, glare, depending on the angle of the incident light, can be more or less subdued, or eliminated completely, with the aid of a polarizer (see p. 55), examples of the effect of which are shown on pp. 264–267.

Space and depth. Reality is three-dimensional but photographs depicting its aspects have only two dimensions: height and width. Depth, extension in space, can only be suggested in symbolic form. Fortunately, a number of expressive symbols exist which can be employed to create effectively the illusion of "depth" in the two-dimensional form of a photograph. Each of these symbols can be controlled to a very large extent. An entire section of this book is devoted to this aspect of photographic rendition. For specific information, see pp. 268–319.

Motion and action. It is characteristic of many photographic subjects that they undergo almost constant change and motion; but a photograph is a "still." As a result, motion can be expressed in a picture only in symbolic form. The nature of the symbols, and how they can be controlled to express specific aspects of motion and action, is discussed and documented in picture form on pp. 320–341.

Timing. A large number of photographs deals with events occurring at a specific instant. This, of course, attaches a special significance to the moment a photographer releases the shutter: too soon or too late, and he misses his best opportunity. Factors that influence and decide the timing of a photograph are discussed on pp. 75–80 and illustrated on pp. 342–349.

Light controls

Every form of creativity has its own specific medium. The photographer's is light. Apart from the obvious fact that without light there can be no picture, light has a greater influence upon the photographic appearance of a subject than any other technical factor. There is an enormous difference in the appearance of a subject if it is photographed in daylight or at night, in bright sunshine or the diffused illumination of an overcast sky, minutely detailed in frontlight or in the form of a backlighted silhouette. Unless a photographer knows how to control light, he is as helpless as a painter who doesn't know how to handle color.

In order to control light a photographer must first understand light in respect to its properties and functions.

The properties of light

As photographers, we must distinguish between three different characteristics of light: brightness, quality, and color.

Brightness is the measure of the strenght of light – its intensity which can be measured with the aid of an exposure meter. It may vary in degree from overpowering brightness to total darkness.

The effects of brightness upon a photograph are twofold: 1. It influences the exposure; the brighter the light, the shorter the exposure and vice versa. 2. It influences the "mood" of a picture; in bright illumination, the same scene appears more contrasty, its colors more vivid, and its "mood" more gay, than in dim, subdued light.

Quality. Independent of brightness, light can be either harsh (emanating from a point-like source) or diffused (emanating from an area source or reflecting surface). Between these extremes, of course, light of any intermediate quality exists.

Light emanating from a point-like source (the sun, a spotlight) is always relatively contrasty, casting strong, black shadows that have sharply defined contours. Conversely, light coming from an area source (the overcast sky, "bounce-light" reflected from a ceiling) is relatively contrastless and casts weak, pale shadows that have softly diffused outlines. Between these extremes, of course, illumination of various qualities exists. A photoflood lamp, for example, produces an illumination that is less contrasty than spotlight illumination but more contrasty than "bounce-light." A lamp in a small reflector produces a harsher illumination that has sharper shadows than the same lamp used in a large reflector. A diffuser placed in front of a reflector lowers the contrast of the illumination. Bright sunlight from a clear blue sky is harsher, and casts "blacker" and more sharply defined shadows, than the same bright sunlight coming from a clear blue sky which, however, has large, luminous, white clouds. The contrast of any kind of illumination can be lowered by "filling-in" the shadows with the aid of auxiliary illumination–flashbulbs, electronic flash, special reflecting surfaces or, if circumstances permit, with photofloods or other forms of incandescent or fluorescent light.

Color. This property of light, although of no concern to the photographer working in black-and-white, is vitally important to anyone working in color. The nature of color film is such that, under normal conditions, satisfactory results can be expected only if the "color" of the illumination coincides with, or at least closely approximates, the "color" of the particular type of light for which the color film is "balanced." Now although special color films exist for use in conjunction with several different types of light (of different "color"), there are innumerable instances when color photographs must be taken in light of a color for which no corresponding color film exists. For example, in comparison to the "average" daylight for which daylight-type color films are balanced, the color of early morning or late afternoon light varies from yellow and orange to red. Similarly, daylight in the shade is generally more bluish or, in the shade of trees, more greenish than daylight in the open. Daylight on cloudy days is often purplish. And so on. As a result, color photographs taken under such "abnormal" conditions are bound to show more or less pronounced color casts unless the photographer controls the illumination and "brings it back to normal" with the aid of the appropriate color-compensating filter. For all the necessary information concerning color rendition and control, the reader is referred to THE COLOR PHOTO BOOK by this author (Prentice-Hall, Inc., Englewood Cliffs, N. J.).

The functions of light

As photographers, we must distinguish between the following three different functions of light:

Light as creator of space-illusions. Most photographers know from experience that the "shadowless" illumination of frontlight (light that comes from the direction of the camera) tends to make a subject appear "flat," whereas sidelight or backlight, because they cast well-defined shadows, make it appear three-dimensional. The fact that light is inseparable from shadow accounts for these effects. Actually, light and shadow are the same insofar as shadow within the picture is merely an area which received less light than the fully illuminated parts. Now, when a three-dimensional subject such as a cube is illuminated with a single source of light, it is not possible to illuminate more than three of its sides at once, the others must invariably remain in shade. On the other hand, we can fully illuminate a flat surface. As a matter of fact, if there is a shadow on a flat surface it is either cast by some object, or the surface is not flat but curved, rippled, etc., in other words, three-dimensional. And since this is so, we associate absence of shadow with "flatness" and presence of shadow with three-dimensionality.

From this it should be obvious that how a photographer handles light and shadow, i. e., how well he controls the illumination, is of vital importance to the space-effect of his pictures.

Light as creator of "mood" and "atmosphere." We speak of the "mood" of a scene or the "atmosphere" of a place, and what we refer to is usually their particular illumination. A brightly illuminated place has a different "atmosphere" from a place that is in semidarkness. An evenly illuminated room (such as an office) has a different "mood" from a room which is sparsely illuminated by a number of small, individual lamps each surrounded by a zone of relative darkness (for example a night club). The interior of a factory, a living room in daylight, a church, a sports arena, a hamburger joint–all have their typical "atmosphere" and "mood" which to a very large extent are created by the particular character of their illumination. And the same is true of outdoor scenes: a landscape, for example, acquires a very different "mood" when seen in bright sunshine, under an overcast sky, on a misty morning, or at sunset. And these differences, too, are largely the result of differences in illumination. Therefore, it should be clear that it is not enough to merely record the external appearance of subjects in terms of perspective, texture, detail, scale, etc., but that we must also strive to recreate the "feeling" which they evoked, their "mood" or "atmosphere" (in the psychological, not the meteorological, sense), if we are to produce photographs with content and meaning – pictures that can communicate our experience to the observer. This is a reminder to those who feel compelled to use flashbulbs whenever a shadow seems a little too dark or the light is insufficient for an instantaneous exposure. In destroying the particular "mood" of the "available light," they also destroy an important characteristic of the subject.

Light as creator of design and composition. It is perfectly admissible to completely disregard the subject matter and meaning of a photograph and to evaluate and enjoy it as a graphic design solely in terms of black and white. As a matter of fact, such an exercise is excellent practice for any photographer who is intent upon improving the design and composition of his pictures.

One should never forget that, in a photograph, light and shadow are identical with black and white and intermediate shades of gray. Now, in a psychological sense, white is basically aggressive and compels attention, whereas black is passive, receding, and quiet. As a rule, in a picture, white areas are the first to attract the eye of an observer. On the other hand, it is usually black which holds a composition together and gives it "substance" and "weight." Emphasis upon white suggests a light, gay, and friendly mood; a preponderance of black symbolizes seriousness, drama, or tragedy. Uniform distribution of white and black usually makes a picture monotonous – something which, however, may occasionally be desirable. In contrast, a predominantly black design with a few, small, well-placed white accents, or a predominantly white design with a few, small, well-placed black accents, can be extraordinarily effective. White appears at its whitest when surrounded by solid black. Black never looks blacker than when completely surrounded by white.

Consideration given to these psychological aspects of light will enable a photographer to improve the graphic effect of his pictures.

Photographs illustrating these and other aspects of light are shown on the following pages.

Light as creator of space-illusions

A most convincing experiment to demonstrate the importance of light upon the spatial impression of a photograph can be made with a white sphere, a plain white background, and two or three lamps. A two- or three-dimensional impression, dark against light or light against dark, can be produced merely by varying the position and intensity of the lights as illustrated in the accompanying photographs.

1. Illuminate sphere and background evenly with a shadowless frontlight so that both appear white. In this illumination, differentiation will be lost, sphere and background will blend, and the picture will appear flat.

2. Shift the main light upward and to the left. The lower right of the sphere will be in shade, and an illusion of three-dimensionality will begin to emerge.

3. Adjust the background light so that the background will be unevenly illuminated as in the third picture, above. Separation between sphere and background will be excellent, and the sphere will seem to stand free in space.

4. Dim the main light in relation to the background light as in the picture at the top, right. A dark sphere will now stand before a white background.

5. Reverse the intensity of the two lamps as shown in the picture at the bottom, right. Now, a light sphere will stand before a dark background.

Light and the importance of shadow

Perhaps to a greater degree than the illuminated parts of the subject, shadows determine the spatial impression of a picture. A good way to study the influence and importance of shadows is to light a work of sculpture in various ways with a single, sharp light which casts well-defined shadows. The point of such an exercise is to learn how to arrange lights so that the shadows cast will organically emphasize the spatial characteristics of a subject and, at the same time, form graphically interesting patterns of black and white.

The pictures on this spread show six different variations of such an exercise. They are the first steps toward "finished photographs," each a potentially interesting representation of the subject that would need for completion a fill-in light, which here was omitted for reasons of clarity.

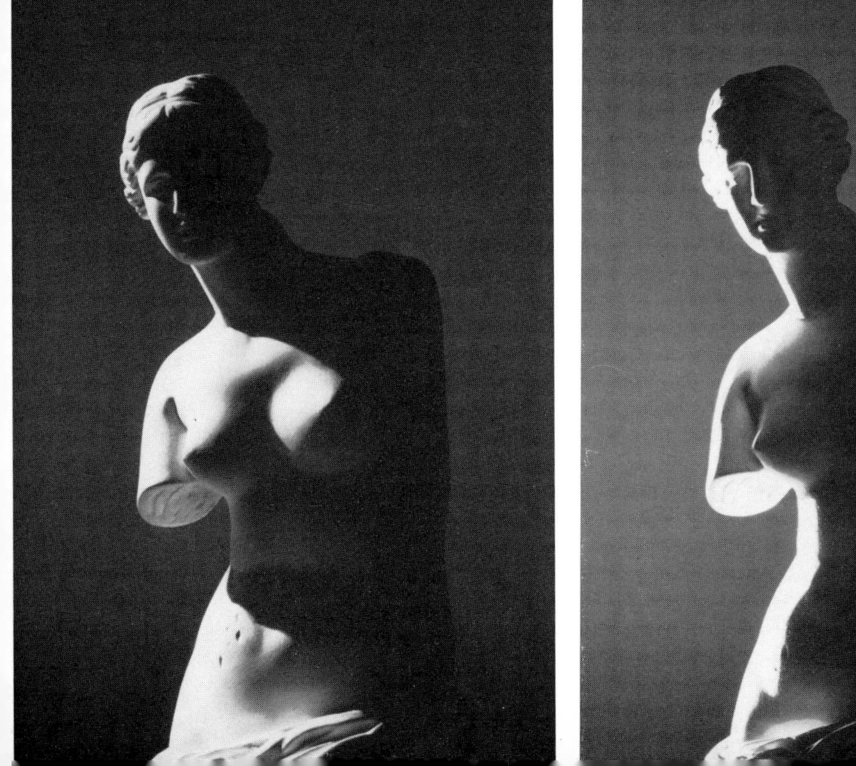

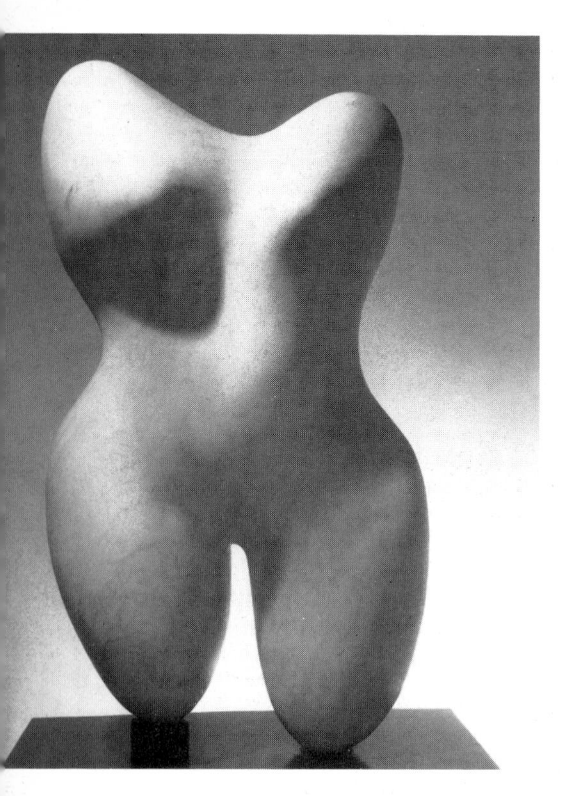

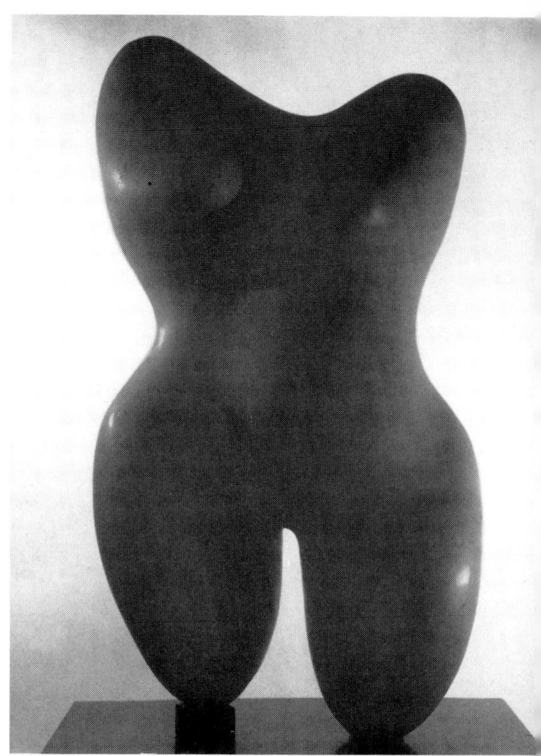

Light and the importance of the shadow

Two photographic versions of a sculpture by Alberto Viani (above) illustrate the application of the principles of lighting shown on pp. 180–183. Neither is "better" than the other, they are merely different. They suggest by their difference the scope of graphic expression which is open to any photographer who uses control.

How important shadow can be to the spatial effect of a photograph is illustrated by the series of pictures at the right, which show the same form photographed from the same direction. The form which actually is concave, as shown in the third photograph, appears either convex (top) or concave (center), depending upon the position of the shadow, i. e., the direction of the light.

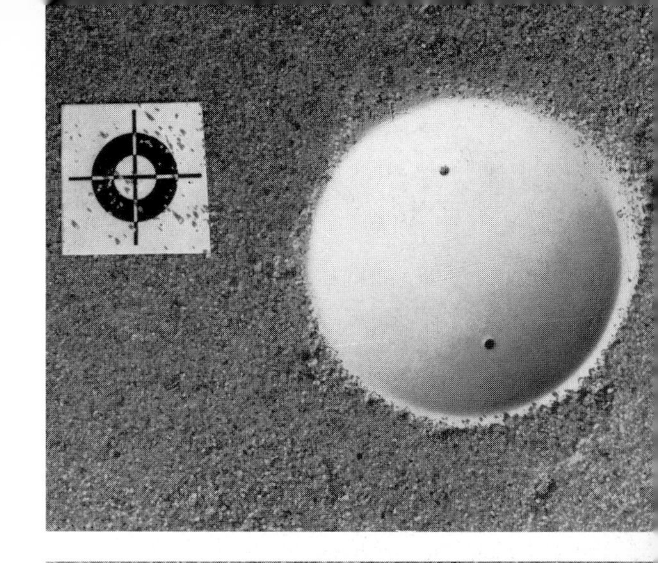

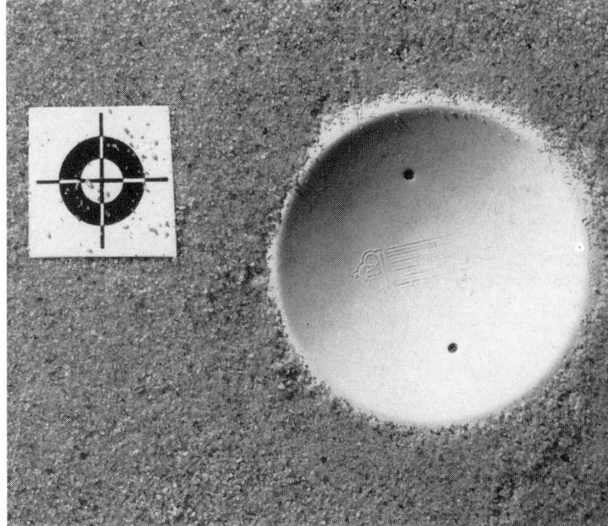

The position of shadow particularly influences the appearance of any relief subject such as a medal, a coin, a bas-relief, and even certain types of aerial photographs which, when taken in low-slanting light may, depending upon the direction of the illumination, show elevations as depressions and vice versa.

Light control:
functions of the shadow

In a photograph, a shadow can have one of three functions:

1. It represents darkness — is part of the black-and-white design of the picture — as in the photograph on the left, bottom.

2. It can be a graphic means for creating an illusion of roundness, volume, or space, as in the charming picture by Erwin Blumenfeld on the opposite page.

3. Finally, shadow can be an independent picture element, as in the photograph of the sculpture above, left, where it emphasizes, by repetition in grotesquely distorted shadow form, the tragic shapes of people fleeing the horrors of war.

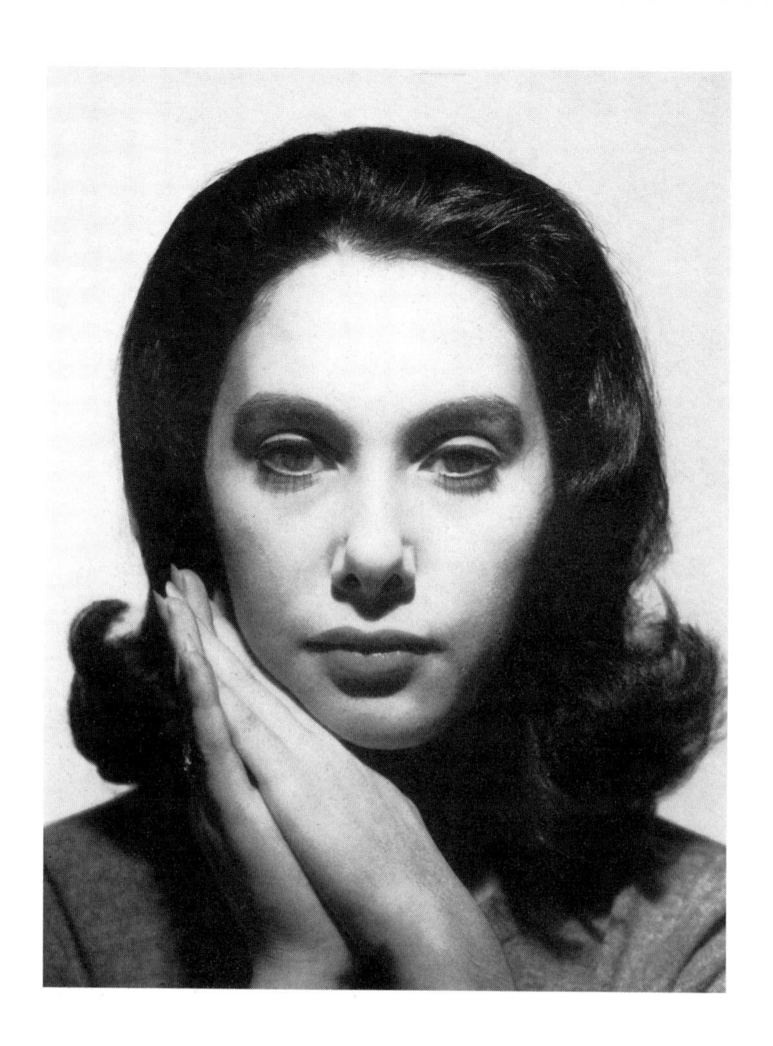

Light of different quality

As far as a photographer is concerned, the two main kinds of light are direct light and indirect light. Direct light is emitted by the sun, incandescent lamps, flashbulbs, and speedlights. Indirect light is either reflected light (for example, bounce-light) or strongly diffused light (such as light from an evenly overcast sky). Direct light casts strong, black, sharply defined shadows which will be the harsher, the more point-like the source of light. For example, the same photoflood bulb will produce a sharper shadow if used without a reflector than if used

with a reflector. And a small reflector will produce sharper shadows than a large reflector. Depending upon its degree of diffusion, indirect light casts either weak and ill-defined shadows or no shadows. The extreme effects of direct and indirect light are illustrated in the photographs above. The left was lighted by a spotlight and the right by light reflected from a large white board. Between these extremes, any type of illumination can, of course, be selected to meet the demands of the subject and the objective of the photographer, through use of different types of lamps, if necessary supplemented by fill-in light.

Light from different directions. Top row: Frontlight; 90 degree sidelight; 45 degree sidelight; three-quarter side-and-top light. Bottom row: Backlight; top light; combination top-and-front light; light from below. Except for the frontlight and the combination top-and-front light, none of these types of illumination is normally

used in portraiture. However, if this series is studied and special attention is given to the shadows around the eyes and below the nose, lips, and chin, it can indicate what the proper position of the mainlight in portrait photography should be — how to proceed in its placement as well as what should be avoided.

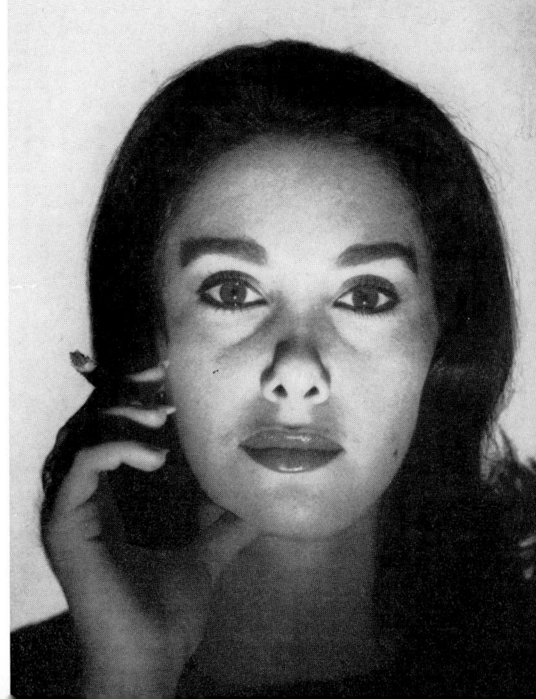

Light control: backlight and silhouette

In pure backlight — light coming from a direction opposite the camera — the side of the subject facing the lens is in shade, and the effect is a silhouette. Provided that its outline is interesting and that it typifies the subject, the silhouette is one of the most powerful forms of graphic expression. The photograph at right shows in pure silhouette a corner of an aircraft carrier at a dock. Above, in semi-silhouette which reveals a certain amount of detail, the painter Lyonel Feininger is depicted at work. Degree of detail, or its absence, within the silhouette can be fully controlled by the photographer through appropriate exposure, negative development, paper gradation, and if circumstances demand, auxiliary fill-in illumination.

Light control: backlight. Backlight is the most photogenic type of illumination because it facilitates symbolization of space by throwing perspective-creating shadows toward the camera; improves the feeling of depth by surrounding (and thus separating from one another) objects at different

distances from the camera with halo-like outlines of light; promotes strong, graphic contrast of light and dark; facilitates rendition of surface texture; accentuates shiny objects with sparkling reflections of light; and, through tonal simplification, strengthens the graphic impact of a picture.

Principles of texture rendition

Good photographic texture rendition depends upon the interplay of two factors: sharpness and contrast. An unsharp but contrasty photograph will reveal as little texture as a sharp but flat picture. The two photographs above illustrate this: In the picture at the left, a total lack of shadow caused by frontlight shows the design but gives no feeling of texture. Conversely, the picture at the right, photographed under identical conditions except that the fabric was illuminated by direct sidelight which casts deep and well-defined shadows, permits one to almost feel the coarse texture of the material.

Opposite page: Sand dunes in Dealth Valley, Cal. This picture was taken within half an hour after sunrise when the low slanting light could be used to bring out texture in the rendition. Later in the day, these dunes appear a solid, glaring, uninteresting white, the texture-giving ripples drowned in floods of uncontrolled light.

Light control: examples of texture rendition. Unless texture is defined in a photograph, it is frequently impossible to distinguish between, for example, a body of water and a meadow; sand and snow; fabric, wood, or stone. Lack of texture tends to make a photograph appear

lifeless and dull. On the other hand, crisp, clean texture rendition gives a picture sparkle and "life." The accompanying photographs show how texture can be brought out through a combination of low, slanting sidelight or backlight (water!) and sharpness of rendition.

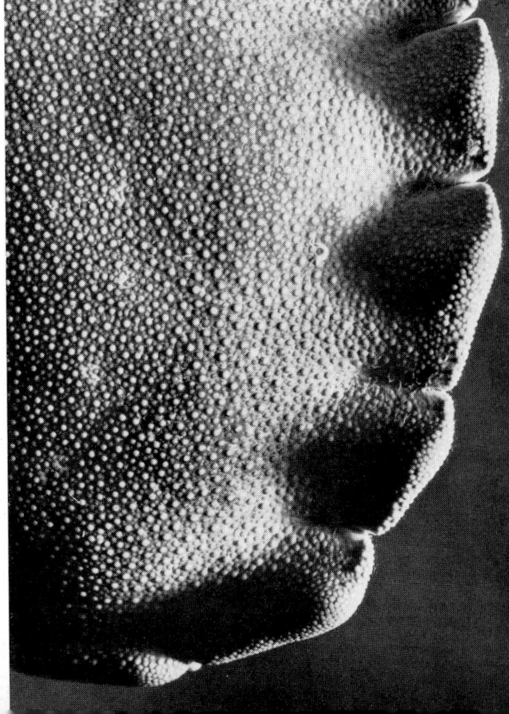

Light control: available light

An ever-increasing number of photographers begin to realize that the character of the illumination is of vital importance for the effective representation of the mood or "feeling" of a subject. As a result, more

and more photographs which previously would have been taken with auxiliary illumination are now being taken in "available light," the light that existed at the moment of exposure uninfluenced by the photographer. This photograph by Wynn Bullock is an outstandingly beautiful example of what a gifted photographer can do with "available light."

Light control: available light

With the aid of fast lenses and high-speed films, photographs can now be made in almost any kind of light, no matter how weak it may be. The pictures on this spread illustrate how even unusual sources of "available light" can be used to characterize a specific "atmosphere" or a "mood." Left: "Florida dawn," photographed by Guy Gillette, effectively

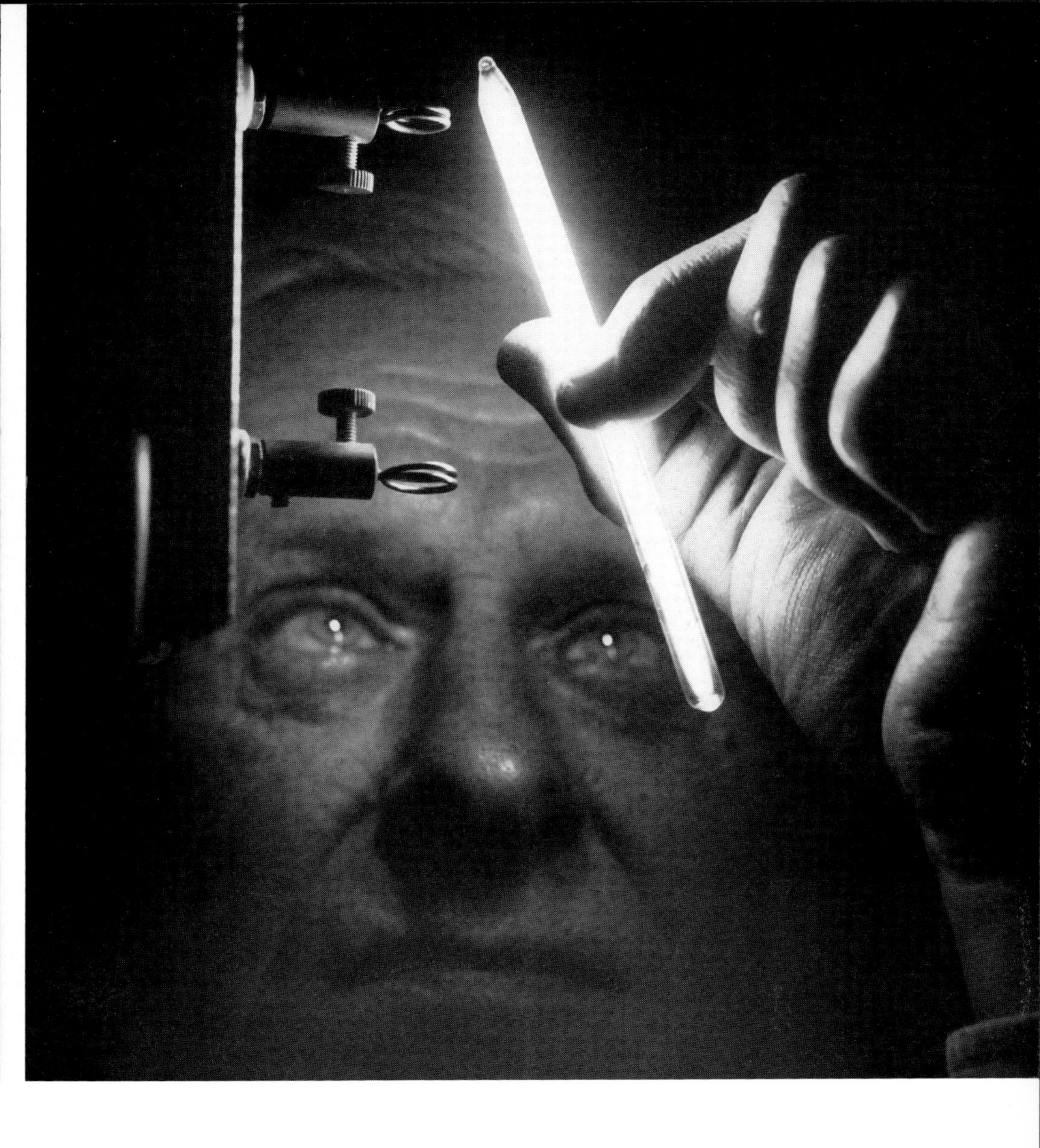

captures the eerie predawn mood of a tree-lined country road. Right: A physicist photographed in light emitted by a tube filled with ionized gas excited by the short-wave generator at the left edge of the picture.

Anyone who lacks the courage to photograph subjects in these and other marginal types of light is bound to miss some of the most unusual and fascinating pictures.

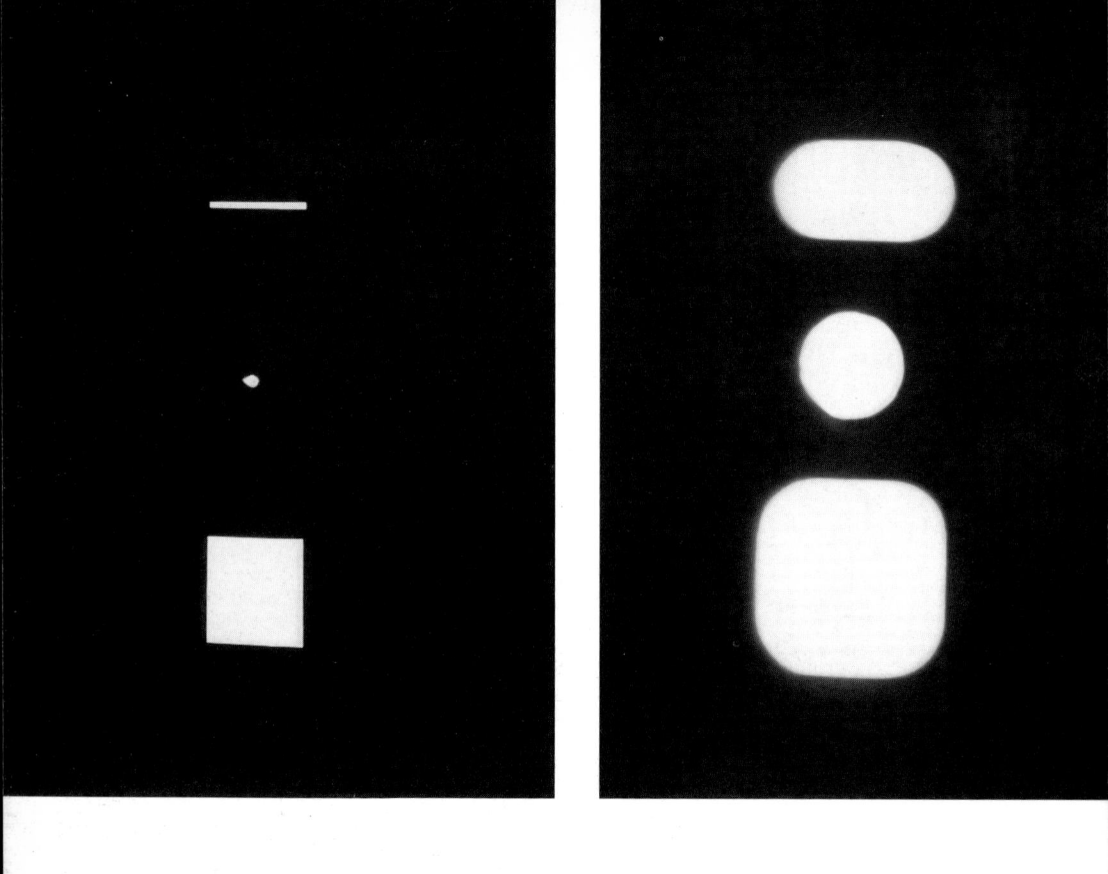

The radiance of direct light: the circle

People respond quite differently to radiant (direct) and reflected (indirect) light. But in a photograph, both types of light appear the same. Like depth or motion, in pictures the radiance of direct light can be rendered only in symbolic form.

Fortunately, several graphic symbols exist that immediately suggest the radiance of direct light. The best known of these is the sparkling, glittering star. Another is the halo. A third is the softly glowing circle associated with certain types of globular lamps or the full moon. Each can be reproduced through photographic means as illustrated on this and the following spreads.

To study these symbols, cut a template from cardboard similar to the one shown at the top of this page, left. Paste a piece of tracing paper which will act as a diffuser behind the slot and the square, but leave the small hole in the center uncovered. Place a lamp behind the template, and photograph it in accordance with the following instructions.

To transform a source of light into a luminous circle, throw the image out of focus. The resulting circles will increase in size as the image becomes progressively out-of-focus and vice versa. This technique was used to make the accompanying photograph of skyscrapers at night.

The radiance of direct light: the halo

To surround highlights and sources of direct light with softly glowing haloes, use a soft-focus lens (such as the Leitz Thambar) or place a diffuser (such as the Duto disk) in front of the lens. The halo effect will be considerably less pronounced than that produced by an out-of-focus image. However, the subject itself will be rendered more sharply since the halo effect is mostly confined to the brightest parts of the subject. For this reason, the photograph above shows only the square of the template photographed through a Duto disk, since the effect upon the slot and the dot-like hole was so delicate that it would have been unnoticeable in the reproduction.

This technique was used by Nina Leen to make the beautiful, almost radiant photograph of a bride which is shown above.

The radiance of direct light: the diaphragm star

If a point-like source of light is photographed with a lens stopped down to f/22 or smaller, in the photograph the source of light will appear surrounded by a star-like pattern of rays which is caused by light reflected from the blades of the diaphragm. This phenomenon will become more pronounced as the length of the exposure and the brightness of the light source increases, as shown in the photographs above.

The star patterns that make these pictures graphically interesting are diaphragm stars. Their origin is explained on the opposite page.

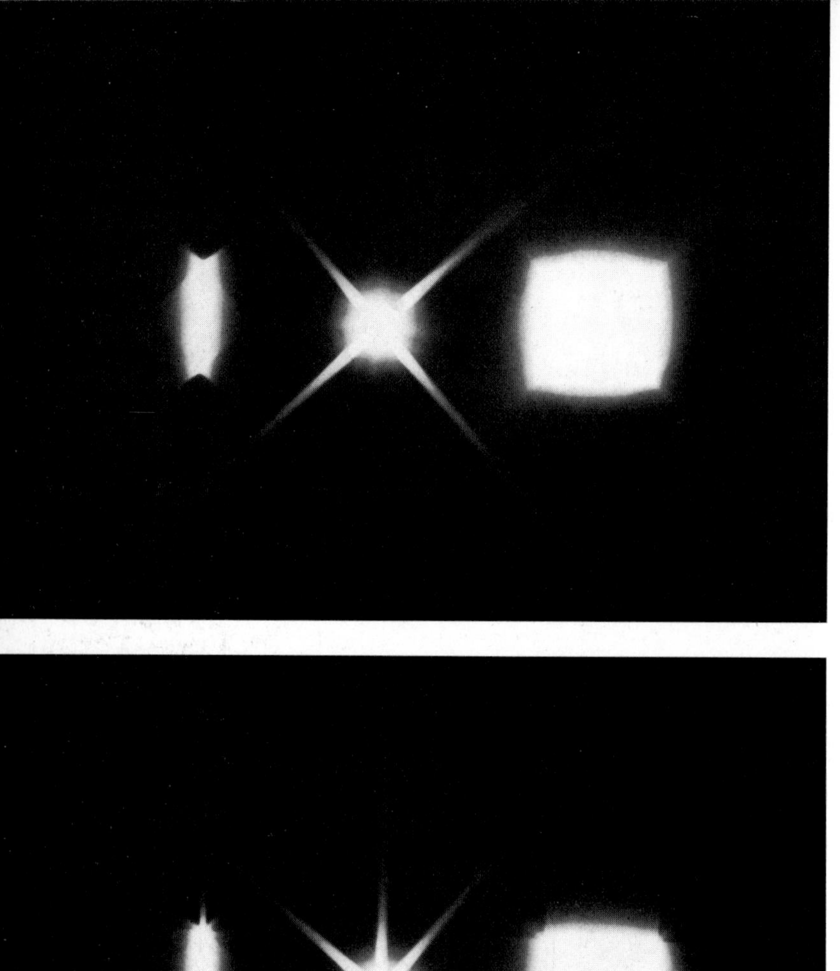

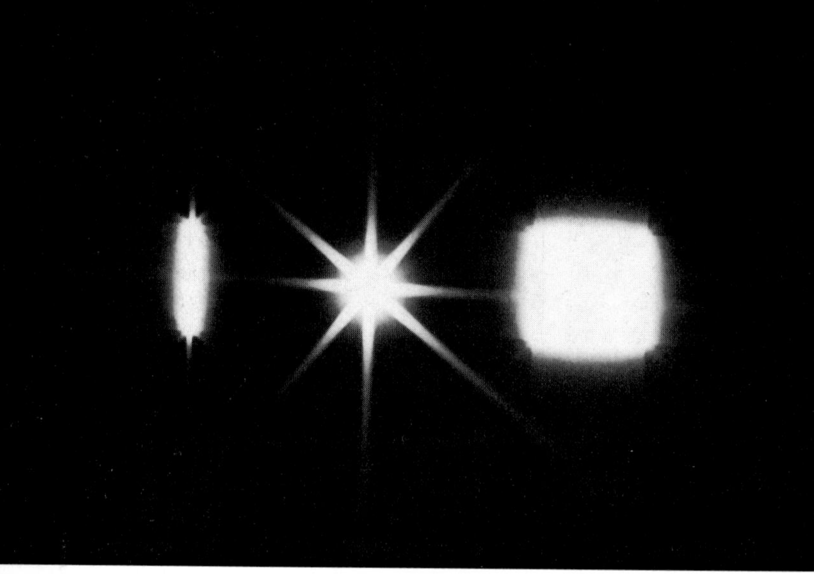

The radiance of direct light: screen-produced stars

Bright points of light can easily be transformed into stars by shooting through fine wire screens. A single screen, placed (as a filter is placed) in front of the lens, produces four-pointed stars (top picture); two screens crossed at 45 degrees produce eight-pointed stars (bottom picture).

The photograph above illustrates how this method, among others, makes it possible for a photographer to symbolize effectively the exhilaration one feels in seeing a big city at night alive with the glitter of millions of lights.

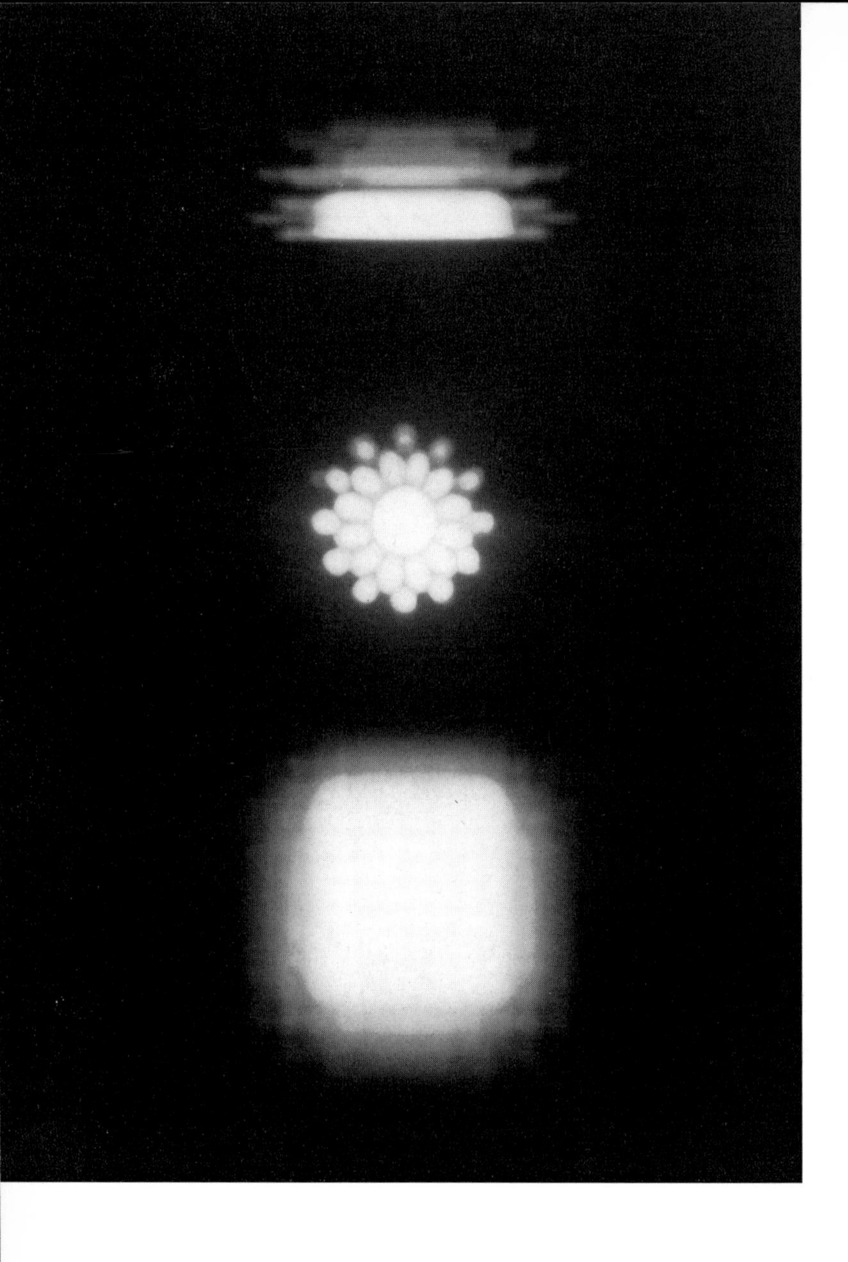

The radiance of direct light: the Imagon lens

An unusual star pattern can be produced by photographing a source of light with an Imagon lens (made by Rodenstock). Its sieve-like daphragm causes each point of light to be changed

into a star pattern that resembles a luminous flower surrounded by a double-row of petals of light, an effect illustrated above which more than any other form of light symbolization suggests the festive glitter of city lights at night.

The radiance of direct light: flares and halations

We shall see, in the case of the grainy negatives, that, occasionally, a fault can become an asset. Here we have another example. In their search for more expressive means, photographers with imagination and daring have even used such obvious faults as lens flares and halations within the negative emulsion to symbolize in heightened graphic form the overpowering brillance of radiant light. How well they can succeed is documented by Ronny Jaques's two photographs of skiers at sunset. Both pictures give an intense feeling of looking into dazzling light.

Sharpness and negative grain

Although normally a fault which should be avoided, under certain conditions graininess can become valuable graphically for strengthening the emotional impact of a photograph. For example, graininess effectively symbolizes concepts such as coarseness, vulgarity, and violence. In interior shots of taverns, cabarets, convention halls, etc., a grainy rendition will better characterize the smoky, dusty atmosphere of such places than a grainless picture. And I have seen any number of war photographs whose impact was partly due to their graininess which vividly suggested grime, smoke, and the violence of combat.

In this photograph by Eric Dyring (Sweden), film grain effectively suggests the hazy atmosphere of a quiet fall morning.

To increase graininess in a print, work with small film sizes and make big enlargements, or greatly enlarge small sections of the film; use high-speed negative emulsions (see p. 60) in conjunction with high-contrast developers (see p. 62); print on paper of contrasty gradation.

Sharpness and reticulation

The extreme in grain pattern can be produced through deliberate reticulation of the negative emulsion. This is brought about by soaking the fixed but not hardened negative for a certain time in hot water. The proper temperature of the water and length of treatment vary from one film type to another and must be established experimentally. Since this process is critical and may result in the destruction of the negative, only duplicate negatives should be subjected to this treatment to avoid possible loss of a valuable original. The simpler the subject is in outline and form, and the more contrasty, the more graphically effective the result of reticulation will be.

Sharpness and unsharpness

Although the vast majority of photographs should be sharp, occasionally a photographer will find that a partially or entirely unsharp rendition will better convey a specific feeling, idea, or mood.

Two methods that can be used to produce controlled partial unsharpness in a photograph are illustrated on this spread.

The picture above was made with a simple meniscus lens (an ordinary, double-convex magnifying lens). The image produced by this type of lens is reasonably sharp at its center but increasingly unsharp toward the edges. The smaller the opening of the diaphragm in conjunction with which the meniscus lens is used, the larger the extent of the acceptably sharp central area and vice versa. (The photographer Nina Leen has made two outstandingly beautiful picture stories for Life Magazine based upon this technique, one on the subject of "Ghosts," the other on "Happiness.")

This photograph by Sharland was shot through a sheet of glass which was partly smeared with vaseline. It is part of a picture story on racial prejudice and the idea behind this picture was to suggest vision blurred by tears — the reaction of the Negro boy rejected by his white "playmates."

Contrast control: devices, techniques, and scope

Whereas in reality visual differentiation of form is based primarily upon color differences and parallax (stereoscopic seeing), in black-and-white photography differentiation depends entirely upon contrast between light and dark. As a result, control of contrast is a most important factor in the creation of effective photographs. Fortunately, the following highly effective devices and techniques for contrast control are available to any photographer who, for pictorial or editorial reasons, wishes to change the original contrast gradient of his subject.

Contrast can be controlled with the aid of:

Films with emulsions of different gradations (pp. 61, 224)
Filters in different colors (pp. 53–55, 226, 242–247)

Illumination of different quality and intensity (pp. 228–231)
Modifications in exposure (pp. 61, 68, 166)
Negative developers of different contrast rendition (p. 62)
Modifications in development (pp. 69, 232)
Sensitized papers of different gradation (pp. 63, 234).

Each of these controls can be used separately or in conjunction with one, several, or all of the others. Thus a photographer can render practically any subject in a contrast gradient that ranges from ultra-low to ultra-high. The comparison pictures above, showing the same subject rendered in two extreme contrast gradients, clearly illustrate the enormous scope of these controls.

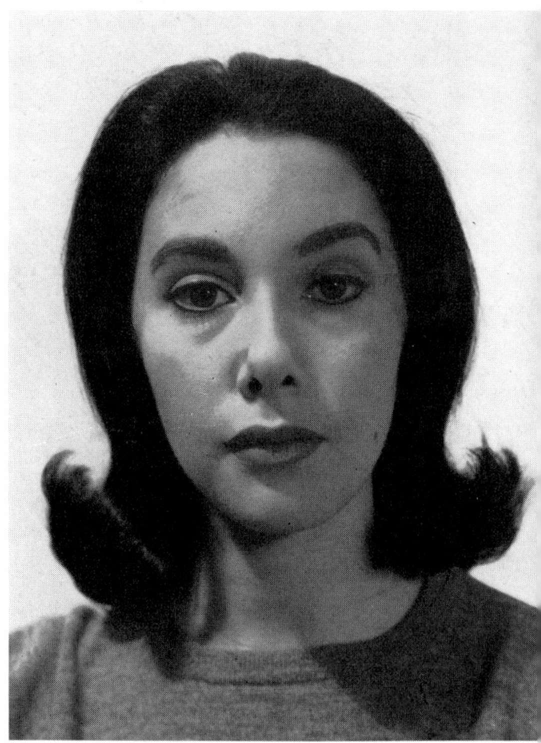

Contrast control through negative emulsions

In regard to gradation (ability to render contrast), photographers must distinguish between three types of film: soft, normal, and hard.

As a rule, the faster a film, the softer its gradation and vice versa. High-speed films with exposure indices of 500 and higher are the least contrasty (softest). Conversely, the most contrasty (hardest) are certain types of very slow, ultra-finegrain process films.

If one were to photograph a gray-scale which ranged in steps from black through evenly spaced shades of gray to white, and if one were to print the resulting negatives on paper of normal gradation, a true

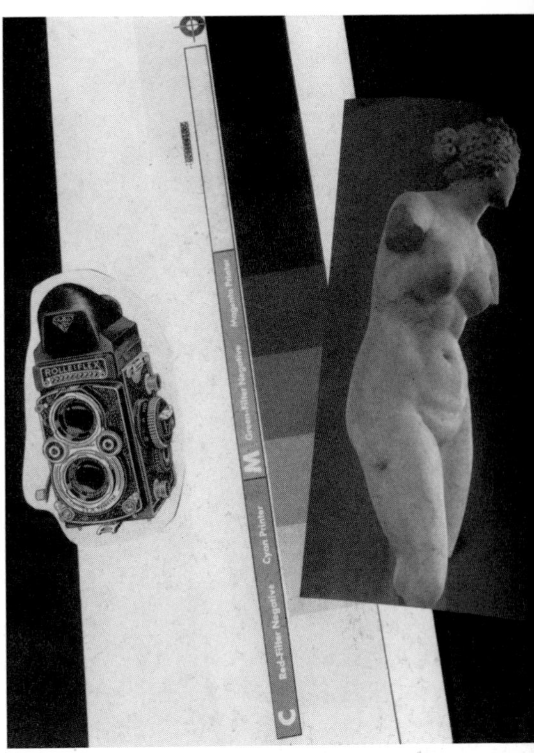

black or white could not be produced from a "soft" film; black would be rendered as a dark gray and white as a light gray. A "normal" film would render each step from black to white in its true tone. And a "hard" film would render black as black and white as white, but would render half the intermediate steps of gray too light and the other half too dark.

The left picture of each of the two pairs of photographs shown on this spread was taken on contrasty process film, the right on a soft panchromatic film. The differences in the gradations of these pictures, all of which were printed on paper of normal gradation, show the available extremes in contrast rendition. Any desired contrast gradient between these extremes can be produced by using the appropriate type of film.

Contrast control through use of color filters

In reality, subject differentiation is largely based upon color contrast. In black-and-white photography, when colors of similar brightness (although of different hues) are translated into terms of gray, they become more or less identical and, consequently, subject differentiation is diminished or even lost. However, this can be avoided if color filters are used to render one color lighter (or darker) than another, and to substitute the graphically effective differentiation of black-and-white for the differentiation in actual subject color.

The illustrations above show how contrast between sky and clouds can be controlled and the sky made to appear in any shade ranging from white through gray to black. From left to right, the pictures were taken through a dark blue filter, a light yellow filter, a red filter, and a combination of red filter and polarizer. Although, in a photograph, it is usually more common to emphasize than to suppress clouds, the latter may be necessary if complex subjects must be photographed against the sky and, for clarity of rendition, a neutral background is needed.

Contrast control through illumination

If it is possible at all, the simplest way to control subject contrast is through control of the illumination: a brightly lit subject will be rendered lighter than the same subject photographed in subdued light. Indoors contrast control is usually easy to achieve. Outdoors it is often possible to control contrast if one has the patience (and time) to wait until the sun reaches a certain position or atmospheric conditions are right.

The scope of this method of contrast control is illustrated by the series of pictures above which show a white statue photographed against a white background so that the subject ranges from white against white to gray against gray to black against black; and from black against white to white against black.

Contrast control through fill-in illumination

Contrast in a photograph is the difference in lightness between the lightest and the darkest parts of the picture. Such differences can be the result of differences in subject color (for example, the colors of skin and hair), or the differences in subject illumination (light and shadow). In the latter case, contrast can usually be controlled by lightening the shadow areas of the subject with fill-in illumination — indoors with additional photoflood or flash lamps, outdoors with flash or large reflecting surfaces.

The photographs above show the degree to which a photographer can control the contrast gradient of his pictures through use of fill-in light. The position of the main light was the same in all four

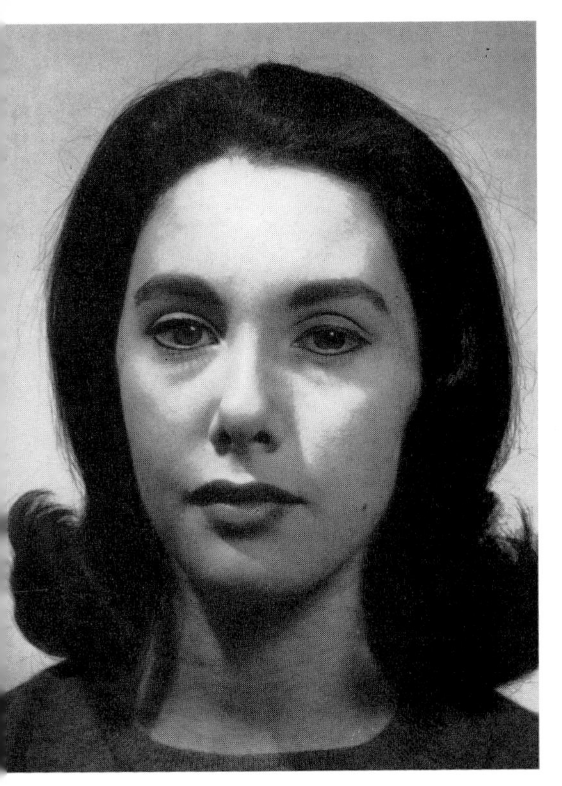

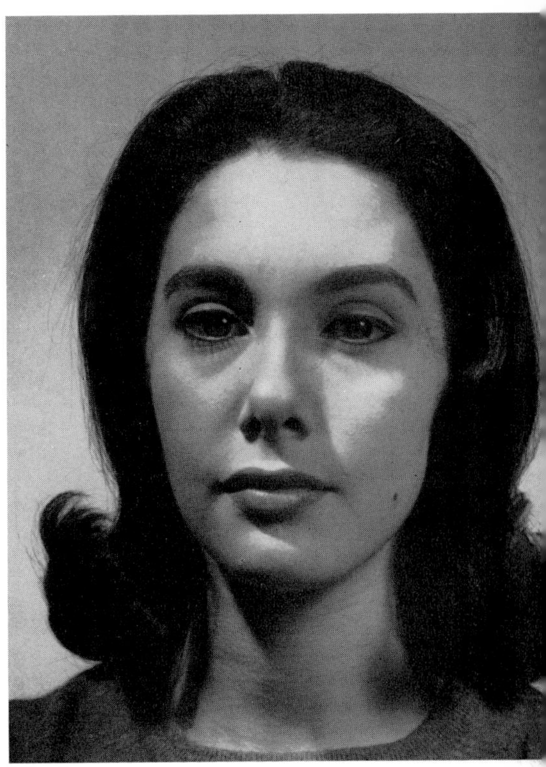

pictures; the subject was illuminated with three-quarter side-and-top light (see p. 191). But whereas the first picture was solely illuminated by the main light, the other three were lighted by a combination of main light and fill-in light, the fill-in light moved closer with each successive shot until in the end the shadow cast by the main light is almost as light as the fully lighted parts of the subject.

The use of fill-in illumination entails two dangers: too much fill-in light, by eliminating shadows, also eliminates the illusion of roundness and depth. And since every source of light casts its own set of shadows, fill-in illumination, improperly used, will produce shadows within shadows as well as shadows which criss-cross one another and create an amateurish look that destroys the picture.

Contrast control through negative development

As a rule, the best way to produce negatives of satisfactory gradation is to develop them by the time-and-temperature method in strict accordance with the film manufacturer's recommendations; if necessary, revising this procedure on the basis of carefully conducted experiments and tests to meet one's own needs.

Occasionally, however, it is desirable to change the normal contrast gradient of a film — to make it softer or harder — to fit the demands of an unusually contrasty or contrastless subject. If such changes are necessary, deviations from the standard procedure of negative development provide a safe and easy way to modify the contrast gradient of a negative: shortening the time of development decreases, and prolonging the time of development increases, the contrast gradient of a negative.

The scope of contrast control through modification of development is illustrated by the three photographs above, the negatives of which were identically exposed. The picture at the left is a print made from a normally developed negative; the picture in the center was printed from a negative developed for half the normal time; and the picture at the right was printed from a negative developed three times the normal time.

Even greater differences in contrast gradient can be produced if modification of development is accompanied by appropriate modifications of exposure. To increase the contrast gradient of a negative, shorten the exposure and increase the time of development; to decrease contrast, prolong the exposure and shorten the time of development. Since data vary with different types of film and developer, exact times must be determined on the basis of preliminary tests.

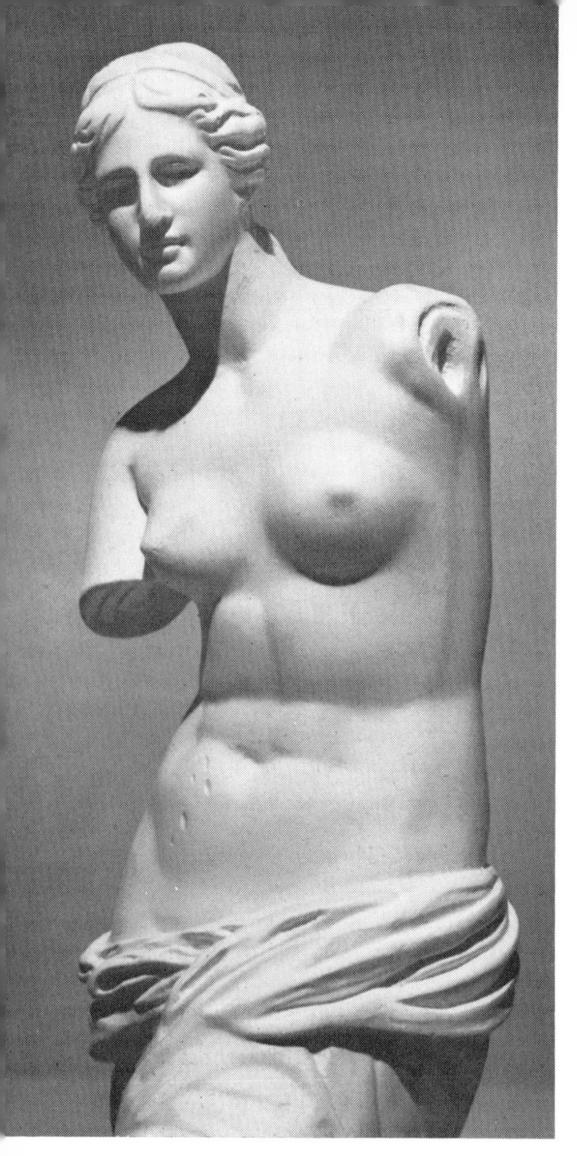

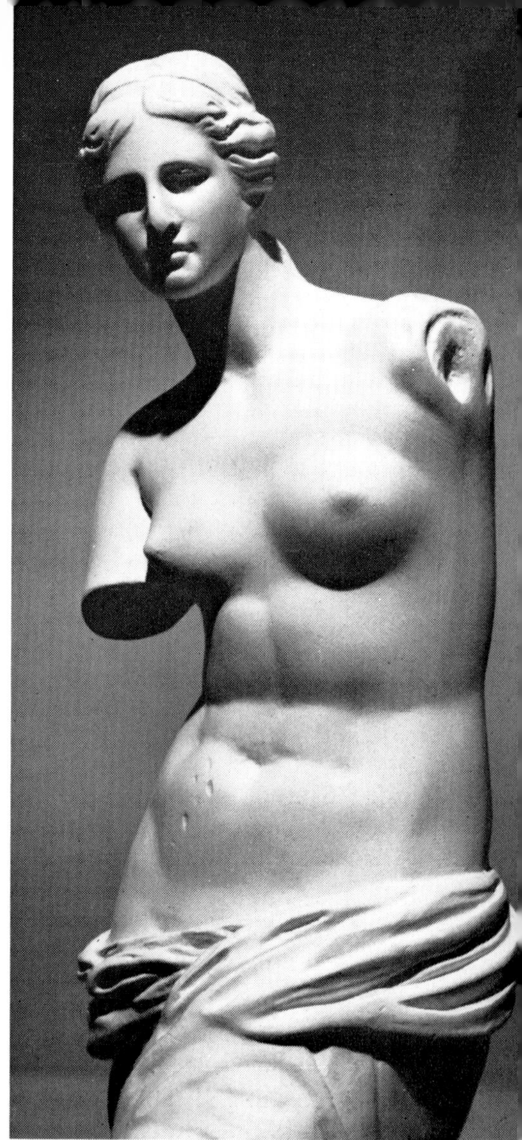

Contrast control through paper gradation

The simplest, although not necessarily the best, way to control the contrast gradient of a photograph is to print the negative on a paper of appropriate gradation. The scope of this method of con-

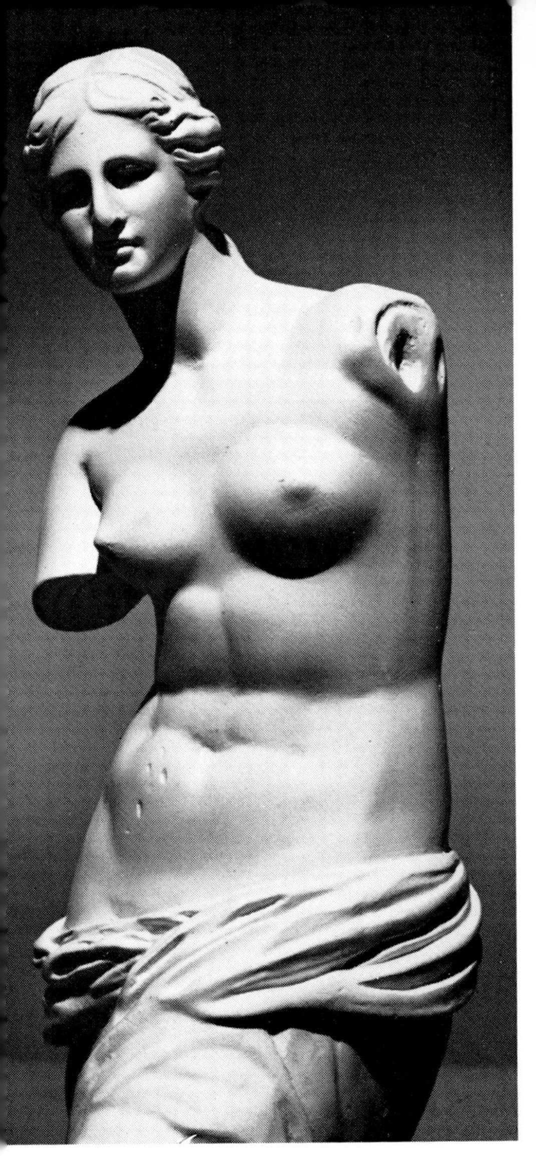
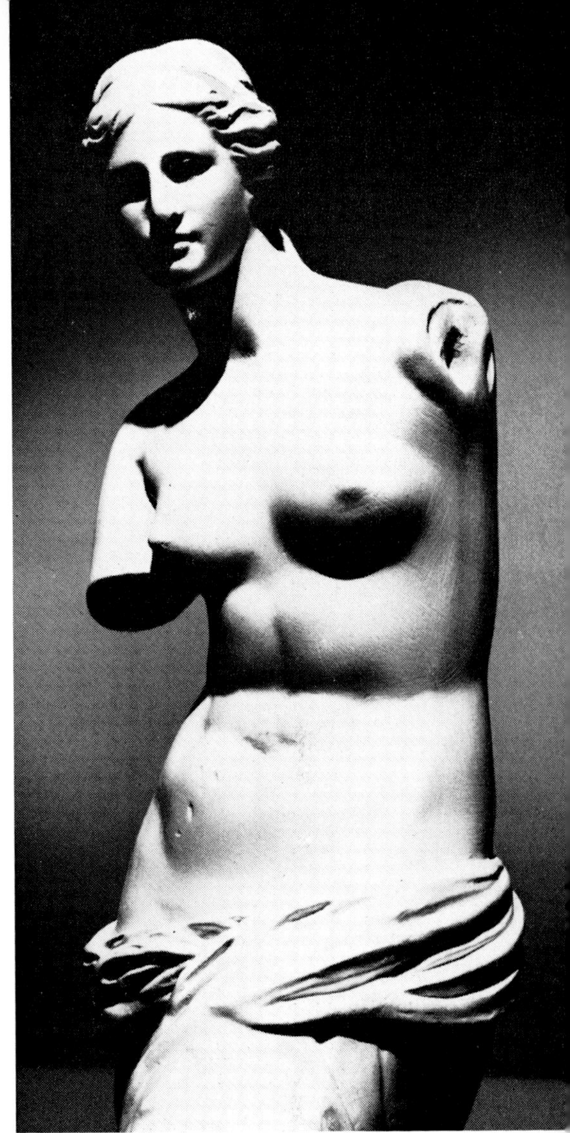

trast control is illustrated by the four pictures above. Prints from the same negative, which has an average contrast range, were made on papers of different gradation: soft, normal, hard, and ultra-hard.

Contrast control: deliberate simplification of tone

Again and again in photography we find that the simpler the means, the stronger the impact of the picture. The two photographs on this spread, examples of deliberate contrast control, effectively prove this point.

Above: The low-key photograph by Harvey Shaman, mainly because of its deliberate restriction to two somber tones, suggests all the loneliness and misery of a drizzling evening in November. Right: The high-contrast photograph by the author, because it consists almost entirely of abstract black-and-white, deliberately "de-personalizes" the face, thereby capturing in graphic form something of the essence of the medical profession.

Contrast control: the beauty of the abstract black and white

Above: "Harlequin" by Zoltan Glass (England); right: sailboats by Josef Scaylea. Both pictures derive their partic-

ular impact from good composition imaginatively brought about through use of powerful, graphic black and white.

Contrast control: the bas-relief process

The ultimate degree of abstraction in black-and-white photography can be reached through the bas-relief process: contact-print a negative on film to produce a diapositive; tape negative and diapositive together slightly out of register; place this "sandwich" in the enlarger and print as usual. If the original negative is sufficiently contrasty

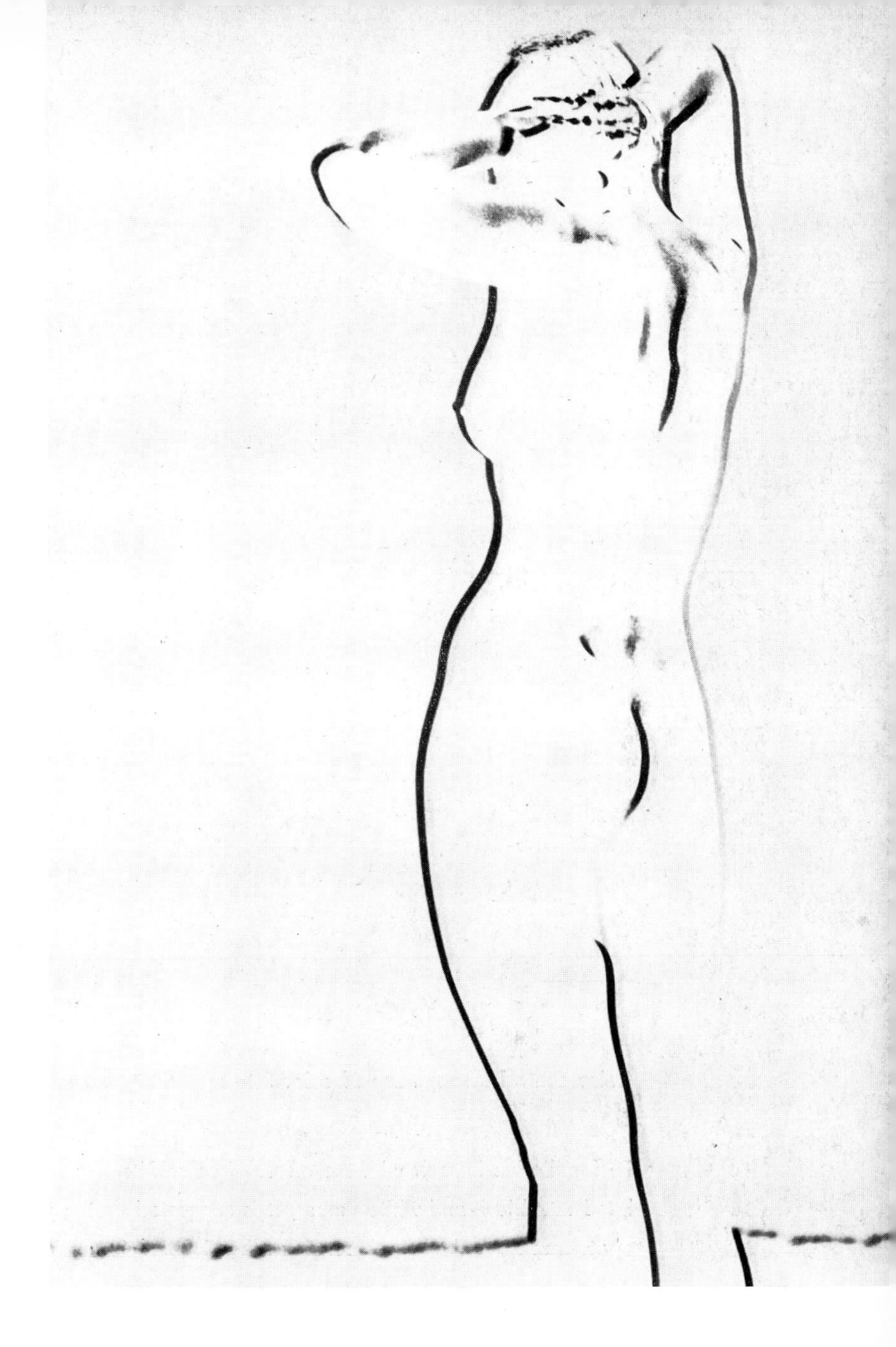

and perfectly sharp, the resulting print will resemble a pen-and-ink drawing or a woodcut. The simpler the subject, composition, and design, the stronger and more impressive the abstraction. If printed on paper of extra-hard gradation, the same stark, graphic black-and-white effect can be achieved as that in the pictures above which, incidentally, derived from the photograph shown on p. 194, top, left.

Color control through use of color filters

To familiarize himself with the effect of color filters upon color translated into black-and-white values, it is suggested that a photographer photograph a colorful subject through all filters from blue to red (as in the series shown above), making careful notes during the procedure. The simplest way to avoid a confusion of data (for confusion would make the whole experiment worthless) is to write such data (for example: b l u e f i l t e r) in India ink on a slip of paper and include the slip in the test setup so that it appears photographed near the margin of the picture.

The pictures above show an identical setup photographed under identical conditions except that each picture was shot through a different color filter. All negatives were printed on paper of the same gradation. From left to right, the filter colors through which these photographs were made are: blue, yellow, green, red. The accompanying sketch indicates the colors of the subject. Note that a filter always renders the subject-color that corresponds to its own color lighter, and renders its complementary color darker than it appeared to the eye in reality. For additional information on color filters see pp. 226–227.

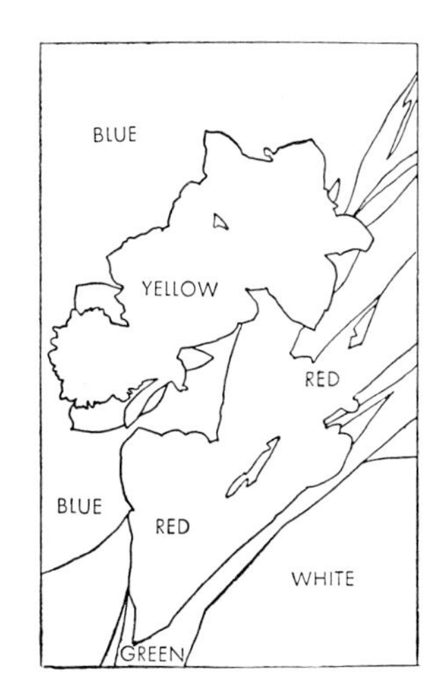

Color control through use of color filters

To further his knowledge of the use of color filters, it is suggested that a photographer make a series of pictures similar to the set shown here: photograph a setup consisting of two subjects which have complementary colors and, by using the proper color filters, photograph these subjects so that their colors appear in the print as white on white, gray on gray, black on black, black on white, and white on black. That this is possible is demonstrated by the accompanying photographs which show a bright red pepper against bright green cabbage leaves. Although, as indicated by the shadows, all the pictures are positives, the differences in color translation are such that the photographs facing one another diagonally in the layout appear as different as positive and negative — which provides convincing proof of the immense scope of this phase of photographic control.

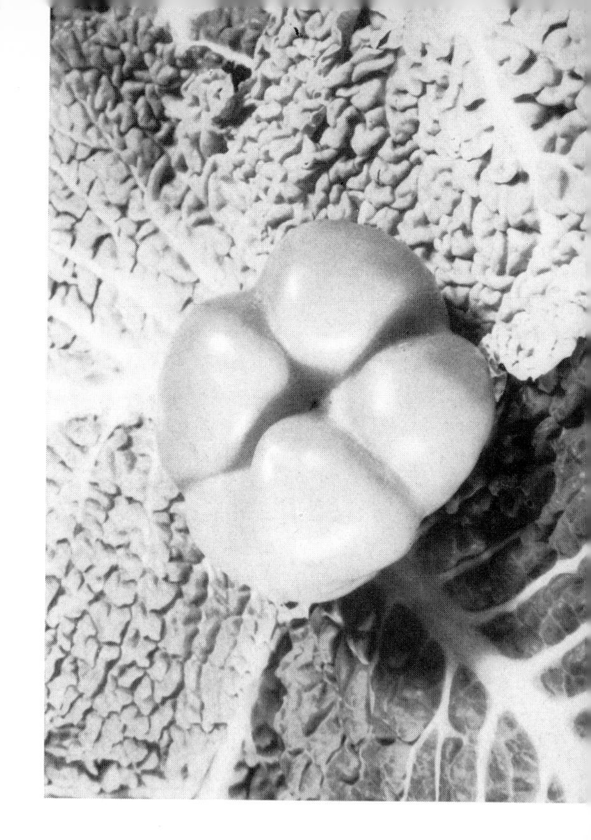

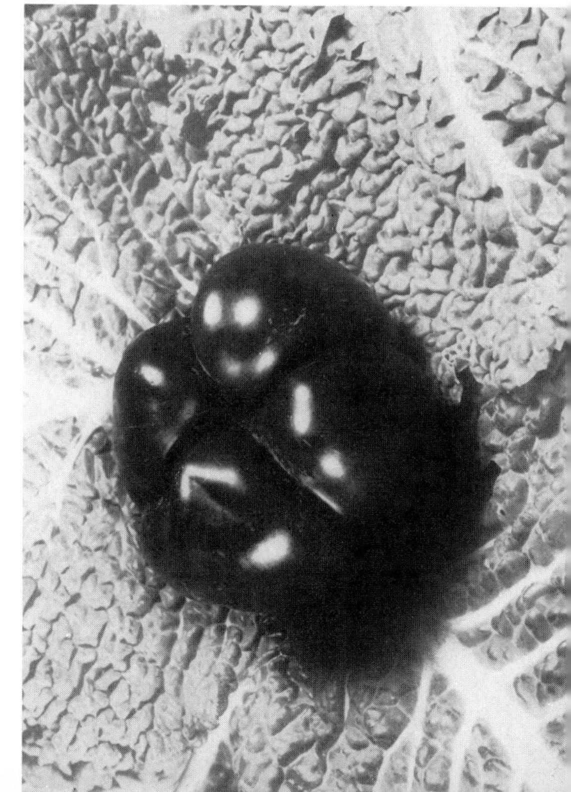

Color contrast through use of color filters

The graphic effect of these two pictures is largely the result of color control through use of color filters.

A b o v e : With the aid of a red filter, the effect of the always present bluish morning haze was deliberately eliminated to increase the contrast of the picture and thus accentuate the rhythm of the composition.

R i g h t : Use of a red filter enabled the photographer to translate the colorful drama of a sunset into equally dramatic shades of black-and-white.

Control in color photography

In all respects except one, the problems that face the color photographer are basically the same as those that confront the photographer who works in black-and-white. Subject selection; sharpness and definition; light and shadow; reflection and glare; perspective and scale; motion and blur and similar factors influence a picture as much if it is photographed in black-and-white as if it is photographed in color. For this reason this book, although it is predominantly illustrated in black-and-white, is nevertheless directed as much to color photographers as it is to photographers who work in black-and-white.

In a black-and-white photograph, apart, of course, from the subject itself, FORM expressed in terms of graphic black-and-white is the most important single factor, whereas in a color photograph the most important factor is COLOR. And in a color photograph, should a choice between form and color be necessary, color must invariably be stressed. This difference in emphasis is the prime factor in which color and black-and-white photography differ.

The problems that relate solely to color are, of course, not possible to present in sixteen pages so that here only an outline of the principles involved in seeing and thinking in terms of color and the means that govern its control is given. Those who wish to know more about this fascinating subject are referred to THE COLOR PHOTO BOOK by this author (Prentice-Hall, Inc., Englewood Cliffs, N. J.).

Although some will doubtlessly disagree with me, the criterion of any g o o d color photograph is whether it is beautiful, exciting, shocking etc.; in other words whether it captures the attention, NOT whether its color is "true." Actually, there is no "true color." Photographs of the same subject shot under identical conditions on color films of the same type made by different manufactures will show totally different renditions of the subject's color, as illustrated by the comparison pictures on p. 252. In addition to color differences that are inherent in the film, subject color is changed by changes in the quality of the illumination and, outdoors, the time of day and atmospheric conditions. Consequently, to be able to make g o o d color photographs, a photographer must cease to be preoccupied with producing "natural" color and approach color with the imaginative eye of the creative artist.

The following sixteen pages illustrate some of the means by which color can be controlled in accordance with artistic demands.

Choice of subject color

Color in a photograph can be either an asset or a liability, depending upon whether it is photogenic or unphotogenic, a fact which makes discrimination, selectivity and taste on the part of the photographer valuable means of color control. Furthermore, since all subjects change in color with changes in the color of the illuminating light, as far as outdoor subjects are concerned, patience and time also are prerequisites for the production of good color photographs.

These illustrations show the extent to which the color of a subject is changed by changes in the color of the illuminating light, the time of day and atmospheric conditions, without any influence from the photographer (for example: use of color filters). All he has to do is wait and choose.

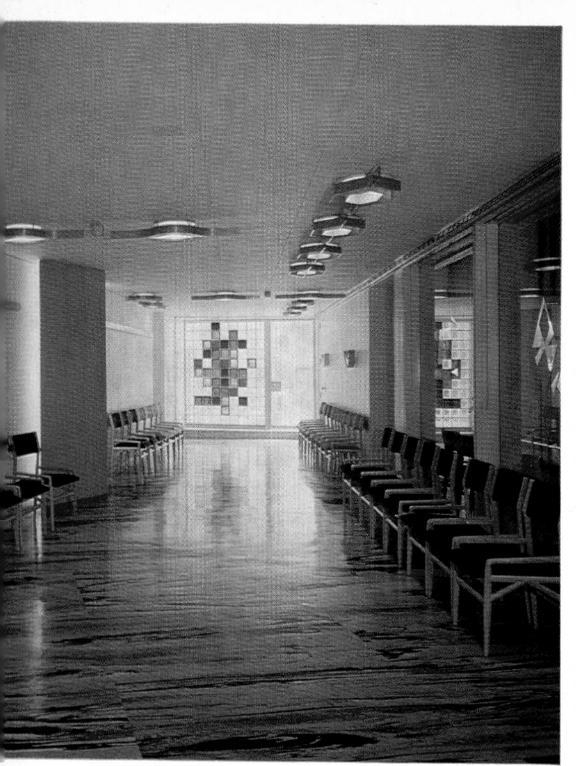

Choice of type of color film

As any color photographer knows, if pictures must be made to appear as "natural" as possible, the color film must correspond to the type of light in which it is used. Usually, the choice is simple: in daylight, one uses daylight type film; in artificial light, one uses the type of film that is recommended for the respective type of artificial light. But what type of film should a photographer choose if daylight and artificial light are mixed?

Since there is no color film for "mixed light," he must use either daylight color film or a color film balanced for artificial light. Neither, of course, will produce color that appears "natural" which is the reason why manufacturers of color film advise against mixing different types of light. On the other hand, precisely because it is different from that which is usual, such highly "unnatural" color can be particularly interesting and beautiful.

Of the two accompanying picture pairs which were taken in a mixture of daylight and incandescent light, the left and top photographs were shot on daylight color film, the right and bottom photographs on color film balanced for incandescent light. As can be clearly seen, in "mixed light" daylight type color film produces warmer, more golden tones and artificial light type color film results in cooler, more bluish shades.

KINSEY
BLENDED WHISKEY
DAYLIGHT TELEVISION
Q-T FROSTING
AUTOMAT
AUTOMAT
Miss Youth Form
Cannot Ride-up
STRAND
ERROL FLYNN
VIVECA LINDFORS
DON JUAN
TOMMY DORSEY
STRAND
make mine
RUPPERT
SLOW-AGED FOR FINER FLAVOR
PEPSI-COLA
PARK CENTRAL HOTEL
HOWARD
TAFT
BRASS RAIL
KO PALACE
GLOBE THEATRE
WHIPLASH
GOTHAM

KINSEY
BLENDED WHISKEY
DAYLIGHT TELEVISION
Q-T FROSTING
AUTOMAT
AUTOMAT
Miss Youth Form
STRAND
ERROL FLYNN
VIVECA LINDFORS
DON JUAN
TOMMY DORSEY
STRAND
make mine
RUPPERT
SLOW-AGED FOR FINER FLAVOR
PEPSI-COLA
PARK CENTRAL HOTEL
HOWARD
TAFT
BRASS RAIL
KO PALACE
GLOBE THEATRE
WHIPLASH
GOTHAM

Choice of brand of color film

These two pictures of the same subject were shot under identical conditions on daylight type films produced by two of the world's foremost manufacturers. No filters were used, and both were developed by the same top-notch color laboratory.

The enormous difference in color rendition results from the inherent characteristics of the two color films (disproving effectively the myth of "natural" color). Conclusion: through trial and experiment, each photographer must find the brand of color film that possesses characteristics which he likes. Choice in this is strictly a matter of one's taste – there is no "best" make of color film.

Choice of color correction filter

The over-all tone of any color photograph can be controlled to a very large extent through the use of special filters. The top picture was shot without a filter; its strong blue over-all tone which is particularly noticeable in the shadows is the normal result of an abundance of light reflected from a deep-blue sky. The lower picture was taken through a filter which eliminated some of the blue, producing warmer, more yellowish colors. Although this color rendition may seem more "natural," the unfiltered version is actually more "true" to reality as it was at the moment of exposure.

Choice of illumination

Since the color of daylight varies considerably, a photographer often has the choice of showing the same subject in one of many different over-all color shades.

The four pictures on this spread were taken on the same brand and type of color film. No filters were used. Differences in over-all tone are the result of differences in the color of the light. Above, the left picture was shot at dusk and the right picture at night. On the opposite page, the two photographs taken in Death Valley, California, show how the over-all color of a landscape changes with the change in color of the light: the top picture was made immediately after sunrise when the light was still reddish; the bottom picture was made two hours later when the light was "white." Later on, during the afternoon, the light would have changed gradually from white to yellow to gold, becoming red at sunset, then fading through pink to increasingly darker shades of blue.

Choice of illumination

Indoors, illumination of any desired type and color can easily be produced by using the appropriate types of lights and, if desired, coloring the illumination by placing colored gelatines in front of the lamps. Outdoors, as these photographs prove, the choice is almost equal, provided that the photographer has enough patience and time to wait for a certain light.

Above: Both photographs were taken within a few minutes. The striking difference in color was caused by moving clouds which cast their shadows upon the middle-ground in one picture, upon the background in the other.

Opposite page: The picture at the top shows a factory "gold-plated" by the last light of the setting sun. The center picture shows a refinery silhouetted against a blood-red sunset sky. The bottom picture shows the actually white structure of a modern house tinted a mysterious blue as daylight fades into night.

In each of these pictures, daylight of an "abnormal" color (i. e. daylight that was not "white") was chosen to give interest to a subject which, if it had been photographed in "normal" light, would have looked commonplace and dull.

The choice of color or black-and-white

Basically, a photographer has the choice of taking any subject either in black-and-white or in color. Unfortunately, amateurs in particular seem to think that "color" is necessarily "better" than black-and-white and shoot subjects in color which would have been more effective in black-and-white.

In contrast to this approach, successful photographers take color photographs only if color is essential to the characterization of the subject. And if this is the case, they are not deterred by whether there are many color shades or few, or whether the subject's color is intense or pale. If rendered in black-and-white, the three accompanying views would have been nondescript and dull. But because color was the most important quality of each subject, they are effective despite (or perhaps because of) the fact that these renditions are practically monochromes.

Choice of usual or unusual color

Most color photographs more or less duplicate what the eye can see and thus they add nothing new to our visual experience. As a result, most color photographs command relatively little attention.

Precisely the opposite is true of photographs in which color is "unusual" (which by no means is the same as "unnatural"). Photographers looking for unusual color have the choice of two color complexes: unusually subtle color (pastel shades) and unusually intense (highly saturated) colors.

The picture above is characterized by unusually subtle color shades. It represents a subject type that many color photographers reject as "not colorful enough." However, in this case, it is the subtle, pearly color shades that contribute so much to the feeling of the winter afternoon. Strange as it may seem, subtleness of color can be an asset in color photography, and the more subtle the color, the stronger the effect.

These pictures are characterized by unusually intense color. In both, the almost luminous effect was achieved through use of backlight. The top picture is based upon complementary colors (contrasting yellow and blue), the bottom picture upon color harmonies (related reds and browns).

Choice of exposure

The contrast range of color films is more limited than that of black-and-white emulsion. As a result, if subject contrast is high, satisfactory rendition of both the lightest and darkest colors is impossible. If such is the case, the photographer has two choices: through appropriate exposure, he can satisfactorily render either the medium and light colors (the dark colors would be rendered black) or the medium and dark colors (the light colors would be rendered white).

The pictures on the opposite page, which were shot under identical conditions, illustrate this choice. The top picture received (in accordance with a meter reading taken of the light sky) a relatively short exposure; the light and medium subject areas are satisfactorily rendered whereas the dark colors and shadow areas appear too dark or black. In contrast, the bottom picture received (in accordance with a meter reading taken of the shadow parts) a relatively long exposure with the result that dark colors are satisfactorily rendered and shadow areas are full of detail; but light subject areas appear either too light or completely colorless.

The shorter exposure enabled the photographer to preserve the particular mood of the scene, the longer exposure to show the stern-wheeler in full detail. Neither picture is "better" than the other, they are merely different. The choice of approach depends upon the purpose for which the photograph is intended. The picture above, a lamp-lighter tending a gas lamp in Independence Hall Park in Philadelphia, was purposely exposed for the lightest colors to preserve the nostalgic mood of the scene.

Picture control through use of a polarizer

In many instances, undesirable glare and reflections can either be toned down in a photograph or completely eliminated through use of a polarizer, placed as a filter in front of the lens. In addition, in color photography, a polarizer can be used to intensify color which is partly or entirely obscured by glare and therefore appears too light or white. Furthermore, a polarizer is the only means by which the blue of a blue sky (particularly near the horizon at right angles to the direction of the incident light) can be intensified in a color photograph. In such a case, a polarizer fulfills a purpose similar to that of a yellow or red filter in black-and-white photography.

The two color photographs on the opposite page were taken under almost identical conditions except that the upper one was shot with, and the lower one without, a polarizer. Glare that in the lower picture washed out the color of the sky and the driftwood is eliminated in the upper picture by a polarizer, and color now appears intense and clean.

Of the two pictures above, the left one was taken with a polarizer. Differences in rendition are so great that one must look at the cars to believe that both were shot only seconds apart.

Glare control through polarizers

Of the two photographs above, the left was made with and the right without a polarizer. Similarly, of the picture pair on the opposite page, the top one was made with and the bottom one without a polarizer. Together, they show some of the effects that can be produced in rendering glass, water, and sky if one knows how to control glare with the aid of a polarizer.

Space controls

Reality is three-dimensional; a photograph is flat. To create the effect of three-dimensionality and space in a picture, depth, the "lost dimension," must be introduced in symbolic form. Fortunately, there are a number of graphic symbols which a photographer can use to express the concept of space. Each of these symbols can either be used alone or in combination with one or several others. Each can be controlled by the photographer and modified to a very high degree to meet specific requirements. Consequently, in a photograph, a feeling of space can be created in an unlimited number of different ways, and a photographer who knows his symbols can express "space" in any desired form.

The following survey lists seven symbols of space rendition together with their controls.

1. **Perspective.** This is the familiar "optical illusion" that makes lines that are actually parallel appear to converge as they recede from the observer. (Perhaps the best known manifestation of this phenomenon is the apparent converging of railroad tracks toward depth.) This illusion occurs regardless of the position of the parallel lines in space, in the horizontal as well as in the vertical or any other plane. However, because daily we look at many things that have great extension in the horizontal plane but few or sometimes none that have great extension in the vertical plane, our eyes "see" and our minds accept as "natural," the apparent convergence in the horizontal plane of actually parallel lines, but reject as "unnatural" or "distorted" the equally natural apparent convergence in the vertical plane of actually parallel lines. Everyone accepts the fact that railroad tracks or the base and roof lines of a row of buildings will appear to converge as they recede toward the horizon (i. e., in the horizontal plane), but many will object to the converging of the walls of a skyscraper in an angle shot because to them this would make the building appear to collapse. In this respect, photography has an educational value for it gradually trains our eyes to

"see" and our minds to accept the phenomenon of "vertical perspective" and to regard it as what it really is, the optical manifestation of "height."

To control "perspective," a photographer must be able in his pictures to control the angle of apparent convergence of parallel lines. This he can achieve through the appropriate angle of view, subject-to-camera distance, and focal length of the lens. In principle, a wide-angle lens used at a short subject distance "exaggerates" perspective by making the angle of convergence more obtuse; conversely, the combination of a telephoto lens and great subject distance minimizes perspective by making the angle of convergence more acute. Furthermore, in certain cases, perspective convergence can be minimized or even eliminated, i. e., parallel lines rendered parallel even in oblique shots, by using the back adjustments of a view camera (see pp. 278–280) or the tilting negative carrier of an enlarger (see pictures p. 281).

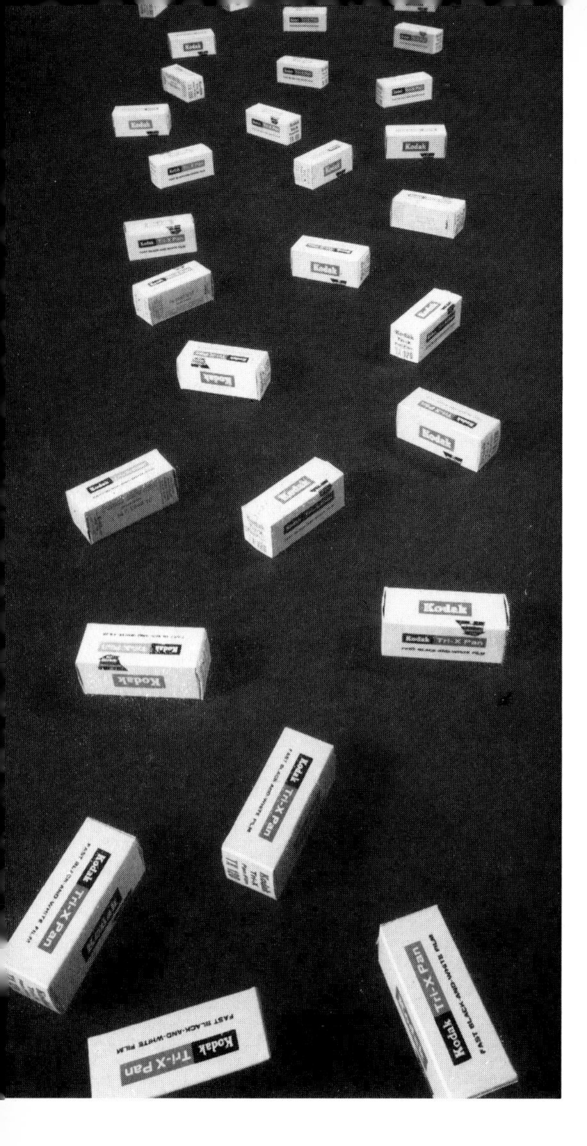

2. **Diminution.** This kind of perspective is an optical illusion which makes an object appear increasingly smaller as the distance from the observer increases and vice versa. Provided that the actual size of the subject which is shown in diminished scale is known to the observer of the picture, diminution is a valuable means for creating an illusion of depth when "perspective" is lacking because no parallel lines exist. For example, in landscape photography, a photographer can advantageously use diminution to create an illusion of space by placing a person (or an object of known dimensions such as an automobile) far away from the camera. Thus, by rendering the person (or the object) very small, he not only provides his picture with scale (see p. 114), but also creates a depth-illusion which will be directly proportional to the apparent size of the figure (or object): the smaller its scale of rendition, the farther away it appears to be and, consequently, the stronger the impression of distance, depth, and space.

The means for controlling diminution are the same as those used for controlling perspective: modification of subject-distance in conjunction with a lens of suitable focal length; for more information see pp. 282–285.

3. **Foreshortening.** This is a third kind of "perspective" which is manifested in the form of "distortion." For example, seen in side-view, a wheel appears "undistorted" or in its true, circular form; seen from an angle, it appears more or less elliptical or "distorted." Seen as a circle, a wheel looks "flat" and lacks "depth"; but seen in elliptical form it acquires depth because we know from its shape that we see it at an angle, receding to a certain degree away from us toward "depth." Because of this association, foreshortening always brings with it the feeling of space and in a photograph it effectively symbolizes extension in depth.

Foreshortening can be controlled through the angle of view: the more acute the angle, the more foreshortened the subject appears and the stronger is the resulting feeling of "depth" and vice versa. Furthermore, to a certain extent, foreshortening can be controlled with the aid of the back adjustments of a view camera: the more the back is turned toward parallelity with the subject, the less the degree of foreshortening. When parallelity of film and subject is established, foreshortening is eliminated altogether and, to return to our example, a wheel then appears in its true circular form *even in an angle shot* (see also p. 278).

4. **Overlapping.** If one subject partly hides another, it is obvious that the partly obscured subject is behind, and farther away from, the subject which hides it. Consequently, overlapping of form in a photograph, by showing that one subject is more distant than another, proves extension in space and is thus a symbol of "depth."

Overlapping may be the only means for symbolizing space when other symbols, such as selective focusing or aerial perspective, are undesirable, and perspective, diminution, and foreshortening cannot be used because there are no parallel lines, objects of known dimensions, or forms that can be foreshortened. For instance, on a beach, there may be no parallel lines; the pebbles may have any size; and their shapes may be so irregular that effective foreshortening is not possible. In such a case, the only acceptable means for symbolizing depth may be provided by overlapping of form coupled with direction of illumination (side- or backlight) that will pick out the individual pebbles and thus make it evident which partly obscures which.

Normally, of course, overlapping will be used in conjunction with some other symbol or symbols for space rendition to further strengthen the illusion of depth in the respective photograph (pictures pp. 314–315).

5. **Subject location** within the frame of the picture. The higher the horizon within the frame of a photograph, the stronger the impression of depth (although not necessarily of space) and vice versa. Consequently, by placing the subject high in the picture, with plenty of foreground in front of it, a photographer can create a stronger feeling of depth than if he were to place the subject low and include little or no foreground.

This is explained by the fact that, in looking at a subject which is placed high within the picture, before we see the subject we must first look at an extensive foreground area, whereas if the subject is placed low there is little or no "ground to cover," and the subject is immediately seen without one having to look any distance in depth to find it.

6. **Contrast between sharp and unsharp.** The eye can focus sharply on only one specific zone in depth at a time, seeing objects beyond and in front of this zone as more or less blurred, increasingly so the farther such objects are from the plane of focus. As a result, in a photograph, contrast between sharp and unsharp, by re-creating conditions associated with actual seeing, becomes a symbol of depth. This depth effect will become stronger as the contrast between sharpness and blur increases and vice versa. The control for this depth symbol is "selective focusing." The larger the relative aperture and the longer the focal length of the lens, and the shorter the subject-to-camera distance, the more pronounced the contrast between sharpness and blur in the picture and vice versa.

7. **Contrast between light and dark.** Trough light-scattering in the atmosphere, objects look lighter, the farther they are from the observer. Lightness evokes an impression of distance, and conversely, darkness evokes an impression of nearness. In a photograph, contrast of lightness and darkness creates an impression of depth.

In outdoor photographs, the juxtaposition of dark foreground matter and light, distant background matter is called "aerial perspective." It can be controlled with the aid of filters. A blue filter, by making distant objects appear lighter, strengthens the feeling of depth; conversely, a yellow and even more so a red filter, by making distant objects appear darker, more or less minimizes aerial perspective in the picture and decreases the feeling of depth.

Rectilinear perspective

These are the rules of conventional, rectilinear perspective rendition:

1. All straight lines are rendered straight (in other forms of perspective (see pp. 302 and 306) they may appear curved).

2. All lines and angles within a plane or planes parallel to the plane of the film (left side of photograph on opposite page, top) remain undistorted and are not affected by "perspective." Parallels are rendered parallel; horizontals are rendered horizontal; verticals are rendered vertical; angles are rendered in their true shapes.

3. All lines receding from the observer appear to converge toward vanishing points (right side of photograph on opposite page, top). If they are parallel, they converge toward a common vanishing point. If they are horizontal, their vanishing point is always on the true horizon.

4. Verticals should not converge in the picture but should appear parallel. This is an arbitrary, artifical rule because in reality receding verticals appear to converge.

The uncontrolled photograph on the opposite page shows perspective "as it really is." Since the camera was tilted, verticals converge. In contrast, in the controlled picture above which was made from the same camera position, verticals are rendered parallel with the aid of the back adjustments of a view camera (see p. 280).

The photograph at the right, a straight downward view, shows that the rules of rectilinear perspective apply regardless of the angle of view.

Space control through the use of view camera adjustments

This series of photographs shows how a photographer can control perspective in a picture. For this experiment one needs a suitable object – a cardboard container or a box – to photograph according to the following instructions (see also pp. 49–52):

1. Aim and focus the camera as usual. Parallel edges of the box will appear to converge on the groundglass (see the first picture).

2. Tilt the back of the view camera backward until it is parallel with the vertical edges of the box. This will restore the vertical lines of the box to parallelity in the image although part of the image will be out of focus. Disregard this unsharpness for the moment (second picture).

3. Without disrupting its verticality, swing the back of the view camera laterally until it is parallel with the front of the box. This will make the horizontal lines of the image of the box parallel. Now, the front of the box will appear on the groundglass in the form of a rectangle, its edges parallel with one another and its corners forming angles of 90 degrees, although the image will be very much out of focus (third picture).

4. Tilt and swing the lens very slowly while readjusting the focus and checking the image on the groundglass until the image appears reasonably sharp. Then stop down the lens as far as necessary and make the exposure. In the resulting picture the box should be rendered sharply from corner to corner and free from "perspective distortion" as illustrated in the fourth photograph.

Similarly, of course, any three-dimensional form can be rendered free from "perspective distortion." For example, the walls of buildings can be rid of convergence and the wheels of an automobile made to appear circular in the picture and not elliptically distorted, see pp. 280–281.

Space control with a view camera

To render a tall building free from "perspective distortion" proceed as follows:

1. Aim and focus the camera as usual. The building will appear distorted on the groundglass as in the picture above, left.

2. Level the camera. In this position, verticals will appear parallel on the groundglass, but the upper part of the building will be cut off as in the picture above at the right.

3. Raise the lens until the building appears on the groundglass as desired; see photograph at right.

Space control through use of an enlarger

To make an "undistorted" print from a negative in which perspective is "distorted" proceed as follows:

1. Place the negative in the enlarger and project it upon the easel. The image will be distorted as in the picture above, left.

2. Tilt the easel until parallel lines appear parallel in the image, and support it in this position. The trapezoid-shaped image will be partly blurred, see picture above, right.

3. Tilt the negative in the opposite direction from which the easel is tilted until, after simultaneously refocusing the lens, the image appears sharp in its entirety; see picture at right.

Space control

The easiest method of space control, and that which supplies the greatest control, is found in the use of a lens of suitable focal length in combination with the most suitable subject-to-camera distance.

The effect upon the picture of the focal length of the lens alone is illustrated by the three photographs above which were made from an identical camera position with lenses of different focal lengths: from left to right, wide-angle, standard, telephoto lens. Since the distance between subject and camera was the same, the perspective (the relative proportions of the individual picture components) is the same in all three photographs; the only difference is in the scale and angle of coverage produced by the different focal lengths of the respective lenses. For additional information see pp. 28–29.

The combined effect upon the picture of the focal length of the lens and changes in subject-to-camera distance is illustrated by the three photographs at the right. From top to bottom, they were made, respectively, with a wide-angle, a standard, and a telephoto lens. Distance between subject and camera was adjusted to make the speed limit sign appear in the same scale in each photograph. Since the subject-to-camera distance is different in each picture, the perspective is different, too. In the top picture the speed limit sign appears larger than the bridge, whereas in the bottom picture it appears smaller.

Thus, by using a lens with the right focal length in conjunction with the appropriate subject-to-camera distance, a photographer can completely control the rendition of space, depth, and the relative proportions of the different components of his picture. For additional information see pp. 26–31.

SPEED
35
LIMIT
STATE TRAFFIC COMMISSION

SPEED
35
LIMIT
STATE TRAFFIC COMMISSION
BRIDGEWATER

SPEED
35
LIMIT
STATE TRAFFIC COMMISSION
BRIDGEWATER
INCORPORATED 1856
TOWN LINE

Space — deep or shallow

Through appropriate choice of subject-to-camera distance and a lens of suitable focal length, a photographer can control the apparent depth of space in his picture, as is illustrated by the space rendition in these two pairs of photographs:

Above: the same scene shot with a telephoto (left) and a wide-angle lens (right). In both pictures, the figures are rendered in the same scale, but the feeling of distance of the opposite shore is different in each.

Opposite page: the same view photographed through a window with a telephoto lens from deep within the room (top) and with a wide-angle lens from close to the window (bottom). In each picture the window itself is rendered in the same scale, but the street in one appears very narrow and in the other rather wide. Which of these (or any other) forms of space rendition to choose is solely up to the photographer.

Perspective "distortion"

"Distortion" increases proportionally as subject distance decreases. The closer the camera is to the subject, the more pronounced the "perspective distortion," i. e., near parts of the subject will be rendered in a larger scale relative to those parts that are farther away. To avoid perspective distortion, the subject must be photographed from a sufficient distance. Naturally, the greater the subject distance, the smaller the scale of rendition. To compensate for decreases in apparent subject size caused by diminution (see p. 270), a photographer must use lenses of increasingly longer focal lengths as he increases the distance between subject and camera.

A b o v e : the Empire State Building in New York, photographed from a few blocks away, appears unproportionally small and "distorted" in scale in relation to nearby, although actually very much smaller, buildings.

O p p o s i t e p a g e : photographed with a telephoto lens from a distance of seven miles, the Empire State Building, free from perspective distortion in relation to its surrounding, appears in its true monumental size.

Perspective and "distortion"

Perspective is controlled by three factors: angle of approach, subject distance, focal length of the lens. Of these, the angle of approach determines the degree of foreshortening. The focal length of the lens determines the scale of rendition (subject size in the negative). But the subject distance — and it alone — determines the degree of "distortion."

Contrary to popular belief, in relation to a lens of standard focal length, a wide-angle lens does *not* "distort" and a telephoto lens does not "compress space," *as long as the three are used in an identical camera position*. The wide-angle lens merely

renders a greater angle of view in smaller scale than the standard lens, and the telephoto lens renders a smaller angle of view in larger scale. But perspective rendition will be identical in all three pictures, a fact illustrated by the photographs on this spread.

The small photograph at the left shows a view of New York taken with a wide-angle lens. The center picture shows the same view taken with an extreme telephoto lens from the identical camera position. And the picture at the right corresponds to the framed section of the wide-angle photograph at the left, enlarged to the scale of the telephoto shot in the center. Apart from differences in sharpness caused by the different degree of negative magnification, the last two pictures are identical in regard to perspective and rendition of space.

Creative use of "distortion"

Perspective, the apparent converging of parallels in the picture, symbolizes extension in space. Now, space extends in all directions, and consequently, perspective can be used to symbolize extension in depth not only in a horizontal direction, but in a vertical direction and in angle shots, too. Here, a pair of pictures taken from the same camera position illustrate the use of the back adjustments of a view-camera to render vertical lines either parallel for a conventional view, or as converging to create a stronger feeling of height — "depth in vertical direction."

The Time & Life Building in New York photographed by Yale Joel with a Hypergon super wide-angle lens which covers an angle of 130 degrees. Radical convergence of verticals here suggests with an almost surrealistic intensity the breathtaking sensation of bottomless depth.

Creative use of "distortion"

Deliberate intensification of perspective convergence through use of short subject distance in conjunction with a wide-angle lens provided these photographs with an unusually strong feeling of height.

Above: an oblique view of a transformer emphasizes "height." Note that the workman suspended in the bosun's chair gives the transformer scale (pp. 114–119).

Opposite page: show-girls photographed by Yale Joel with an extreme wide-angle lens. Deliberate use of "distortion" re-creates the impression for the sake of which aficionados compete with one another for the first rows of seats.

Space control: the four basic types of perspective

Photographers have, in theory if not always in practice, the choice of four different types of space rendition which correspond to the four types of perspective illustrated above. All photographs were made from the same camera position.

1. **Academic rectilinear perspective.** Straight lines are rendered straight in the picture. With the exception of verticals which are always rendered parallel, straight lines that are not parallel to the plane of the film converge toward vanishing points. The angle of coverage is usually (though not necessarily) limited to approximately 50 degrees. The photograph above, left, which illustrates this type of perspective, was made with a lens of standard focal length and a view-camera whose adjustments were employed to create such perspective.

2. **True rectilinear perspective.** Straight lines are rendered straight in the picture. Straight lines that are not parallel to the plane of the film, whether they are in the horizontal, vertical, or any other plane, converge toward vanishing points. The angle of coverage may reach 90 degrees or more. The photograph above, right, was made with a 35 mm camera and a wide-angle lens of 21 mm focal length.

3. **Cylindrical perspective.** This form of space rendition is produced by all cameras whose lenses swing through an arc, "scanning" the film during the exposure (and by the old-fashioned panoramic "Circuit-cameras"). In the picture, actually straight lines appear either straight or curved, depending upon whether the lens of the camera scanned the picture horizontally or vertically. The angle of coverage in the principal direction of the picture is generally 140 degrees. The photograph above, left, was made with a Panon camera, scanning vertically.

4. **Spherical perspective.** This form of space rendition is typical of the "Fish-eye" cameras which produce circular pictures. All straight lines appear curved except those parallel with the optical axis which, appearing as radii in the picture, are rendered straight. The angle of coverage is 180 degrees plus. The photograph above, right, which covers an angle of view of 180 degrees, was made with a Japanese Nikon Fish-eye camera.

Space control: composite panoramic views

Lacking a Panon or a similar type of panoramic camera, a photographer can produce a pretty good approximation of a panoramic view with an ordinary camera by taking a progression of pictures from left to right and mounting them together in the form of a "panorama." For best results, two conditions must be fulfilled:

1. The camera must be set up perfectly level, otherwise the effect of perspective in the vertical plane will make it impossible to accurately fit the individual shots together. Consequently, a good tripod and, if possible, a level, are needed for successful "panoramic" shots of this kind.

2. Each negative must overlap the next to a certain degree, otherwise it may be impossible to accurately fit the prints together later.

The photograph above is a night view of New York's Polo Grounds stadium. It consists of three individual pictures taken with a Rolleiflex. The camera position and the direction of view of each of the three pictures were chosen so that the joints would coincide with the upright supports of the stadium's roof. Since in the photograph these appear as straight, wide, black lines, joining the three pictures presented no problem and the joints themselves are invisible.

Synthesis of a "true" perspective

Rectilinear perspective is only o n e type of perspective; two others are cylindrical and spherical perspective. Although, at first, they may seem "unnatural," they are actually more "real" or "true" than rectilinear perspective, as the following discussion will prove.

Imagine that you are facing an "endless" building that extends from left to right from one horizon to the other. Directly in front of you, you should see a section of this building in the form of a rectangle. Its roof and base lines should appear straight, horizontal, and parallel to one another, similar to the picture at the top of p. 300.

If you turn your head to the left and look at the building, you should see it stretching toward the left horizon, its roof and base lines converging toward the left as a result of perspective. And if you turn your head to the right, you should likewise see the building "in perspective," its horizontal lines now converging toward the right.

Now, if you can imagine having eyes (like certain fishes, insects, or the lens of a Nikon Fish-eye camera) which are capable of encompassing an angle of vision up to 180 degrees, and if you then faced the building at right angles, with such vision you should be able to see it in its entire extension from one horizon to the other. And this is what you would see:

Far away to the left, out of the corner of your eye, you would see the building emerge from the horizon as very small because of perspective diminution. In the center of your field of vision, the building would look large and high because this part of it is so close to you. And far over to the right, you would again see the building becoming progressively smaller as it recedes toward the other horizon.

Now imagine the shape of the two horizontals that constitute the building's base and roof. Obviously, although they are actually parallel, these lines cannot *appear* parallel since they converge toward vanishing points at your left and right, respectively. On the other hand, they cannot appear straight since then there should be a break in the lines, an obtuse angle in the center of your field of vision where the lines from the left meet those from the right. And obviously, since there is no such break (remember, these lines appeared to stretch smoothly from one horizon to the other), the only possible conclusion is that "actually" these straight lines appeared as curves!

And the second conclusion, of course, is that your first head-on view of the building could not have been a rectangle since it is an integral part of the entire 180 degree view, and, therefore, its top and bottom lines must also curve, regardless of how slight this curve may be.

Following this, the third conclusion will scarcely be surprising: since the laws of perspective apply regardless of whether perspective is manifest in the horizontal, the vertical, or any inclined plane, the apparent convergence of straight vertical lines in angle views must also be in the form of curves. And, whether or not it seems difficult to believe, it is true.

The photographs on the following spread illustrate step by step the emergence of this type of true perspective.

Synthesis of a "true" perspective

T o p : rectilinear perspective. Straight lines are rendered straight. Since the planes of subject and film were parallel, "distortion" was avoided. Horizontals appear horizontal and parallel. Verticals appear vertical and parallel. Angles appear in their true shapes. This photograph appears "true" according to the rules of academic perspective rendition.

B o t t o m : composite picture made from two photographs taken at a 30-degree angle toward the left and right, respectively. Straight lines are straight. Verticals appear parallel because they were parallel to the plane of the film, but horizontals converge toward two vanishing points because their planes inclined toward the plane of the film. The angle at the junction of the two picture-halves is artificial and did not exist in reality.

Top: composite picture made of three photographs eliminates the center angle but introduces two new angles which, though less acute, are nevertheless not true to fact. The "curving" convergence of receding parallel lines characteristic of "true" perspective begins to emerge.

Bottom: photograph taken with a Panon camera (see p. 302). Perspective is "cylindrical": verticals are still rendered straight, but horizontals appear curved. This photograph corresponds to the impression one gets in turning one's head from one side to the other when looking at a subject of exceptionally great horizontal extension.

Space control: cylindrical perspective

The photographs on this spread were made with a Panon camera which, because of its swinging lens, produces pictures in which perspective is cylindrical. They clearly illustrate the two characteristics of this type of perspective:

1. The unusually wide angle of view of 140 degrees can be covered in one picture.

2. Straight lines that are parallel to the plane of the sweep of the lens appear curved. If the lens sweeps horizontally (as in these views), all horizontals, except the one bisecting the picture, appear more or less curved — increasingly so, the closer they are to the edge of the picture. And if the lens sweeps vertically (as in the view on page 295, left), all verticals except the one bisecting the picture appear in the form of curves.

However, if the subject does not contain any straight lines, this particular type of pseudo-distortion (see also pp. 120–121) will usually go unnoticed as demonstrated by the landscape photograph above which also was made with a Panon.

Synthesis of a cylindrical perspective

The composite picture at the left illustrates why straight lines must of necessity appear curved in all super wide-angle renditions. Each of its three components was taken with an ordinary camera and a lens of standard focal length. The perspective of each is "normal": with the camera in level position (center), verticals are rendered parallel; with the camera pointed upward (top), verticals converge toward the top of the picture; with the camera pointed downward (bottom), verticals converge toward the bottom of the picture. Each of these photographs encompasses an angle of approximately 47 degrees. Now, if all three were combined in one single shot encompassing three times 47 degrees, or approximately 140 degrees, how would perspective be manifest? It would appear as in the Panon shot on the opposite page which encompasses an angle of 140 degrees in which the actually straight verticals of the skyscraper are rendered as curves.

Synthesis of a spherical perspective

The two photographs on this spread look almost identical. However, upon closer examination, one will see that the camera and tripod in the left picture do not appear in the shot at the right. This is the clue to their difference: the left picture shows the scene reflected in a large, mirror-plated glass sphere, and the camera with which this picture was taken is, of course, reflected in its center. The other photograph was made with a Fish-eye camera from the position of the sphere.

The most interesting feature of this pair of pictures is that perspective is manifested in both in identical form, from the distortion-free center to

the violent curving of actually straight lines near the edge of the circle. The angle of view encompassed by the reflection in the sphere is approximately 220 degrees, whereas the Fish-eye camera covered "merely" an angle of some 180 degrees.

Originally, fish-eye lenses were designed for meteorological photography, permitting photographers to show the entire expanse of the sky in one shot. Today, fish-eye lenses, although still expensive, and the less expensive slip-on lenses which convert standard lenses temporarily into fish-eye lenses, have made "fish-eye photography" accessible to many amateurs. To see how the above scene appears in "ordinary" photographs taken with standard and wide-angle lenses, turn to p. 152.

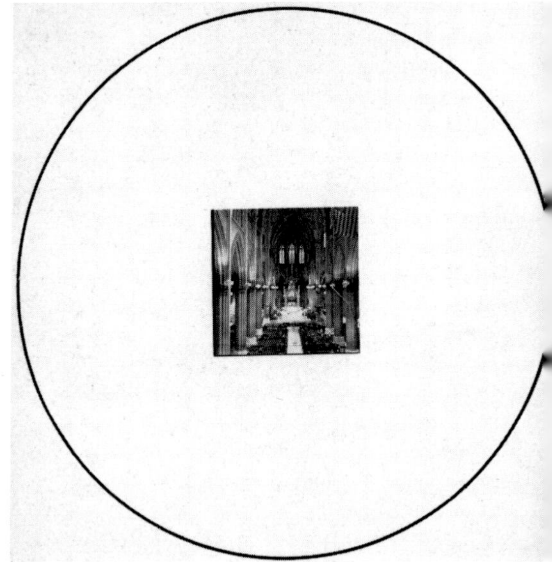

Space control: spherical perspective

The picture at the left is a 180 degree view of St. Patrick's Cathedral in New York made with a Fish-eye camera. The angle of coverage is so enormous that even the photographer who was standing to the left of the camera appears in the picture, near the edge of the circle at approximately "8 o'clock."

The picture at the right is a comparison view taken with a Rolleiflex from the same camera position. It is reproduced in the same scale as the Fish-eye picture. The surrounding circle corresponds to the additional subject area which a Fish-eye camera would have covered.

A Fish-eye camera view of Rockefeller Center, New York. The strange shape of the large building at the left (which looks as if it were made of wax that had begun to melt) is the natural manifestation of spherical perspective as explained before. Anyone who has the opportunity to frequently see "Fish-eye pictures" soon gets used to their curving lines and, particularly if he thinks of reflections in a mirrored sphere, learns how to "read" them correctly. He will find that the strangeness of their perspective is more than offset by the fact that they literally show in one single picture one half of the visible world.

Space control: diminution

Any object appears smaller as its distance from the observer increases. And if the observer knows the actual size of an object, its *apparent* size will make it possible for him to judge the distance between the object and himself.

From this it follows that, if a photographer shows an object (whose dimensions are generally known) either in smaller or larger scale in his picture, he can make depth appear either more or less extensive and space either great or small as illustrated by the photographs on this spread: although no other manifestations of space rendition are present in these pictures — no "converging parallels," foreshortened forms, overlapping, contrast between sharp and unsharp, haze or "aerial perspective" — the fact that the car and the ships are rendered relatively small in comparison to the surrounding landscape makes the landscape appear big and wide and produces a pronounced feeling of depth. Space is thus symbolized through subject diminution.

Foreshortening and distortion

Although it may not be generally realized, "perspective" and "distortion" are inseparable. Without some degree of distortion, there is no "perspective" and consequently no feeling of "depth." Seen head-on in its true, undistorted form, a circle appears "flat." However, seen at an angle as "distorted" in the form of an ellipse, even a (two-dimensional) circle acquires a certain degree of "depth" because it then seems to be part of three-dimensional space (as illustrated in the picture above.)

"Distortion" is a relative concept. At least some degree of distortion is essential for the symbolization of space with two-dimensional means. In a photograph, only excessive distortion is commonly regarded as a "distortion" of reality. A photographer has full control over the degree of distortion he wishes to create; his means: appropriate choice of angle of view, distance between subject and camera, and focal length of the lens. Basically, the greater the degree of distortion, the more pronounced the feeling of depth in a picture and vice versa. This, incidentally, explains why (the relatively "distortion-free") photographs taken with super telephoto lenses, in which space appears "compressed," always appear curiously "flat."

This photograph of a window cleaner at work on the facade of the United Nations Building in New York illustrates how "distortion" (here: the distortion of actually rectangular windows) can be deliberately used to give even such a flat subject as this facade a feeling of "depth."

Overlapping of form

If in a photograph, one thing is partly hidden by another, it was obviously farther away from the observer (the camera) than the one that hides it. Thus, overlapping is another graphic symbol for expressing "depth" photographically.

In the absence of other depth-symbols (as in these two pictures), overlapping was the only means for creating impressions of space. It becomes particularly effective if, as in the picture of racing cars by Earl Seubert, the partly hidden (farther) object is larger than the (nearer) one which partially abscures it. Normally, of course, one would assume

that, because of diminution, the larger object is closer to, and the smaller farther away from, the observer (the camera). As in this case, overlapping may then be the only possible means for preventing such an erroneous conclusion. In addition, the "inverted perspective" which in such a case results from overlapping makes for a particularly spectacular picture.

Space control: contrast between sharp and unsharp

The eye can focus on only one zone in depth at a time. Objects in front of or behind that zone appear increasingly unsharp as their distance from this zone increases. As a result, contrast between sharp and unsharp is associated with the sensation of depth. This feeling can be produced in a photograph through use of the technique of selective focusing (see pp. 154–159), examples of which are shown on this spread.
In the comparison pair of photographs above, the picture at the left (shot at f/3.5) in which sharpness is deliberately restricted to the foreground, produces a much stronger sensation of depth than the picture at the right (shot at f/22) in which foreground and background are rendered equally sharp. And on the opposite page, Grey Villet deliberately used selective focusing to single out one student in the group of children, simultaneously providing his picture with depth.

Space control: aerial perspective

Outdoors, as distance from the observer increases, intervening masses of atmospheric haze cause objects to appear increasingly light. This phenomenon, aerial perspective, can be exploited and controlled with the aid of color filters to influence the impression of depth in a picture as illustrated by the photographs on this spread, all of which were shot one after another on a somewhat hazy summer day. In the first

picture the scene is shown approximately as it appeared to the eye. The second picture was shot through a yellow filter; contrast is improved and the scene appears less hazy. The third picture was shot through a blue filter; contrast is reduced, the haze effect is heightened and veils the distant parts of the scene. The fourth picture was shot through a red filter; contrast is excessively strong, the haze effect is almost eliminated, and detail is rendered crisp and sharp throughout the entire picture.

Motion controls

A large number of photographic subjects, animate as well as inanimate, are subject to motion or change, but a photograph is a "still." Motion, like "depth," can be indicated in a photograph only in symbolic form. Fortunately, there are a number of different, expressive motion symbols that can be used to indicate any desired degree of motion, action, or speed in graphic form. Each of these can be fully controlled and, in many cases, modified in an almost limitless number of ways. The following survey gives nine effective motion symbols and their controls.

1. **"Freezing."** A single, significant phase of motion is selected and the moving subject sharply rendered. Although this method destroys the "feeling" of motion, in a photograph it is an excellent graphic solution for the rendition and study of subjects in motion when it is evident that the depicted subject was in motion (for example, a horse in mid-air over a hurdle) and no additional indication is needed.

Motion can be "frozen" either by using a sufficiently high shutter speed or, if circumstances permit, electronic flash.

2. **Blur.** Motion is synonymous with change of position in space. This fact offers a photographer an excellent opportunity for symbolizing motion through graphic means by showing his moving subject, so to speak, in many positions at once: by selecting a shutter speed a little too long to "freeze" the motion, he can render his moving subject somewhat blurred, such blur literally consisting of many slightly different images almost superimposed and forming a synthesis of motion.

Blur is proof of motion — either motion of the subject or of the camera. If both subject and camera are motionless, a photograph can never be blurred although it may be unsharp, i. e., out of focus. Blur is "unsharpness in a single direction" — the direction in which the subject or camera moved.

Blur is perhaps the most expressive photographic symbol of motion. It can be easily and fully controlled: the slower the shutter speed relative to the apparent speed (the angular velocity) of the subject, the more pronounced the degree of blur and vice versa.

3. **Multiple exposure.** Instead of indicating motion through a continuous sequence of subject positions resulting in blur, a photographer can reduce the continuity of the motion to a definite number of sharply rendered, individual phases exposed one after another on the same sheet of film. The result is a sequence of sharp, slightly different, often partly overlapping images of the subject caught in different phases of motion which together symbolize in clear and graphically elegant form the concept of motion.

If this method is to be successful, the subject must be relatively light in tone and the background very dark or black. Otherwise, the background would "burn through" the subject, obliterating most of the subject's image in the picture and making the rest appear transparent. If subject motion is relatively slow, the individual exposures can be timed manually with the shutter. If subject motion is fast, exposure and timing must be done automatically with repetitive electronic flash.

4. **Multiple printing.** The principle of this kind of motion control is the same as that of multiple exposure, but the technique is different. In this case several individual negatives, each showing one specific phase of the motion, are printed together on one sheet of paper to form a single, composite picture of the motion.

Provided that the number of individual picture components is small — four or five being the maximum — this method has two advantages: The position of the individual picture components can be visually controlled during the printing or enlarging; and if one of the negatives is unsatisfactory, it probably can be eliminated and the sequence still be saved, whereas if anything goes wrong in a multiple exposure the entire effort was a waste.

5. **Time exposure.** In this case, the exposure time (shutter speed) is very slow in relation to the speed of the subject in motion. As a result, the subject itself will appear completely unrecognizable in the picture and be represented only by a graph of its motion, its path being rendered in the form of a more or less continuous line or smear.

Well-known examples of such motion symbolization are time exposures of automobiles in motion at night represented in the picture by bright, continuous lines. Although, in such cases, the subject itself is totally unrecognizable, the picture fulfills its purpose through association: we know that these traces were made by the headlights of cars. Consequently, we reconstruct an image of the traffic, although no cars are seen in the picture.

6. **Panning.** In principle, this is the reversal of blur. There, the moving subject was rendered blurred against sharply rendered stationary picture elements. Here, the moving subject appears sharp in the picture and the stationary objects appear blurred.

The technique of panning is similar to shooting a flying duck with a gun: the image of the moving subject is picked up in the view finder, held there by following through with the camera, and the shutter released in swinging.

The uniqueness of panning is that it enables a photographer to show the moving subject in relatively sharp rendition while still conveying, through contrast of sharpness and blur, an intense feeling of motion. This method is particularly effective in creating impressions of speed when photographing automobile and horse races.

7. **Open flash.** This technique is a combination of time exposure and instantaneous exposure and is accomplished as follows: in very subdued light against a black background, a time exposure is made of a subject in motion, recording its track on the film. At the peak of motion, a flash is fired at the subject and a sharp image recorded upon the "track"

while the shutter of the camera remains open. It should continue to remain open an additional moment or two so that the "track" is continued beyond the flashed image of the subject. The result is a graph of motion at the peak of which the subject itself appears in crisp and sharp form. Often, to strengthen the clarity of such a graph, small, battery-fed flashlight bulbs can be attached to important parts of the moving subject to better trace its path. The darker the background is in relation to the tone of the subject, the more effective the resulting picture will be.

8. **Picture sequences.** This is a variation of multiple exposure. But in this case, instead of superimposing several sharp images of a moving subject on the same film, the photographer records each image on a separate sheet of film. Motion is thus subdivided into a number of phases and presented in the form of a picture sequence which, in its entirety, is a record of the motion. This method is particularly well suited to recording relatively slow motions, or progress such as the different stages of a building under construction, the seasonal changes in a landscape, or the growing up of a child.

9. **Composition.** A photographer can suggest motion in symbolic form even in the way that he arranges the elements of his picture. For example, by slightly tilting the image of a subject in motion within his picture, he can convey an impression of movement, whereas the same subject, printed from the same negative in a straight position, would induce no feeling of motion. Furthermore, the image of a subject crowded into one corner of a picture unfailingly suggests motion; whereas if it were more or less centrally positioned, the same image would appear motionless. And finally, whereas a composition which depends largely upon horizontal or vertical lines is always static, denoting equilibrium and rest, a diagonal composition is always dynamic, suggesting motion either in real or latent form.

Photographs illustrating these and other means of motion control are shown on pp. 324–341.

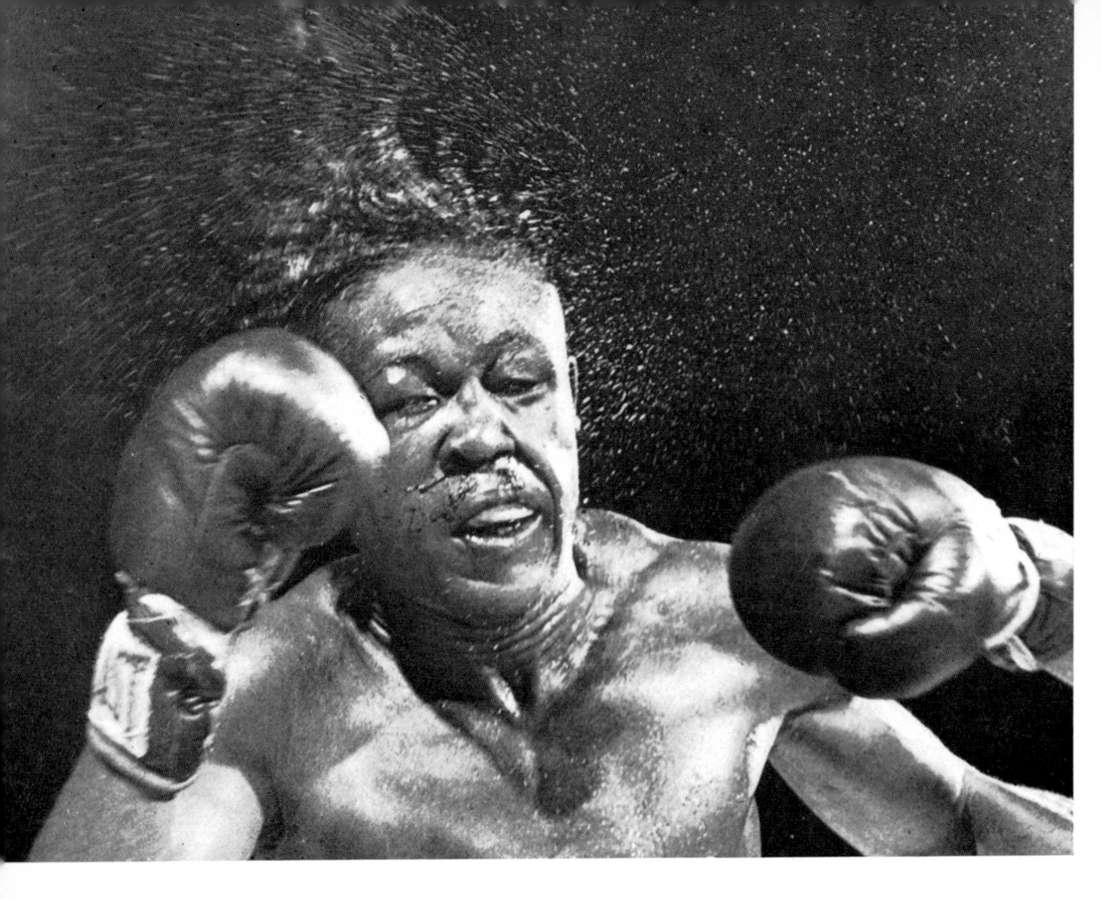

Motion control: "freezing"

In a photograph, to sharply render a subject in motion, i. e., to "freeze" it on the negative, the exposure must be so short that the image of the moving subject moves only an unnoticeable distance across the film during the exposure. This can be accomplished in two ways:

1. By photographing the moving subject with a sufficiently high shutter speed. This method is limited by two factors: shutter speed and illumination. Very few camera shutters in general use are equipped to make exposures of 1/1000 sec. or shorter; on the other hand, very few subjects usually photographed move so fast that 1/1000 sec. is needed to "freeze" them. Naturally, the higher the shutter speed, the more light needed to prevent underexposure.

2. The moving subject can be photographed with speedlights, the flash duration of which ranges from 1/800 to 1/1,000,000th of a second. This method is limited by the subject-to-speedlight distance and the cost and bulk of the flash equipment.

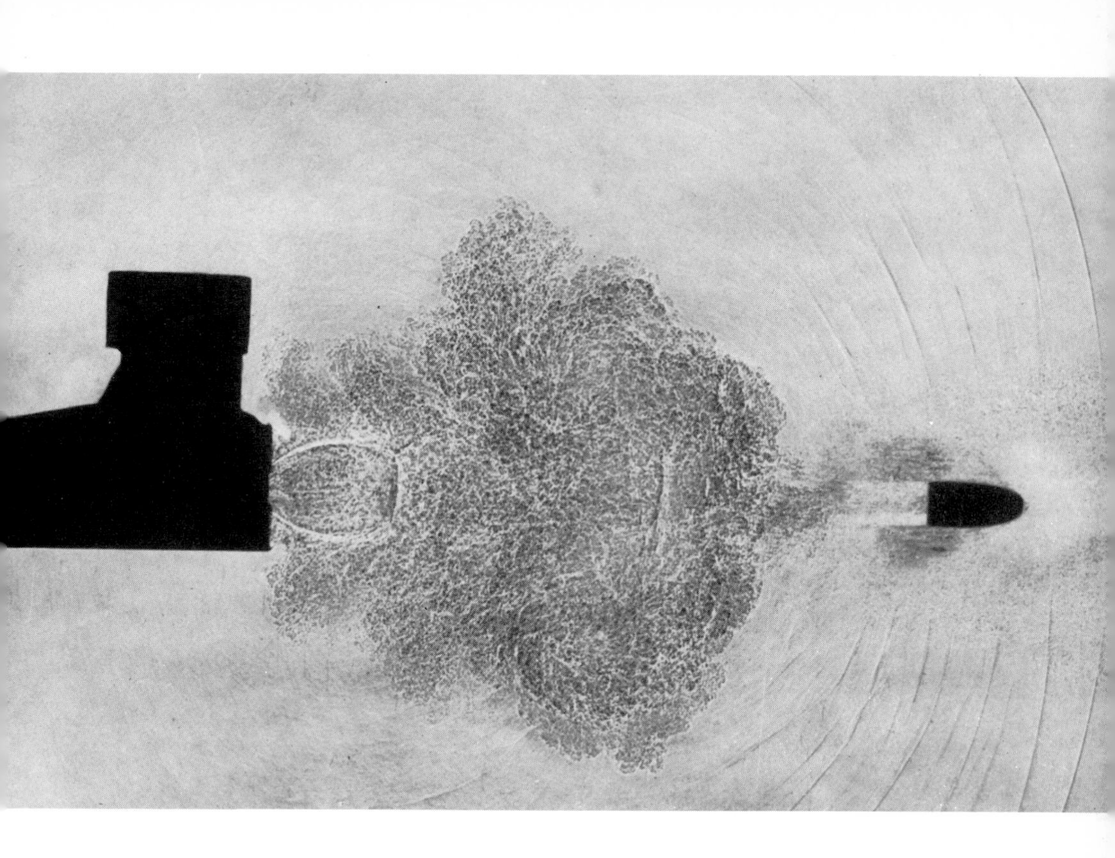

All of the accompanying photographs were made with speedlights. Note, in the boxing picture (New York Daily News) the drops of sweat sent flying by the blow; in the ballistic photograph above (Remington Arms Company) the shock waves in the air; and in the picture at right (A. G. Spalding & Bros.) that, at the moment of greatest compression, the apparently iron-hard golf ball assumes the shape of half an apple.

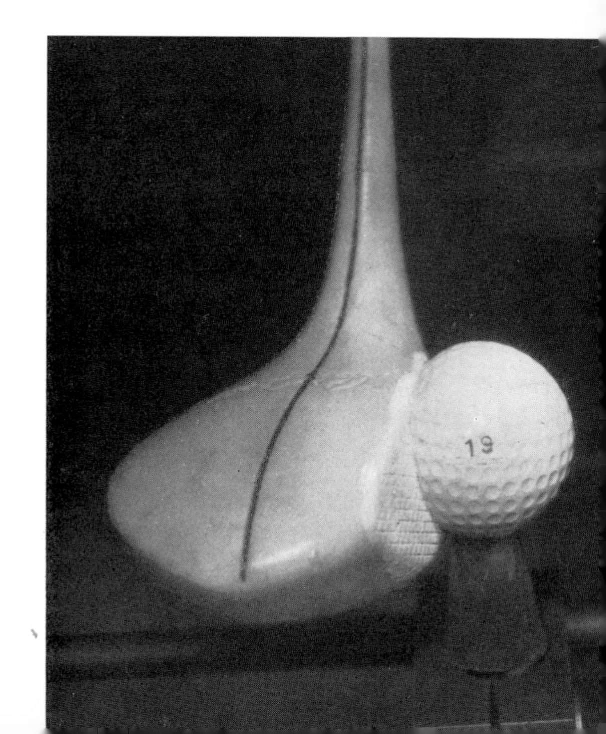

Motion control: blur

If the exposure is not sufficiently short to "freeze" a subject's motion, the rendition will become more or less blurred; increasingly so, the longer the exposure is in relation to the apparent speed of the subject. Thus a photographer can render a moving subject with any desired degree of blur and create any desired impression of speed.

To render a moving subject with a predetermined degree of blur, a photographer must know how to adjust his shutter speed in relation to the angular velocity of his subject. It makes a great difference whether the moving subject is close to the camera or far away, whether its direction of movement is toward the camera, away from it, or at right angles to the line of sight because these are the factors that determine the angular velocity (apparent speed) of the subject which is in turn the decisive factor in determining the most desirable shutter speed. For example, photographed at 1/25 sec. from a distance of several miles, a plane

flying at a speed of 400 miles per hour will appear sharp in a picture whereas a pedestrian crossing right in front of the camera at a speed of only 3 miles per hour will appear blurred.

To become familiar with the concept and nature of angular velocity, it is suggested that a photographer shoot a few picture sequences at different shutter speeds of different subjects in motion such as pedestrians, automobiles, children playing, dogs running, pigeons flying, etc. similar to the picture-sequence of skaters shown above, the individual shots of which were exposed at 1/100 sec., 1/25 sec., 1/5 sec. and one full second, respectively. Note that in the first picture 1/100 sec. stops all motion but the fastest; that in the second shot 1/25 sec. stops motion parallel to the line of sight (toward and away from the camera) but not motion at right angles; that in the third picture contrast between blur and sharpness graphically indicates which skaters were moving and which were not; and that the fourth picture, because it has the highest degree of blur, suggests the highest rate of speed.

Motion symbolization through blur

The photograph above taken by the Swedish photographer Hugo Lundberg is so vibrant with life and motion that one can almost physically feel the power behind the downthrust of the paddle and the foreward surge of the canoe. And in Paul Schutzer's photograph on the opposite page, the deliberate use of blur to express motion vividly conveys the swirl of the dance as the couples swing around the placid caller.

This is the secret of expressive motion rendition through blur: select a shutter speed that is long enough to produce sufficient blur to indicate the subject's motion, but not so long as to render the subject unrecognizable through excessive blur. If motion is uneven, the fastest moving elements show the highest degree of blur. For best results, the most important elements of the picture must also be the slowest; as long as they appear recognizable in the photograph the rest can be a frenzied blur.

Motion symbolization through panning

Blur is the symbol of motion and in a photograph, contrast between sharpness and blur suggests movement, action, and speed. Now it does not matter whether the moving or the stationary picture elements are rendered blurred, as long as one is blurred and the other sharp. Normally, of course, the moving subject is rendered blurred, and the stationary background appears sharp. However, this effect can be reversed through panning, i. e., centering and holding the image of the moving subject stationary in the view finder by swinging the camera as a gun is swung in shooting flying game, and releasing the shutter while the camera is in motion. In this way, the background moves relative to the subject as a result of which, in the picture, the moving subject will appear relatively sharp while the stationary background will appear blurred.

The picture of a pickup truck above and the photograph on the opposite page taken by Hugo Lundberg, illustrate the creative potentialities of this technique.

Motion symbolization through time exposure

A b o v e : the traffic pattern of incoming aircraft at night is traced by their landing lights. R i g h t : an expert simultaneously juggling 14 hula hoops, photographed by Joe Clark of Detroit, Michigan. A tiny flashlight attached to each hoop traces its path in the form of a fine white line. At the height of the action, a couple of electronic flash lamps were fired to superimpose the image of the boy upon the time-exposure.

In both cases, the moving objects themselves — the airplanes and the hula hoops — are invisible, lost in the long exposures. But this loss, so easily filled by the mind through association, is more than compensated for by the creation of something new, something which in reality the eye could not have seen in this form: the patterns of light, the visual experience of graphs of motion, space, and time created by the camera.

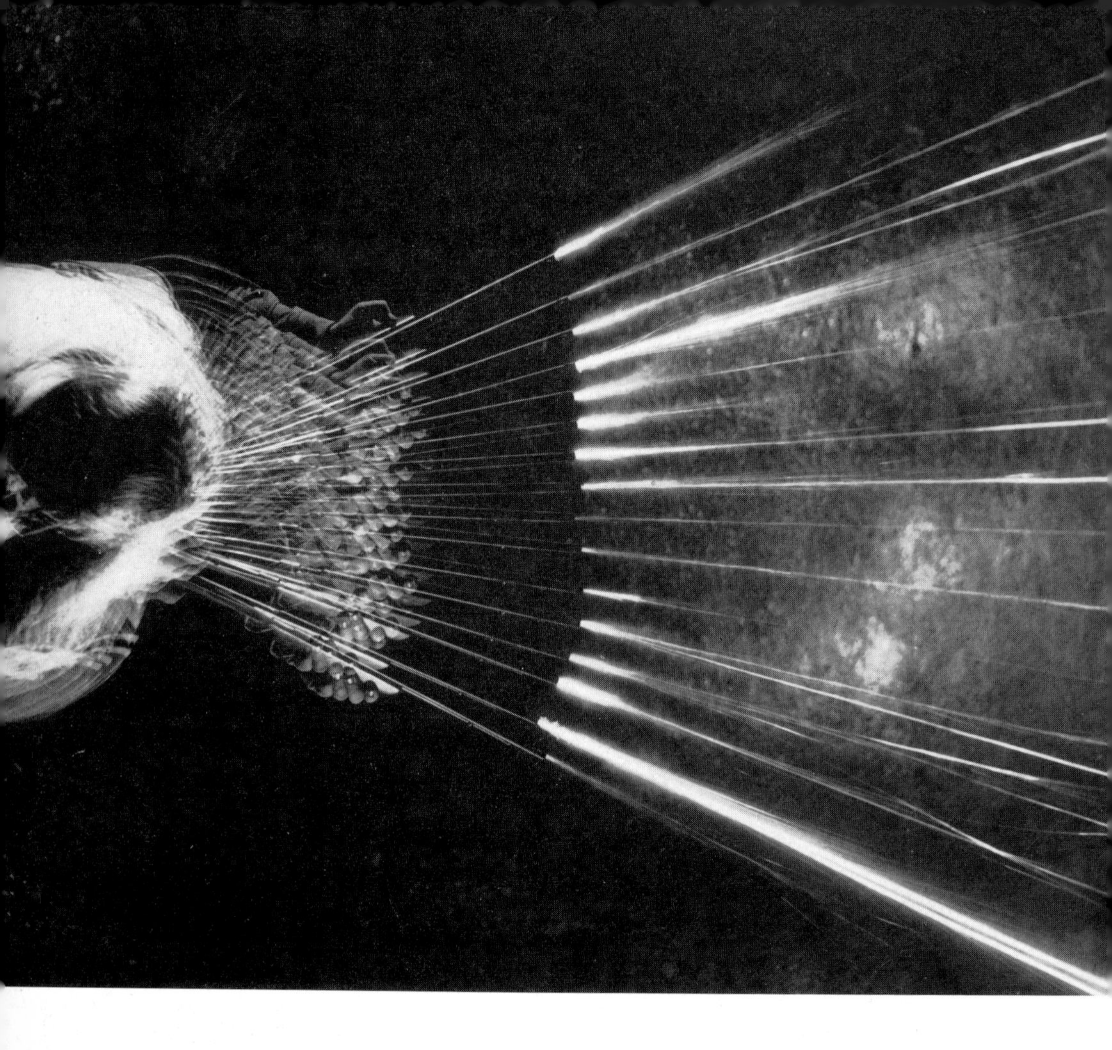

Motion symbolization through multiple-exposure

Frequently, instead of trying to capture the essence of motion in a single impression, a photographer can advantageously divide the flow of motion into different phases and register each separately, sharply superimposed upon one another on the same sheet of film.

Above: a multiple-exposure convincingly demonstrates the enormous firing power of a modern semi-automatic rifle. This photograph was made at the Winchester Plant in New Haven, Connecticut.

In a demonstration designed to show the great tensile strength of Mylar, an athlete performs on a trampolin made of this new plastic material. Triple-exposure with electronic flash recorded three positions — the jump, the impact, the rebound — on the same sheet of film.

Motion symbolization through multiple-printing

Occasionally it may be desirable to show two stages of a motion, perhaps the beginning and the end, in one picture. Often this can be done by photographing each stage separately on its own sheet of film and printing the two negatives together in the form of a "sandwich" on a single sheet of paper.

The accompanying pictures were made to illustrate the enormous, 30-foot tides at Passamaquody Bay in Maine. A row boat was tied to the pier and photographed at high tide and again at low tide (pictures above). Subsequently, the two negatives were taped together, their stationary images in register in the form of a "sandwich," and enlarged on the same sheet of paper.

For satisfactory results, two conditions must be fulfilled: the camera must be in precisely the same position for both shots; and the moving subject must be outlined against a dark or, still better, black background. Otherwise, the subject would appear transparent, and the background would be visible through it.

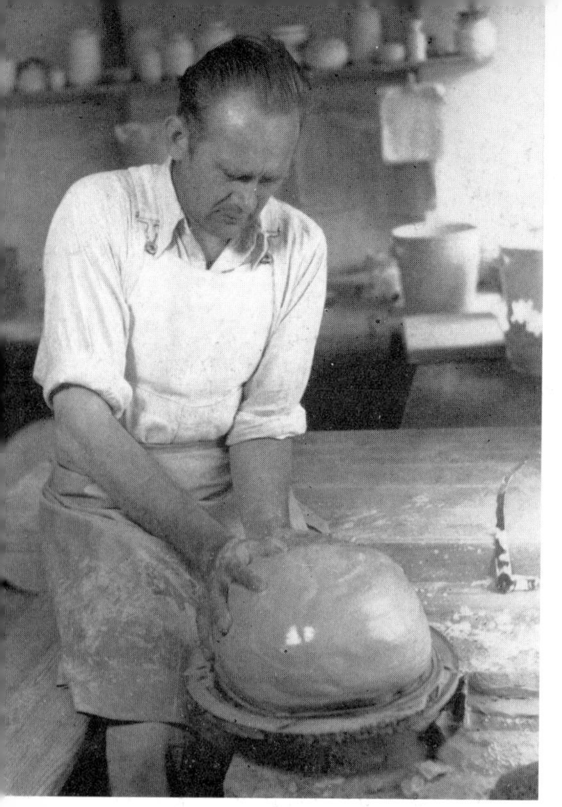

Motion symbolization through picture sequence

Instead of trying to condense the total impression of a subject's motion into a single picture (whether in the form of a single or multiple image), a photographer can at times advantageously depict a number of its most important phases in separate photographs and thus present his impression in the form of a short sequence — a strip — of related progress shots.

This technique is particularly well suited to illustrate relatively slow motions such as the making of the large ceramic vessel shown on this spread. In this particular case, the camera position remained the same throughout the entire sequence. Although this is usually desirable, it is not always necessary. When a motion or change is extremely slow, as in the growing up of a child, it is, of course, impossible to maintain the same camera position throughout the entire strip.

Motion symbolization through composition

Motion can be implied through composition. By placing the moving subject at a diagonal in his picture, a photographer can create an impression of motion through association: seeing the subject tilted in the picture, the observer has the feeling that at that angle it will slide, and sliding is a form of motion.

The photographs on this spread illustrate this effect. Although there is no trace of blur, each conveys a strong feeling of motion which directly results from the diagonal composition of the picture.

NEW YO
SAVING
BANK

Timing

Perhaps more than any other contributing factor, it is the accuracy with which an exposure is timed that determines the effectiveness of a photograph. The main goal of any photographer engaged in pictorial pursuit of the ever-changing aspects of the world must be to capture what Cartier-Bresson calls "the decisive moment." No matter how costly his equipment, how accomplished his technique, and how superior the quality of his prints, unless accurate timing enabled him to capture the "decisive moment" his pictures are bound to miss.

The main aspects of timing have been discussed on pp. 75–80. Some of them are illustrated on the following pages. Here I wish to add some considerations which are often overlooked.

Timing is important even in the studio when a still life is photographed. I have seen photographers slam in a film holder, cock the shutter, and press the cable release to make a time exposure without waiting for the resulting vibrations to cease. Naturally, pictures taken in this way are not as crisp as they should have been — their timing was off. Other photographers forgot to consider that people walking in the room, or trucks passing in the street, may cause vibration, and that exposures must be timed to coincide with a moment of quiet.

Even a seasoned photographer will often find it difficult, if not impossible, to capture the "decisive moment" at first try. Whether he is making a portrait and wishes to catch the one significant expression, or photographing a tumultuous rapidly changing event, he cannot foretell exactly when the decisive moment will occur. If such is the case, the only way to insure its capture is to take many pictures. Amateurs often complain that if they could afford to shoot as many pictures of one subject as some professionals do, they, too, would be bound to have a "hit" among their usual "misses." Of course, no professional photographer of worth shoots roll upon roll of pictures in the hope that one of his shots may "turn out all right." No, each of his many shots is carefully timed, for in each there was a reason to shoot. This method provides the only way to be sure not to miss the decisive moment. Our best photo-journalists subscribe to it, and its use is one of the reasons for their success.

To accurately time the peak of a rapidly developing event such as the tackle illustrated above, a photographer must be able to anticipate what's coming and trip the shutter a fraction of a second in advance of the climax. If he delays and waits until he sees what he wishes to depict, it will be too late. His own reaction time and the mechanical inertia inherent in his equipment will cause him to miss the significant shot.

Timing: the psychological moment

This famous photograph by Paul Schutzer (copyright Time, Inc. 1958) which shows Vice President Nixon admonishing a heckler in Lima, Peru, is a perfect example of split-second timing. A fraction of a second earlier or

later and the "decisive moment" would have been missed and a great picture lost. This photograph, shot with a 35 mm camera (see pp. 37, 146), is a tribute to Schutzer's ability to "see," his alertness, and his lightning-fast reflexes — qualities which a successful photo-journalist must have.

Timing: seasonal and atmospheric factors

Photographers too often record their first impression of a subject, giving no thought to the possibility that that particular time may not have been the best. These pictures illustrate what I have in mind: it makes an enormous difference whether one photographs a tree, for example, in summer or in winter, foliated or bare; a thing which, of course, is a matter of timing.

Another example: the concept of a skyscraper is best illustrated if its top disappears in the clouds — the building then is literally "scraping the sky." And this also presupposes proper timing, the choosing of a rainy day when the "ceiling" is low enough to envelop the top of the structure.

Timing: compositional factors

Timing means waiting until the time is right to release the shutter. One of the many factors that influence timing is composition, illustrated here with photographs by David Moore of Sydney, Australia (above), and Robert M. Mottar of New York. Closely watching their slowly moving subjects, both photographers patiently waited until all the picture elements had arranged themselves compositionally in the best position, not releasing the shutter until the time was right.

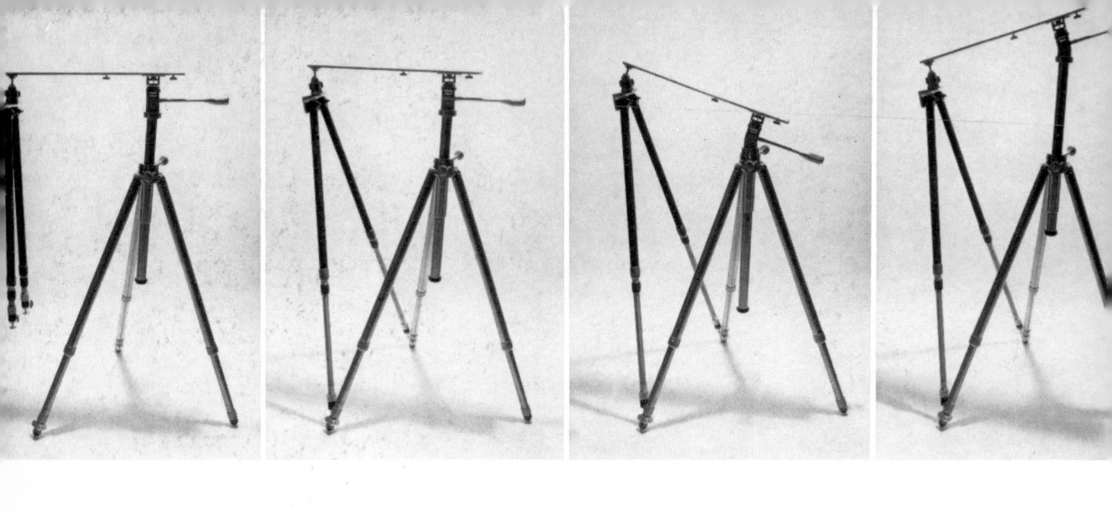

Appendix: how to construct a "five-pod"

It is an axiom of telephotography that the longer the focal length of the lens, the more rigidly the camera and lens must be supported to avoid unsharpness caused by vibration or movement of camera or lens. Unfortunately, the most common of all methods of camera support — supporting a long telephoto outfit at its center of gravity — is, in my opinion, the worst, since it permits the system to vibrate freely at both ends. The only technically sound way to support a long telephoto system is to support it simultaneously at both ends (and if necessary in the middle as well). The simplest device to use is a five-pod.

A five-pod, which is my own invention, is a tripod with five legs. However, these five legs touch the ground at only three points, making the system rock-steady and easy to erect. Basically, a five-pod consists of three parts: a regular tripod equipped with a center post and pan-head; a pair of auxiliary legs taken from a discarded tripod; and a flat piece of aluminum rail approximately 20 inches long, 2 inches wide and 1/4 inch thick which supports the telephoto camera.

To build a five-pod, start with a sturdy tripod equipped with "elevator." (I prefer the Tilt-all tripod because of its fine workmanship and exceptional lightness and sturdiness, and the fact that it can be levelled laterally with a single adjustment.) Then, take two legs from an old tripod and bolt them to an L-shaped piece of aluminum 2½ to 3 inches long, the top of which should be fitted with a strong universal joint as illustrated on the opposite page, top right. Fit the lower end of each auxiliary leg with a small universal joint; these joints will be used to attach the auxiliary legs to the "front legs" of the tripod by means of small, drilled and tapped lugs clamped to each of the two tripod front legs as illustrated in the picture on the opposite page, bottom right. Next, drill and tap the flat aluminum rail at both ends to receive the screws of the tripod head and the universal joint; in addition, drill a hole through the aluminum rail through which the screw will go which secures the camera to the rail. Finally, fit your telephoto lens near its front end with a quarter-inch aluminium pin which, riding back and forth on the flat rail, will support the front end of the lens as illustrated in the photograph on the opposite page, top right.

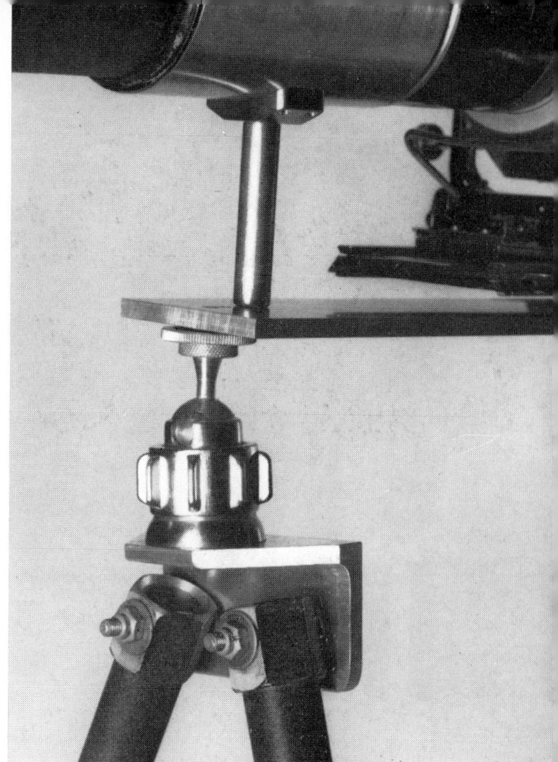

To assemble the five-pod proceed as follows (see illustrations on the opposite page):

1. Set up the regular tripod, raise its "elevator" approximately 5 inches.
2. Attach one end of the flat aluminum rail to the tripod head.
3. Attach the auxiliary legs to the other end of the flat rail by means of the screw of the universal joint, allowing the legs to dangle for the moment.
4. Extend the auxiliary legs and screw each to the respective lug at the lower end of each of the two tripod front legs.
5. Attach the camera to the flatbed rail.
6. To point the lens upward, lower the center post of the tripod.
7. To point the lens downward, raise the center post of the tripod.

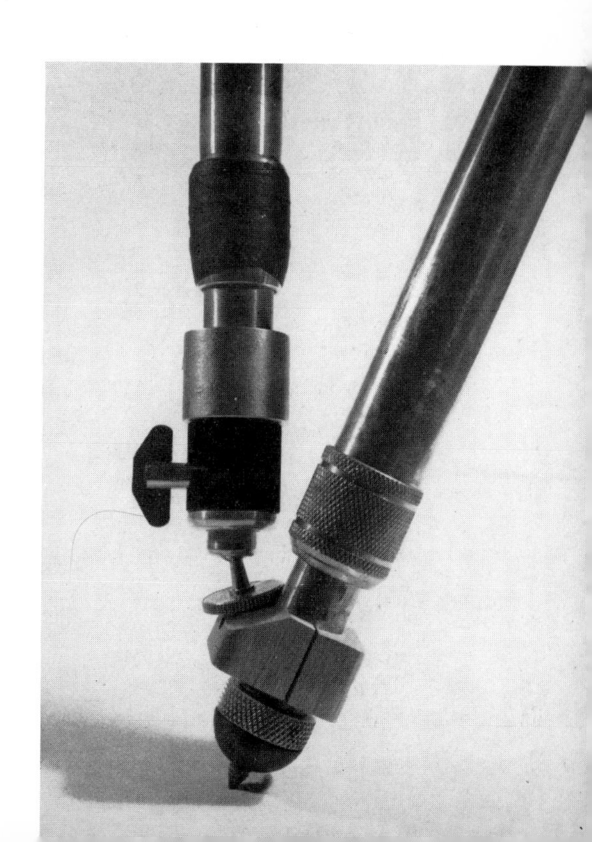

Index